PERIOD POWER

PERIOD POWER

A MANIFESTO FOR THE MENSTRUAL MOVEMENT

NADYA OKAMOTO

SIMON & SCHUSTER BFYR

NEW YORK LONDON TORONTO SYDNEY NEW DELHI

An imprint of Simon & Schuster Children's Publishing Division
1230 Avenue of the Americas, New York, New York 10020

This publication contains the opinions and ideas of its author. It is intended to provide
helpful and informative material on the subjects addressed in the publication. It is sold
with the understanding that the author and publisher are not engaged in rendering
medical, health, or any other kind of personal professional services in the book. The
reader should consult his or her medical, health, or other competent professional
before adopting any of the suggestions in this book or drawing inferences from it.
The author and publisher specifically disclaim all responsibility for any liability, loss,
or risk, personal or otherwise, which is incurred as a consequence, directly or
indirectly, of the use and application of any of the contents of this book.

Text copyright © 2018 by Nadya Okamoto
Jacket illustration copyright © 2018 by Rebecca Elfast
Interior illustrations by Rebecca Elfast
Interior images on pages 83, 86, and 88 courtesy of the US Patents Office.

For information about special discounts for bulk purchases, please contact
Simon & Schuster Special Sales at 1-866-506-1949
or business@simonandschuster.com.
The Simon & Schuster Speakers Bureau can bring authors to your live event. For
more information or to book an event, contact the Simon & Schuster Speakers Bureau
at 1-866-248-3049 or visit our website at www.simonspeakers.com.
Book design by Krista Vossen
The text for this book was set in Sabon.
The illustrations for this book were rendered digitally.
Manufactured in the United States of America
First Edition
2 4 6 8 10 9 7 5 3 1
CIP data for this book is available from the Library of Congress.
ISBN 978-1-5344-3021-1 (hc)
ISBN 978-1-5344-3020-4 (pbk)
ISBN 978-1-5344-3022-8 (eBook)

To my most cherished menstruators—
my mom, Sophia, and my two younger sisters,
Ameya and Issa

ACKNOWLEDGMENTS

I decided to embark on this journey of writing my first book in the summer of 2016, right after I graduated high school. On the first day of that summer break, I moved to Los Angeles with a few suitcases, tears in my eyes from my first breakup, a mind set on figuring out what I wanted to focus my energy on, and excitement about moving to a city I had never been to, with a family I had never met before. I had no idea what the process for publishing a book was, so naturally I googled it!

After writing my book proposal, I pulled an all-nighter to learn what literary agents were and, using a combination of Google and Twitter, found the email addresses of close to one hundred literary agents I admired. A few weeks later, after many submission rejections and even more ignored emails, I received an email from my dream literary agent, Lindsay Edgecombe, who had recently worked on one of my favorite young adult feminist books. Over the past year, Lindsay and Kerry Sparks of Levine Greenberg

Rostan Literary Agency have guided me through my first journey of publishing a book. They have been the friends I needed most when I questioned every draft I submitted because I often felt like my writing wasn't good enough. They have been the educators and advisers I have needed at every step to define words I had never heard before but which are used commonly in the publishing world. And they have been an inspiration for me to keep writing and have faith in this Menstrual Movement and what role I can play in it.

We took almost an entire year to refine my book proposal to match what we felt the world could use, and what felt the most authentic to me as a new writer. In the fall of 2017, my book was picked up by Simon & Schuster, my dream publisher—something I am still trying to wrap my head around. From the moment my editor, Liz Kossnar, and I hopped on the phone, I knew it was meant to be. We talked at similar speeds, she is a young up-and-coming editor in the industry, and our initial call felt effortless—we talked mostly about the Menstrual Movement, and our shared passion for intersectional feminism, youth activism, and this potential book. After signing with Liz, I took a couple months to write this book, knowing how urgently I wanted a manifesto like this to exist in the real world, geared specifically to young people. Liz has exceeded all expectations in terms of supporting this book and bringing it to life, and I am forever grateful to her for taking a chance on and believing in an extremely inexperienced author like me and a rather daring book like this one.

Thank you so much to publisher Justin Chanda for stepping up and supporting *Period Power* as a non-menstruating ally of this movement. Thank you to designer Krista Vossen and managing editor Dorothy Gribbin for making this book beautiful and ready to be seen and read. And thank you to Lauren Hoffman, Chrissy Noh, Anna Jarzab, Lisa Moraleda, and Milena Giunco—our marketing and publicity team—for helping to share this book and in turn, this movement, with the world.

Thank you to the PERIOD fam—my cofounder, Vincent; trusted board members; valued chapter leaders and members; and our partners, sponsors, and volunteers—for being a part of this Menstrual Movement and making the success of a book like this possible. And, finally, thank you to my family and friends for the constant support and unconditional love, and for believing in me even when I didn't believe in myself.

CONTENTS

INTRODUCTION

It came on December 26, 2010.

I was pretty sure I was dying. For the whole week, I had been dealing with a stabbing pain in my stomach. And when you constantly feel like someone is poking you in the gut with all their strength, it's hard to focus on anything else. My mom thought it was just a stomachache, but I knew she was wrong. I had just learned about appendicitis in school, and I was convinced I had it. I told her this, and in response she explained what "hypochondriac" means.

My sisters and I were on our way to visit our father in New York City from Portland, Oregon, where we lived with our mom. With only two hours before our flight's departure time, my mom rushed around the house helping us finish our last-minute packing. She made sure we had all of our essentials for travel: toiletries, enough pairs of underwear, and the appropriate number of Pillow Pets (the animal pillows that my sisters and I were obsessed with at the time). Suitcases finally packed, Pillow Pets in hand, we started to bundle up and head out the door.

But before we left, there was one thing I had forgotten about in all the rush: I needed to pee.

I scurried to the bathroom, pulled down my pants, and sat down. I shivered out a sigh and felt the familiar shudder of warmth leaving my body. For a second I felt relieved . . . but then I looked down.

Brownish blood covered my inner thighs and underwear.

Blood. From *inside* me.

I was *bleeding out*. I started to panic.

Without wasting a second to think about what was happening, I jumped out of my pants, tore off my underwear, and ran into the living room. Through tears I started to apologize for my impending death. I hugged my sisters and told them how much I loved them and that I wished I didn't have to leave the family so soon. But all they seemed to focus on was avoiding the gory underwear, still in my hand.

To my total shock, my loving mother broke into a know-it-all sort of smile. I stood rooted in my living room as she placed her hands on my shoulders and lit up with excitement. My twelve years of life were nearly over, and my mom *found it funny*?!

Wasn't the *blood* proof enough that I was DYING?

Jumping up and down, my mom started a celebratory chant: "You're a woman! You're a woman!"

Yes, I had gotten my first period.

Menstruation. Let's talk about it.

You may have a menarche story too and may be able to relate to this with a traumatizing or celebratory experience of your own. Perhaps you are hearing a menarche story (or are hearing period talk in general) for the first time. And that's great. Before we move on, though, I want you to sense if you're feeling squeamish or uncomfortable by my opening with a period story . . . because the goal is to get comfortable with it as you read on, with the hope that by the end of this book, we will have worked through the discomfort.

I'm from a family that talks about body parts and puberty. Whether in family conversations or one-on-one, my younger sisters, my mom, and I never shy away from talking about bodies, in all their gory glory.

When I was around seven years old, my mom would pick me up from piano lessons and sometimes take me to a restaurant nearby called Route 66, where she would answer my prying questions. It was sitting there, eating with my mom, that I learned where babies come from, how to tell when you're pregnant, and yes, even about *periods*. Every time my mom told me a new detail or fact about the female body or reproductive health, I felt a little bit more grown-up. It was like I was part of a special club or had some valuable secret that I couldn't yet share with my younger sisters. On several occasions my teachers sent me to the principal's office for taking the liberty of educating my peers about how they were made (and with what body parts). I have always found the capacity to create life unbelievably beautiful.

"Route 66" actually became a code phrase for me and my mom. When I had questions about bodies or sex but we were around my younger sisters, my mom would say "Route 66," and I knew that we would be sure to talk about it the next time we could grab dinner together.

Clearly I have always wanted to know about the human body. My parents and peers got used to constant streams of questions about puberty and sexuality. I wondered what boobs were and when I should expect my own. I looked at my full-body profile daily to see if I could notice any changing shape in my breasts, convincing myself every few months that I needed bigger bras (wishful thinking, completely). I noticed the physical differences between grown-ups and kids and was so excited for my own body to develop.

My mom bought me my first packet of panty

liners when I was in fourth grade. At the age of nine I *insisted* that I could already sense my period coming. Every time I cried, I credited it to premenstrual syndrome (PMS). But that was three years before I actually experienced my first period. In December 2010 I knew what a period was and felt genuine excitement in anticipation of my own big transition into womanhood. So why did I have that morbid and fearful reaction when I finally got my period?

Bottom line, getting your period for the first time is *scary*. No matter how mentally prepared you are, it is rare to be *emotionally* prepared for that moment. You can know the details of menstruation and have period products ready to go, but you still don't know what it feels like until it actually happens. I was so used to looking down at my underwear and seeing nothing that when one day there was suddenly blood, it was *shocking*.

Even though I had already asked my mom many, many questions, when I finally got my first period, there was still so much I didn't know—so much I didn't even know that I didn't know. I wasn't prepared at all to navigate those strange moments between discovering my period and actually securing a period product—and then somehow putting it inside myself, another foreign concept. If anything, I'd been expecting only a few drops of blood—not the brownish massacre that had happened in my underwear.

My experience is a unique one, and so is my relationship with my mom. I know this from what I've seen with and heard from my peers. Some of my friends in middle school got their periods before I got mine. Some were so scared and ashamed that they hid their periods from both of their parents. My best friend at the time was so embarrassed to tell her mom that she spent her allowance buying her own pads.

When I got my first period, my family was financially stable enough to always have basic necessities around the house. My having access to pads when I first needed them was a privilege, but it shouldn't be.

A few years after my first period, at a time when my family was experiencing housing and financial instability ourselves, I began to talk to homeless women living in much worse situations than I was in, women whom I saw on my way to and from school. I would meet them on my bus commute, most of them traveling to the shelters and soup kitchens downtown to get a meal, or killing time by waiting under the short awning of the rental car shop near my bus stop. Our conversations started casually, usually about the weather or about the loud music from the clubs down the street that started at around eight p.m., when I'd be coming home from school club commitments. We became sort of accidental friends as I saw these women more often, and as we became more comfortable with one another and as the winter months caused more bus delays, our topics of discussion got deeper.

In talking to these homeless women and with other women I met while volunteering at a local homeless shelter washing dishes and singing at morning church services, I felt immensely privileged. Unlike many of the homeless women, who were often squatting on the streets, I had my family, I had educational opportunities, I had a roof over my head, and I had a mother who I knew would always make sure that I had access to those things.

Unlike food or shelter, the issue of menstruation is ignored so significantly that these women sometimes had to use trash—such as newspaper, brown paper bags, and cardboard—to meet their basic hygiene needs. Hearing the stories of these women using such items stirred something in me: anger at the unfairness of it, and confusion at my own feelings of privilege in comparison, when I'd felt a lack of privilege elsewhere in my life. I felt a sense of duty to these women and their stories.

Over the course of several weeks, I became obsessed with periods. Using every free moment I had, I searched the internet for more information about the lack of access to menstrual hygiene. I wanted to know how it affected people differently—from all socioeconomic, racial, and religious backgrounds, and around the world.

Starting with the local homeless services in downtown Portland, I asked why none of these nonprofits had permanent services to provide period products to homeless menstruators. I usually got two answers: there was either a lack of funds or a lack of displayed need. There was a never-ending cycle of organizations not prioritizing menstrual hygiene, and thus not feeling any need to invest in tampons and pads. On the other side, homeless menstruators did not feel comfortable advocating for their menstrual needs, because menstruation is something that most want to hide.

I began passionately questioning why people were so afraid to talk about menstruation. I even reflected on why I felt so comfortable talking about it with menstruating peers and strangers but was terrified to bring it up with any cisgender men around me.

I continued filling my journal with the anthology of stories I heard from women, and at night before going to bed, I would add newly discovered facts found through Google about inequities and activism around menstruation. For example, periods are the number one reason why girls miss school in developing countries, partly because of a lack of access to adequate menstrual hygiene.[1] But also, in some countries a girl's first period signifies the transition from girlhood to womanhood, when she is ready to take on the roles of wife and mother—and this can mean child marriage, female genital mutilation, and even social isolation. I learned that in the United States, a majority of states still have a sales tax on period products because they are considered *luxury* items. Meanwhile, products such as Rogaine and Viagra are not.[2] My general reaction to this newfound knowledge: ARE YOU &@%*$&# KIDDING ME?! OLD-MAN HAIR GROWTH AND ERECTIONS ARE MORE OF A NECESSITY THAN FEELING CLEAN ON YOUR PERIOD? HOW?

In December 2014, a few months after my family got back on our feet, I founded what would become PERIOD, a global youth-run nongovernmental organization (NGO) that celebrates menstrual health through service, education, and policy. Within our first three years we grew to be one of the largest youth-run NGOs for women's health in the world, and the fastest-growing one in the United States. In just three years we addressed more than two hundred and fifty thousand periods through period product distribution to people in need, and registered more than two hundred campus chapters at universities and high schools around the United States.

When I started PERIOD, I worked with unrelenting passion, fueled by the inequalities I saw. With this feeling of purpose, I felt a hunger to do whatever I could, with whatever I had, to push forward access to period products for all. From what I could tell at the time, no one else was talking about the need for period products. I felt like I had something new to offer the world and a duty to speak up. I felt *empowered*. I talked to anyone who would listen about what I was trying to do—bring products to people who needed them in my own local community. What kept me going was realizing the power of my speaking up, finding peers to collaborate with, and hearing the stories of more homeless women as I continued to listen. I had no idea that PERIOD would grow into this larger movement for social and systemic change powered by youth—but I am thankful every day to play a part in the Menstrual Movement.

When it comes to breaking down the stigma around menstruation and fighting for equitable access to menstrual hygiene, we have serious work to do. Menstruation has been a part of the human experience since the very beginning of our existence. Yet as a global community we have still not acknowledged access to menstrual hygiene as a universal natural need—or, TBH, acknowledged menstruation at all. It is a human right for every individual to feel equally capable and confident, respected, and even empowered, regardless of whether one is menstruating or not.

But we must not be impatient and must instead stay persistent. Progress happens piece by piece, and it's easy to feel overwhelmed by this seemingly slow pace. I like to remember all the work we've done already as being as strong a part of the work as what we still need to do. All the work we do factors into the bigger picture, a future where equitable access to menstrual hygiene is not just a possibility or privilege but a right.

The movement for menstrual health is *not* just a "women's issue." Equitable access to menstrual hygiene intersects with other issues of social justice— whether we're discussing infrastructural development around the globe, creating equity in education, or breaking the cycle of poverty for those who feel economically trapped.

The Menstrual Movement is the fight for equitable access to period products and the fight to break down the stigma around periods—and it is just now starting to move into mainstream media and into popular conversation, especially among young people. It is up to us to start conversations and change the narrative around periods, so turn to your neighbor and ask, "Why are we so afraid to talk about something so natural?"

We need to feel comfortable talking about periods. We are all familiar with how taboo this topic still is, even here in the United States. Most of us menstruators share the experience of using code words to hint at the fact that we're menstruating, because we're uncomfortable just saying, "I'm on my period." Or we hide a period product in a pocket or sleeve before running to the bathroom, so that no one will know it's our "time of the month." I applaud you for simply picking up this book and taking a big step toward becoming what I call a "Period Warrior"—someone ready to fight the stigma around periods and start conversations about menstruation, regardless of how many giggles you may spark.

It's important to change the culture's view of menstruation, because some people continue to believe that because women menstruate, they are not as capable as men when it comes to holding positions of power or otherwise participating in society. We saw this recently in the 2016 presidential election. Many people said that Hillary Clinton could never be president because of her period (even though she was sixty-nine and presumably was done menstruating).

People claimed, *She can't be trusted. What if she's on her period and starts a war?* There are many reasons to criticize a politician, but having a period (even a fictional one) is not one of them.

My blood also boiled during a 2015 Republican presidential debate when one of the moderators, Megyn Kelly, pressed then presidential candidate Donald Trump about past misogynistic and sex-ist comments he had made about women. She cited instances in which he had called women "fat pigs" and "disgusting animals." He responded by saying that her questions were unnecessary and "ridiculous."[3] Perhaps in reference to her determination to find an explana-tion for his misogyny, Trump later said that he could see there was "blood coming out of her eyes . . . blood coming out of her wherever."[4] Her *wherever*? Trump discounted the legitimacy of her role as a moderator and disrespected her questions because of the possibil-ity that she was menstruating?!

Trump's comments were condemned for obvious reasons—and this wasn't the first time that Trump had referred to menstruation as a cause for what he perceived as a woman's crazed and overly emotional behavior. On Twitter, Donald Trump later tried to say that his comments had related to Kelly's having a bloody nose,[5] and he slammed "'politically correct' fools in our country. We have to all get back to work and stop wasting time and energy on nonsense!"[6]

This sort of language and period "humor" come from people in the highest positions of power. From the Oval Office to the hallways of elementary schools, menstruators are made fun of for possibly being on their period, as if menstruation lessens a person's emotions or intelligence. We *still* hear twisted humor in classrooms and on mainstream media that jokes about "manstruating," a term that implies that men and boys who express emotions and fears are probably "on their period."

I am not the first person to stand up and vocalize the need to change the way we think about periods; in fact, this is a movement that has been brewing and escalating for centuries. However, as a menstrual rights activist I have a fierce passion for bringing young voices to the forefront of this movement—and I strongly believe that we young people have a unique ability to do just that. In our digital, fast-moving world, this movement needs all hands on deck, and I have devoted my efforts to recruiting young people to join the army of Period Warriors.

Simply put, young voices matter. Politics and other conversations about social and systemic change focus on how to better our future, for everyone. And, well . . . who better to participate in those discussions than the *future* leaders of our world? Young people can make significant contributions toward both creating and implementing solutions to current problems, and we will be the ones to carry on the legacy of changing ideas.

Finding a purpose in the Menstrual Movement ignited a passion within me to advocate for and empower others who have not yet found their voice, especially relating to such a basic need as menstrual health. Leading PERIOD has taught me the power of organizing at a grassroots level, and it has given me a glimpse into the magic that can happen when young people are inspired, unite around a common mission, and activate a tapestry of collaboration and shared passion.

I really do think of my leadership of PERIOD as a lifesaver. I founded the organization, and in turn I found my own voice, immediately following a time when I had felt quite voiceless because of my family's and my own experience facing instability and abuse. This Menstrual Movement has pushed me to reclaim my body and my powerful voice, something I struggled with for so long. I am writing this book as a determined #PeriodGirl who is ready to get to work. I hope that this book will act as the cape, crown, and manifesto you may need to find your voice as a Period Warrior and superhero, because this movement is universal, and we need all menstruators and non-menstruators ready to fight the stigma. Let's show the world that periods are natural and that we all have PERIOD POWER!

CHAPTER ONE

•

THE BLOODY TRUTH

Periods are *powerful*. Human life would literally not exist without them. They are what make reproduction possible and keep our wombs ready to bear children, if or when we choose to do that.

The common experience of menstruation connects people all over the world. Think about it: if you were assigned female at birth, most likely you *will* get your period on a monthly basis for around forty years of your life. It doesn't matter where you are from, how you identify, or what access to resources you have. And if you don't get your period during menstruation age, it means that your body is telling you either that you are pregnant or that your health needs attention. Though, it's also important to know that when birth control is used without breaks, menstruation may stop as well.

To strengthen the way we advocate for periods,

we need to understand what a period is in the first place. In the United States we still live in a culture where there is no expectation that we'll learn about periods. Even when it is taught (in schools, by parents, by friends), it's often taught in a way that limits our understanding of what we might call the *menstrual experience*.

Basic sex education—if available—usually starts in the final years of elementary school and continues into middle school. For those of us who have already experienced it, we might have cringe-worthy memories of our teachers holding up bananas or wooden models of penises to demonstrate how to properly roll a condom on. My favorite memory is of when my eighth-grade science teacher took a red condom, blew it up, and shouted, "See? It works for *any* size!"

My experience with sex education in elementary and middle school was in gender-segregated classrooms. Teachers often shuffle boys into one classroom and girls into another. In the boys' classroom the health teacher might explain that the boys' voices are going to get lower, their testicles will descend, and hairs will grow in unfamiliar places on their bodies.

In the other classroom the girls are learning about their bodies too. They will learn about their own hair growth, about the development of boobs, and about hormones and the new emotions that they might start to feel. This might also be the first time periods are brought up in the classroom. The teacher will hold up a tampon and pad and explain what products are available and the basics of how to use them. But the *experience* of actually menstruating will not be covered. You won't find out what the blood will actually look like or what to do if you feel extreme pain while menstruating. The teachers won't tell you what you should do if you stop menstruating suddenly. The option of using sustainable alternatives such as menstrual cups and reusable pads, rather than a typical tampon or pad, will not be discussed.

From the moment the classroom separates into boys and girls, the girls learn to feel shame about openly talking about menstruation, and this prevents future conversations and questions from surfacing. Girls learn that the topic of periods is something you either keep to yourself or you mention only to other girls, in private circles. And boys often don't formally learn anything about menstruation. They are taught that it isn't any of their business, that it's weird to even be curious.

Menstruator or not, you still have to share spaces with many people who are. Everyone, regardless of sex or gender identity, should know what periods are and should feel comfortable talking about them—this is *necessary* in order to build inclusive and egalitarian communities. So, let's dive in.

• WHAT'S THE DIFFERENCE BETWEEN A PERIOD AND A MENSTRUAL CYCLE? •

"Period" and "menstrual cycle" are two terms that are used to indicate the time of the month when the body excretes blood, but the words don't mean exactly the same thing. The "menstrual cycle" refers to the approximately twenty-eight-day process during which the body prepares for pregnancy. A "period" is just one brief stop in a much larger menstrual cycle.

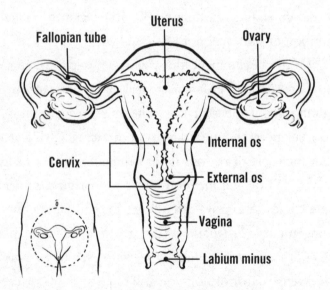

The diagram above gives us a look into a menstruator's pelvic area, right between the hips. The two ovaries hold the eggs, and the whole menstrual cycle is directed by two of our hormone friends: estrogen and progesterone.

At the beginning of each cycle, estrogen and progesterone trigger the creation of the endometrium, which is a lining on the inside walls of the uterus. Made of tissue and blood, the endometrium is spongy enough to make a perfect landing place for a fertilized egg. When pregnancy does occur, the uterus is often referred to as the womb.

Ovulation happens when a menstruator's ovaries release a matured egg about halfway through a menstrual cycle. As you can see from the diagram, in order to get to the uterus, the matured egg travels through the fallopian tubes. The egg basically just sits in the fallopian tube or the uterus and waits, hoping to be fertilized by a sperm cell. Most of the time pregnancy does not occur, which causes the uterine lining to break off from the uterine wall and exit the body through the vaginal canal. This action is what we call a period.

• THE BLOODY TRUTH ABOUT PERIOD BLOOD •

When I first got my period, I was scared. I knew what menstruation was, but no one had ever told me how period blood would look, smell, and feel. So, here it is—the bloody truth in all its glory:

What period blood actually looks like, how it smells, the color, and how much of it comes out will vary across menstrual experiences. There is no "normal" version of menstruation. All bodies are different, so period experiences will also be different. Yes, the menstrual cycle is approximately a twenty-eight-day interval, but the cycle is rarely precisely twenty-eight days—and some menstruators sometimes will bleed between periods.[1]

On average a menstruator will lose anywhere from five to twelve teaspoons, or about thirty to seventy-two milliliters, of blood in one menstrual cycle.[2] Sixty milliliters of blood or more is considered a heavy flow. But how can someone measure the amount of blood? Each regular-size tampon holds about five milliliters of blood;[3] so this means that if you are using more than twelve tampons per period that are getting fully soaked, then you should go see a doctor. Another way to figure out how much blood you are expelling is to use menstrual cups, which often have marks for measurement on their sides.

When period flow gets very heavy, more than eighty milliliters per cycle, it's called menorrhagia, and losing this much blood can cause one to feel tired and short of breath—both of which are symptoms of anemia. Having such a heavy flow is not only a hassle because more period products are needed, but it can also be extremely painful. The opposite of this condition, a very light period of less than twenty-five milliliters of blood lost, is called hypomenorrhea.[4] So what causes some of us to have only light spotting once a month, and others to experience prolonged menstrual cycles that involve changing pads multiple times in an hour?

Menstruators who have had children or are in perimenopause (the phase right before menopause) typically have heavier flows because menorrhagia can be caused by hormone imbalance—high estrogen and low progesterone leads to more bleeding and clots (passing more than one per day)—but menorrhagia can occur for a number of different reasons, such as certain medications that interfere with blood clotting, uterine fibroids (benign tumors), and polyps (benign growths).[5,6] What can you do to regulate or help lessen the pain of period flow? Use the right products for you, eat well, and exercise in a healthy way.[7]

The color of period blood can also be anywhere from dark brown or even black to a very vibrant red color. This difference in color does not necessarily have any implication for one's health when within the red spectrum. The color of the blood is dependent on how long the blood, tissue, or even clots have been exposed to oxygen. It's similar to how your blood changes color if you cut your skin. When you first start to bleed, the color is this very bright red. After letting the cut heal a bit (hopefully with a bandage and disinfectant), the scab that forms is very dark, almost purple. The color of blood darkens with more exposure to oxygen because the pigment concentrates as the water in the blood evaporates.[8] The brighter the period blood, the less time it has been in your uterus. The blood flow tends to get a bit heavier on day two or three of your period, so this is when the color of one's period blood might become brighter.[9]

The consistency of period blood is probably what people are most in the dark about. No one really tells you what your period is going to feel like, much less what the actual blood is going to be like. Most of my guy friends assume that period blood is watery, like when you get a bloody nose. *Incorrect.* Your menstrual blood might be watery some of the time, particularly in the first few cycles or in the final days of your period, but it won't only be like that—and it might not be like that at all for some menstruators. Since vaginal mucus also comes out during a period, the discharge is sometimes slippery and feels a bit like jelly. It's also pretty normal for period blood to look a little clumpy, from small blood clots. There is nothing to worry about if any clots appear on a period product or in the toilet. This just means that your body is pushing out the menstrual blood faster than your body can break down the clots. Clots are a concern only if they are the size of a quarter or larger.[10]

Do not feel embarrassed about how your period blood smells, and definitely don't try to fix it by douching. Douching and forcibly cleaning out your uterus can actually be very unhealthy because it changes the uterus's natural acidity. It is totally normal for your vagina and period blood to have distinct odors. In fact, menstrual blood is supposed to have that smell. Some might describe this smell as a bit metallic. It isn't just blood you're smelling; it's also mucus and tissue from the lining, as well as bacteria and other fluids. And the smell is stronger when these things sit in your uterus for longer.

If your vaginal discharge or period blood starts to have a fishy scent, that's when you should see a doctor. There are some common infections, such as bacterial vaginosis and trichomoniasis, that are known to have a fishy scent. Luckily, these infections can be easily cured with antibiotics.[11] The truth is, after the first few times, you'll get familiar with your period, and the smell of your own period blood and vaginal discharge will become completely recognizable. So, if you suddenly start to notice that it smells different, then you know to go to the doctor and ask questions.[12]

Pooping more during your period? Also *totally* normal. When progesterone levels suddenly drop immediately after your period starts (after reaching maximum production right before), that sort of release can cause your bowels to open up a bit more.[13]

• WHO MENSTRUATES? •

Menstruation usually starts when a person is between ten and fifteen years old, with the average age of menarche being twelve years old. There is no "correct" age when someone should get their first period, and there are a lot of biological and environmental factors that affect when menarche begins.[14] Usually, in the six months leading up to menarche, a menstruator will notice more vaginal discharge than usual.[15] Vaginal discharge is absolutely normal: it's a sort of housekeeping function where glands in the vagina and cervix produce fluids to help carry dead cells and any bacteria out of the body. The discharge can vary in color and texture but is usually a white or cloudy-colored thick paste.[16]

There are theories about the age at which menarche occurs and what it can tell you about your future and current life, especially since studies have shown that both hormones and stress can influence when you get your period. Some of these theories say that an early first period can signify an unsettled childhood, and that if menarche occurs at either a very young age or a very late age, that can mean a higher chance of heart disease.[17] Another observation is that experiencing menarche at a younger age is linked to breast cancer.[18] But ultimately the most important thing is that the first period (when blood actually comes out of the vagina) indicates that a menstruator has the ability to get pregnant.

The menstrual career (a term that we'll use to refer to the years when menstruation happens) extends until menopause occurs. After menopause happens, a person can no longer get pregnant.[19] There is no process to determine when a menstruator can expect to experience menopause, but in the United States the average age is fifty-two.[20] The process of menopause can be a strenuous one that may involve vaginal dryness, hot flashes and chills, abrupt mood changes, trouble sleeping, lower energy, and so on. Of course, different people will experience different symptoms, but having irregular periods during perimenopause is very common. A menstruator is considered to be in menopause when a full twelve months have passed without a period.[21]

It is not only women who menstruate. Some transgender men and people who identify as nonbinary or genderqueer (or others) but who were assigned female at birth might still experience periods. For many readers this may be the first time you've thought about the intersectionality of gender and periods before, but it is an extremely important discussion to have early on, to ensure that the Menstrual Movement is inclusive of all period experiences. I will admit that in my early days of menstrual activism, I did not consider that anyone other than women could experience menstruation. However, since learning about it, gender inclusivity when talking about periods has become one of my priorities.

It's important to use language that is inclusive of all menstrual experiences. For transgender men and genderqueer people (and others) who still experience menstruation and have uteruses, vaginas, ovaries, and fallopian tubes, periods can be very difficult—not only because of menstrual health management, but also because menstruation is a reminder that their sex (assigned at birth) does not match their gender identity. As you may have noticed, I avoid using terms such as "feminine hygiene" and "feminine products" in an effort to be gender-inclusive.

• WHEN YOUR PERIOD DOESN'T COME •

The word "menarche" is made up of two Greek words: "men," which means "month," and "arche," which means "beginning." So the term literally means "the first occurrence of a monthly event." It is the beginning of something that starts when you're young and continues through much of your life.

"Amenorrhea" is the word used to describe when menstruation is absent for someone who is of menstruating age—when they have missed three or more of their periods or haven't gotten their period before the age of fifteen. Amenorrhea is usually caused by pregnancy, breast-feeding, or menopause. When someone gets pregnant, they do not experience menstruation because the uterine lining is needed to cultivate the fertilized egg.[22] Amenorrhea can also be caused by a problem with the reproductive organs or unregulated hormone levels, or disruption of normal hormone levels as a result of birth control.[23]

Periods are sort of magical in the way that they can tell us when our bodies need a bit more attention. For example, I ran for city council in Cambridge, Massachusetts, when I was nineteen years old. Doing so was one of the most exhausting experiences of my life—from how emotionally draining it was to be under scrutiny at all times, to the physical fatigue of canvassing for at least four hours per day.

I did not get my period for the *entire* duration of my campaign—literally from the week before I announced my candidacy in March, all the way until the day after Election Day, November 8. My doctors could explain my period's break only in relation to the stress and perhaps increased and abnormal (for me, at least) activity that canvassing so often requires.

• WHAT IS PMS? •

In anticipation of a potential sperm cell that can fertilize the egg, two weeks prior to menstruation, estrogen and progesterone orchestrate premenstrual syndrome, more commonly referred to as PMS. It is not irregular to meet someone who doesn't fully understand what a period is but is *definitely* familiar with PMS—especially men who use the term "PMS" to refer to that "time of month" when they perceive women as more emotionally on edge.

Who hasn't heard jokes about PMS? When I was growing up, boys and girls being moody or overly emotional were called out for being "on their period." My sisters and I would also tease my mom about menstruating when she had odd cravings or would start randomly crying about things that seemed trivial to us. I heard these jokes on my favorite television shows and in school hallways as boys competed with one another to see who was more "manly." While all these jokes exacerbate the stigma around periods in a very negative way—by painting periods as something that makes women perhaps less stable and thus less capable—these assumptions are based on very real symptoms of PMS.

PMS symptoms, which affect an estimated 75 percent of menstruators, include "mood swings, tender breasts, food cravings, fatigue, irritability and depression."[24] Other symptoms include social withdrawal, having trouble concentrating, crying spells, heightened anxiety, muscle pain, and so much more. Though the list of potential symptoms is long, most menstruators experience only a few of them and not severely.[25] PMS is very normal, and symptoms can be reduced and even stopped with basic nonsteroidal anti-inflammatory drugs (NSAIDs) like Advil and Motrin, or basic hormonal therapy like birth control (which can help regulate or healthily stop periods).[26]

If the PMS symptoms are extreme, even to the point where the menstruator can't get out of bed, then they could be suffering from a condition such as endometriosis (which we will explore in a bit) or premenstrual dysphoric disorder (PMDD). PMDD is a severe form of PMS that induces a lot of pain, like strong menstrual cramps and headaches. Severe PMS like this is difficult to handle every month and can lead to poor mental health— the cramps and negative moods can seriously affect a menstruator's confidence and perception of their own ability.[27]

• DOES GETTING YOUR PERIOD HURT? •

> If you have to miss something because you have
> bad cramps, tell someone that is why! The more
> we legitimize periods and period pain, we will help
> people think of it as something that happens to
> everybody, which it does.
> —Elizabeth Yuko, sex educator and writer[28]

As I said, it's very common to experience some degree
of pain during your period. Most of the time it's perfectly normal and fine, even if it's unpleasant. At other
times the pain can be an indication that something is
wrong, so we do need to pay attention. Here are various kinds and causes of menstrual pain. I hope this
information doesn't scare you but rather empowers
you to know your body!

MENSTRUAL CRAMPS (DYSMENORRHEA)
Painful menstruation, also known as dysmenorrhea, is
the number one cause of absenteeism in menstruating
adolescents and in menstruators younger than thirty
years old.[29] Up to 80 percent of menstruators struggle
with varying levels of menstrual pain in their lifetime.[30]
At least 10 percent of these menstruators are tempo-
rarily physically disabled by extreme symptoms.[31]

Because menstrual cramps are so common,
young menstruators often assume it to be a natural
part of having your period—even when the cramps

are debilitating. While there are no cures for cramps, there are remedies that can reduce the severity of the symptoms, but in order to find the right treatments, menstruators have to speak out about their period experience. As more young women have come forward with their personal stories of feeling incapacitated by menstrual pain, dysmenorrhea has increasingly been recognized as a serious medical condition. It is important to talk about period pain—not only because it may help lead to more menstruators finding effective remedies, but also because severe menstrual cramps could actually be endometriosis, which is much more serious (and, if left untreated, can cause more permanent damage to internal tissue), rather than simply normal cramps.[32]

Menstrual cramps are caused by chemicals called prostaglandins, which are produced by the uterine lining that grows during the menstrual cycle. These chemicals cause surrounding muscles to contract, triggering sharp pains in the lower abdomen and lower back areas, similar to labor pains. The cramps usually start a few days before menstruation begins and last for up to four days. Other symptoms of dysmenorrhea include "nausea, vomiting, sweating, dizziness, headaches," and sometimes diarrhea.[33] These cramps usually start when puberty begins and will last for around a decade, so younger menstruators are more at risk for painful periods. Cramps also tend to be worse for those who have never given birth or who naturally have heavy flows.[34]

Nonsteroidal anti-inflammatory drugs (NSAIDs) such as Advil, Motrin, and generic ibuprofen can be used to block the production of prostaglandins—and these drugs are often more effective for period cramps than other basic painkillers, like Tylenol.[35] Some menstruators have their own home remedies for preventing painful periods—whether that be taking warm baths or using heating pads or sipping certain favorite decaffeinated teas. Menstrual cramps can also be lessened with a healthier diet that lowers the intake of fat, alcohol, and caffeine; and by engaging in less stressful and more active lifestyles.[36]

Cramping pain that is caused by a specific condition is called secondary dysmenorrhea, and an estimated 5 to 10 percent of menstruators suffer from these conditions.[37] These include endometriosis, uterine fibroids, and pelvic inflammatory disease.[38]

ENDOMETRIOSIS

Endometriosis is a gynecological disorder and chronic condition that makes menstruation a very painful and difficult process, with heavier flows, extreme fatigue, and chronic pain around the pelvis. Those who suffer from this condition may experience congestive dysmenorrhea, a fancy term for *really painful periods*, where the pain is a deep, constant severe aching. This intense pain usually begins before and ends after one's period. While endometriosis can typically occur in menstruators between the ages of fifteen and forty-four, the symptoms are more apparent for women in their thirties and forties.[39] Endometriosis may also cause deep dyspareunia, which means that sex is extremely painful—usually triggered by pressure on the cervix. Even going to the bathroom might be painful.[40,41] And it is not guaranteed that symptoms of endometriosis will stop after menopause, when menstruation no longer occurs.[42]

Endometriosis is a condition in which the uterine lining (the endometrium) grows outside the uterus.[43] The endometrial tissue will act normally and will thicken, break down, and bleed as it usually does during menstruation. However, when the tissue isn't in the uterus, there is nowhere for the blood to exit the body, so it gets trapped. This irritates the surrounding body tissue and can cause the tissue to scar and stick together. Too much adhesion of the tissue can even cause the pelvic anatomy to distort (like the colon sticks to the back of the uterus or an ovary).[44] In some cases of endometriosis, endometriomas (ovarian cysts made of endometrial tissue) may form.[45] These cysts are associated with heightened pain during menstruation.[46]

Endometriosis is also directly linked to infertility. A study conducted in 2009 found that about 47 percent of infertile menstruators had endometriosis.[47] Unfortunately, the condition never disappears once you have it, but the symptoms may be less severe at certain points.[48] Most symptoms will subside when menopause occurs, because endometriosis is an "estrogen-dependent disease."[49]

Endometriosis is extremely hard to diagnose because many of its symptoms are extreme versions of a usual menstrual experience. On average, someone with endometriosis goes seven years before any formal diagnosis.[50] The only way to diagnose endometriosis is with a laparoscopic inspection of the pelvis—an invasive procedure that uses a video camera to examine internal organs.[51] Another issue that may prevent a diagnosis is the fact that period pain is so common and there is no "normal" level of pain. Many menstruators underestimate the severity of their condition, and it's also difficult for doctors to gauge when period pain becomes serious enough to demand the laparoscopic surgery.[52] In 2011 a study found that 11 percent of all menstruators who had not already been diagnosed have endometriosis, and 6 to 10 percent of all menstruators of reproductive age have the disorder. If this holds true for the general population in the United States, then it is estimated that more than 6.5 million menstruators suffer from endometriosis.[53]

There is no cure for endometriosis, and there are limited options for treatment. Hormone therapy and some surgery are usually used to reduce the severity of symptoms.[54] In very extreme cases of endometriosis—where having your period may be absolutely debilitating—having a hysterectomy (an operation to remove the uterus) is a last resort. However, even then, endometriosis symptoms can reoccur because of tissue lesions that still exist.[55]

Lowering estrogen levels in the body by using birth control and other drugs also hinders ovulation and will likely compromise fertility, and the painful symptoms of endometriosis will recur as soon as drug usage ceases.[56] Fortunately, surgical treatment of endometriosis has been found to improve pregnancy rates for previously infertile women.[57] Lowering body fat percentage (eat well and exercise more!) and limiting the amount of alcohol and caffeine you consume can also help decrease estrogen levels, which helps decrease the severity of symptoms.[58] If these medical interventions do not improve the condition, there are also alternative methods such as acupuncture, naturopathic medicine, homeopathy, chiropractic treatments, and energy therapies to reduce pain.[59]

ADENOMYOSIS

Adenomyosis is a condition more prevalent in older menstruators closer to menopause age, when the endometrial tissue that normally lines the uterus actually grows into the muscular wall of the uterus. This makes periods increasingly painful because the tissue continues to act as it normally would—thickening, breaking down, and bleeding—but while embedded in the uterus. Symptoms include heavier and longer periods with much more cramping, and painful sex. The treatments that exist are anti-inflammatory drugs and hormone therapy.[60] The cause of adenomyosis is unknown, and the only known cure is a hysterectomy.[61]

UTERINE FIBROIDS

Uterine fibroids—also known as leiomyomas or myomas—are noncancerous tumors that "grow from the muscle layers" of the uterus.[62] Fibroids are not associated with any form of cancer, and their presence does not mean that a menstruator has a higher chance of developing uterine cancer, but they can cause period-related pain and other unfortunate symptoms. Uterine fibroids are surprisingly very common. By the age of thirty-five, about 30 percent of all women have fibroids, and 20 to 80 percent of women will have them by the age of fifty.[63]

The size of uterine fibroids ranges from undetectable

to the naked eye to much bulkier growths that can enlarge or distort the shape of one's uterus. Most people who have fibroids do not suffer any symptoms besides heavier flows and increased pelvic pressure and pain. However, in some cases—depending on the size, location, and number—fibroids can cause difficulty peeing or pooping, and increased back and leg pains. Because fibroids often don't cause any particular symptoms, it's sometimes really hard to tell if you have them. They can be found only if a doctor actively looks with a pelvic exam, ultrasound, or further confirming tests.[64]

Uterine fibroids are the leading single reason why a hysterectomy—the surgical removal of the uterus—is performed. The hysterectomy is the "second most frequently performed surgical procedure (after cesarean section) for US women who are of reproductive age."[65] More than six hundred thousand hysterectomies are performed every year in the United States alone, and "more than one-third of all women [aged sixty or older] have had a hysterectomy." And it is estimated that "approximately 20 million American women have had a hysterectomy."[66] There are four different types of hysterectomies, involving partial or total removal of the uterus, cervix, ovaries, and fallopian tubes. There is still a chance of pregnancy when only one ovary or fallopian tube is taken out.

However, for a total hysterectomy—which is the removal of the uterus, cervix, both ovaries, and both fallopian tubes—there is absolutely no chance of pregnancy.[67]

Two other less-invasive surgical procedures that do not involve removing the uterus are called a myomectomy (removes just the fibroids and keeps the uterus intact) and a myolysis (an electrified needle shrinks the fibroids and their blood supply).[68] Neither a myomectomy nor a myolysis affects a woman's fertility, but it is possible that after a myomectomy a doctor will recommend that the person give birth only through a cesarean section.[69]

Additionally, uterine artery embolization (UAE) is a minimally invasive approach to treating fibroids. In UAE an interventional radiologist uses local anesthesia so that a catheter can be inserted into the uterine artery (which supplies blood to the uterus) through a tiny cut made right at the top of your leg.[70] Through this catheter "small plastic or gelatin particles"—called polyvinyl alcohol (PVA)—are pushed into the blood supply. The PVA then "creates a clot that blocks the blood flow to the uterus and fibroids," which causes the fibroids to "shrink and die."[71]

Though any human with a uterus can have uterine fibroids, African American women tend to have more, get them at an earlier age, and suffer from more severe symptoms. Black women are also more likely to experience painful symptoms for longer before seeking any sort of treatment—and studies have shown that it is significantly harder for these women to find valid information on the effects of treatment options.[72] African American women are also 2.4 times more likely to have a hysterectomy than a woman from any other group.[73] And as women grow older, the risk of developing uterine fibroids decreases overall for most women but not for African American women.[74]

Lynn Seely is the CEO of Myovant Sciences, a biotechnology company that is working to develop "innovative therapies for heavy menstrual bleeding from uterine fibroids and endometriosis-associated pain." Companies such as Myovant are striving for a future where menstruators do not have to "suffer in silence, unable to realize their full potential," but can have their pain recognized and "treated with a pill, instead of invasive surgeries." Seely says that breaking the silence around menstruation is part of the journey to alleviating intense period pain. Talking about menstruation helps medical professionals diagnose conditions, it raises awareness about the demand for more research into solutions, and most important, it contributes to a future where people feel empowered to "speak openly about their experiences [and] to seek help if needed."[75]

PELVIC INFLAMMATORY DISEASE (PID)

More than eight hundred thousand menstruators are diagnosed with pelvic inflammatory disease (PID) every year in the United States. PID is "an inflammation of the female reproductive organs" that causes chronic pain around the pelvic area and difficulty with fertility. One in eight women who have been diagnosed with PID have difficulty becoming pregnant.[76] PID is usually caused by untreated sexually transmitted diseases (STDs), such as chlamydia and gonorrhea.[77] PID may be prevented by reducing STDs—so use condoms!

PID is curable once it is diagnosed. However, there is no treatment to fix the damage already done by the infection to the reproductive system. Once you are treated, you also have a higher chance of getting it again. If PID is not treated early, complications that may arise include the formation of scar tissue surrounding the fallopian tubes, long-term pain, infertility, and even ectopic pregnancies (when a fetus grows outside the womb, often in fallopian tubes).[78] Everyday symptoms of the infection include general pain in the lower back and abdominal area, longer and heavier periods, fever, painful sex, and a burning sensation while peeing.[79]

We as a society need to talk more about periods *and* about the related conditions, so that menstruators are better able to know their bodies and regulate their own health. We need to create an atmosphere in the medical field (and also with the general public) that encourages finding solutions to painful period-related infections. We need to educate others about these different health risks, and create an environment where menstruators aren't afraid to ask questions about their periods and talk about their menstrual experiences, so that we can collect more information to actually find solutions and make diagnoses much earlier and more accurately.

We have just begun to tap into the potential of how better understanding menstruation can improve daily life. There is a slowly growing wave of menstruators who are using their menstruation cycles as a way to plan out their social and work calendars. Some people are even relying on their cycles when making life plans, because they are more in touch with how hormones affect them. A good friend of mine, Mara Zepeda, an entrepreneur in Portland, Oregon, introduced me to this concept of planning around periods—which she learned from Miranda Gray's book, *The Optimized Woman: Using Your Menstrual Cycle to Achieve Success and Fulfillment*. Mara thinks of her menstrual cycle as having four seasons, each with its own energy, and plans how she works around this—from the number of hours she works or meetings she has scheduled, to how much social time she allocates for herself to tend to relationships. She says this understanding has allowed her to be more in touch with "what type of self-care and support was needed, and what was possible energetically."[80]

In order to increase equitable access to menstrual hygiene and education, it is essential that we understand what stands in our way. Our capacity to innovate and find solutions around problems related to menstruation is hindered by our inability to comfortably talk about and understand periods. We still live in a society where simply whispering the word "period" or "menstruation" can trigger a hailstorm of giggles and redden the cheeks of spectators from discomfort and embarrassment. This taboo and stigmatization of menstruation and associated pain creates a status quo that needs to change.

CHAPTER TWO

●

THE STATUS QUO

> Shaming processes run deep, not only among men, not only in inter-gender conversations, even among women.
> —Dr. Alma Gottlieb, co-editor of *Blood Magic*[1]

In the previous chapter we talked about what periods actually are and some complications menstruators can face. I hope that you are feeling better equipped to answer simple questions about the biology of menstruation. Now we get to work. I hope you're ready to confront that taboo!

"Taboo" literally means "banned on grounds of morality or taste" or "banned as constituting a risk." It is obvious that menstruation is *taboo*, but you don't yet know why. Prepare to have your mind blown. . . .

The word "taboo" comes from the Polynesian word "*tapua*," which means "menstruation." The word "tapua" more literally means both "sacred" and "menstrual flow," which leads to the thought that periods were considered "too powerful or horrible to even talk about."[2] Therefore, tapua was also considered a sort of "sacred law," often associated with customs on "menstrual seclusion rites," linking the word to the "male abhorrence of the menses," which refers to the utter disgust that men had (and have) for periods and to the "primitive fear of blood."[3] Throughout the last few centuries, these seclusion practices often "include three basic taboos: the menstruating woman must not see light, she must not touch water, and she must not touch the earth."[4] Forced social isolation practices like this still exist today, and in some parts of the world this extreme form remains.

A quick note: the words "vulva" and "vagina" also have etymologies that link back to patriarchal views of womanhood and bodies in general. I spoke with Annabel Kim, an assistant professor of Romance Languages and Literature at Harvard, about these words. "'Vulva' is Latin for 'womb,' but its etymological meaning is that of 'envelope,' or 'wrapper,' as in the envelope of the fetus. 'Vagina' is also Latin, and it means 'sheath.'" So the word "vagina" is meant to describe a cover to protect a sword, a.k.a. a penis. Professor Kim pointed out that these are problematic etymologies because they "conceive of the female sexual organs as being defined completely by the fetus or the penis and not having a proper identity of their own." She says that it is important to be conscious of the language that we use because although words such as "vagina" and "vulva" may seem completely neutral, in fact they have an inherent "misogynistic charge." Professor Kim asks, "If slang terms like 'woke' or 'lit' can become so thoroughly entrenched in our language, why can't new words for our genitals that don't partake in or reproduce sexist significations, explicit or implicit?"[5] (End of note.)

The menstrual taboo that we talk about today usually refers to the societal fear of talking about periods. Because of this universal understanding that people should *not* talk about periods in public, there are many code words that exist to refer to menstruation: "Aunt Flow," "Shark Week," "Strawberry Week," "the Rag," etc. It's hard enough to even get people to be comfortable with saying the word "period," let alone talk about its intricacies.

The effect of this established taboo is that if we do talk about periods, we usually do so only with other people who get their period. This in turn perpetuates the idea that only those who menstruate need to be responsible for learning about and discussing periods, and this ignorance by those who don't (and who tend to be in power) can then be held against those who do. This movement to break the silence around menstruation is not just for menstruators but for all humans. Our goal is gender equality, and fighting for the Menstrual Movement is one of the ways to reach that goal, and thus we need all gender identities to participate.

• SO WHY IS MENSTRUATION TABOO IN THE FIRST PLACE? •

Let's get one thing straight—period shaming and the stigma in general are straight up *misogyny* (prejudice against, dislike of, or contempt for women). So, thinking that something like menstruation, a natural process that is inherently associated with the female body, should be considered dirty and worthy of shame is misogynistic. Period.

There are several theories as to why periods are taboo. The theory that feels most true to me is the one that says periods make people uncomfortable because of how closely they are related to sex and pregnancy.

With changes in diet and health care over the decades, the menstrual career has gotten longer—menarche happens earlier and menopause happens later—which means there is a greater period of time in which pregnancy can occur. Until the twentieth century "most women spent the years between their first menses, around the age of 14, to their menopause, at age 35 or 40, either pregnant or breast-feeding."[6] Similarly, it's been shown that girls who get their first period earlier tend to lose their virginity earlier as well.[7]

The connection between sex and menstruation is also central to another, more controversial theory explaining the origin of the taboo, known as the "sex-strike" theory. In 1991 Professor Chris Knight (who teaches social anthropology at University College London) wrote the book *Blood Relations: Menstruation and the Origins of Culture*. In it he explained his controversial sex-strike theory that says *women* are responsible for advancing the taboo, which in turn created the male-dominated and -led patriarchal society. Knight believes that women didn't want their bodies touched during menstruation and hence they went on a sort of sex strike. So "only later did this taboo transform into something that compromised female autonomy."[8]

We may never know when period shaming and the overall taboo began. Because menstruation predates language, we do not have a record of what period talk might have been like before it could be documented.

Perhaps the earliest recordings of a word referring to menstruation are in the Kahun Gynecological Papyrus (an ancient Egyptian medical text written around 1825 BCE) and the Ebers Papyrus (from around 1550 BCE).[9,10] In both texts the word "*hsmn*" appears to refer to menstruation; some argue that the word also means "purification" in a positive light. In these texts there were even recipes for ointments that used menstrual blood to offer solutions to bodily conditions, including one "for saggy breasts."[11]

References to menstrual periods can also be found throughout religious texts such as the Bible and the Koran. Overwhelmingly these texts discuss menstruation as a reason why women are or should feel unclean or impure, especially while on their periods. The Koran, the sacred book of Islam, expressly instructs men to "go apart from women during their monthly course," and to avoid "them until they are clean" (Koran 2:222).[12] The Koran does not say that menstruating women cannot participate in usual religious practices during their cycle, but it is customary that they often sit out when they are menstruating. At first glance some might think it's misogynistic to not allow women to perform certain prayers, recite verses, enter a mosque, perform a pilgrimage, or participate in fasts, but when we look more closely, we see that these common prohibitions arise out of respect for the woman's preference.[13] The woman's body is focusing on cleansing itself, and until the cycle is completed, she does not have to participate in religious practices.

The Bible similarly refers to the monthly event of "menstrual impurity for seven days" in Leviticus 15, in which women are "unclean." In the case that a man comes into contact with menstruation, he shall also be considered "unclean and shall wash his clothes and bathe in water and be unclean until evening."[14] Everything on which a woman lies or sits during her time of menstrual impurity shall be considered "unclean until the evening" after washing both their clothes and own bodies. If "any man *lies* with her and her menstrual impurity comes upon him, he shall be unclean seven days, and every bed on which he lies shall be unclean" (Leviticus 15:19–24).[15] If period sex were to happen, then "both of them shall be cut off from among their people" (Leviticus 20:18).[16] So the taboo that establishes menstruation isolation is socially enforced by portraying periods as a sort of contagious disease of uncleanliness.

The taboo that encourages isolation and silence around menstruation has formulated and strengthened a persistent stigma. The word "stigma" means "a mark of shame." A stigma is an identifying characteristic associated with a particular quality or individual. We have created a society in which menstruators are taught to feel less confident and are too often considered less capable, simply because their bodies menstruate.

The period stigma tells us that menstruation makes women crazy, moody, and irresponsible. Suddenly our opinions and emotions are less legitimate because we have *raging* hormones. We have to refrain from participating in educational, professional, extracurricular, and social activities because we are considered weaker or because we might make others uncomfortable. The stigma causes people with periods to feel ashamed and embarrassed about their bodies and menstrual cycles.

The effects of the stigma are deep. It is common to experience heightened anxiety during menstruation—a time when an overcautious mind (especially in young menstruators) may be swarming with concerns such as: *Can someone smell and detect my period? What if someone notices that I'm wearing a pad? What if I bleed through my clothes?* God forbid that anyone finds out that you menstruate and has an opinion about it!

If the combination of the taboo and stigma tells us that periods are something menstruators should keep quiet and feel ashamed about, then to reverse the taboo and the stigma, we need to do the exact opposite. We will not be quiet. We will talk about periods openly and proudly—we will organize and talk about cycles and period products and menstrual health through megaphones on stages, and advocate for the Menstrual Movement to rooms full of initially uncomfortable listeners, who can then go on to do the same thing. BREAK THE SILENCE.

When I founded PERIOD in 2014, our original name was Camions of Care. The following year, 2015, was declared the year of the period by many news outlets, including NPR, BuzzFeed, and *Newsweek*, because of the seemingly sudden surge of activists demonstrating and speaking out about the persistent menstrual taboo and stigma. Since then, interest in this topic has skyrocketed. The media and the public are talking more about periods and the importance of menstrual health, as a need and as a human right—and that energy is why organizations like my own have been able to grow so rapidly.

My original goal for the organization was to have a mobile service that carried tampons around in a sort of truck and distributed them to homeless people on the streets who might need them. As an overly excited sixteen-year-old ready to get started with the project, I was desperate for a name for the organization. So I typed the word "truck" into a thesaurus and got "camion"—which apparently means "truck" in Latin, Spanish, and French. I tacked an *s* on to the word, and we got Camions of Care. Even then I was too nervous to have the words "menstruation" or "period" in my organization's name, because when I started telling people about what I was trying to do, I usually just got giggles in response. People couldn't get past the taboo.

After a year as a global organization, our board of directors started pointing out how much time we seemed to be wasting, both in press interviews and pitch competitions, just trying to explain what the name meant. We quickly landed on the new name "PERIOD" for our organization because we wanted to break the taboo around periods and just get people to talk about them. Consequently, throughout 2017 we had a campaign called Let's Talk about It, PERIOD.

For the campaign we worked with a digital agency called Swift, based in Portland, Oregon, to make some really cute GIFs that made fun of different euphemisms for the word "period," such as "Aunt Flow" and "Strawberry Week," and we would share them over social media on the twenty-eighth day of each month. The GIFs would begin with an image having to do with the euphemism, and it would morph into our logo: PERIOD. The goal? Just to get people to *read* the word, *say* the word, and *share* the word.

It's not a bad word! Yet it's treated like one. In conversations people *whisper* the word "period," like they have something to hide. When I spoke to homeless women, menstruation almost always came up. But even if no one was around, their shoulders would rise, they would look around nervously, and they would sometimes even cover their mouth to whisper the word "period." The obvious shame and embarrassment that they conveyed when talking about periods angered, stunned, and energized me. I realized that I had never thought about how nervous I myself felt when talking about periods openly. I had been so conditioned to accept that menstruation wasn't an appropriate conversation topic.

Talking about periods can be nerve-racking, especially when it involves advocating for menstruation to people who you *know* are going to be made uncomfortable by it. Many of our calls with chapters are to get them over the initial fear of just getting started on campus. It is very common to feel a bit afraid of how people are going to think of you after you start talking about menstrual blood, tampons, and pads so openly. Some chapter leaders can't get past the fear, and their career as a chapter leader might be short-lived because of that. I hope to not hear any more stories of Period Warriors' careers being cut short, because we're all needed in this Menstrual Movement. We should recognize the taboo—what we're up against—and understand the roots and persisting reasons for it, so that we can fight it, often by just talking.

Then again, it doesn't totally matter if *you* as an

individual are shamelessly comfortable talking about periods to anyone and everyone; at the end of the day, we still live in a society that as a whole considers the topic vulgar and off-limits. Young children quickly become familiar with the concept of "bathroom talk"—the discussions about poop, pee, and anything toilet-related. They're told that it's unacceptable to talk about these things at the dinner table, to strangers, and in public. These are the topics that prepubescent kids usually find hilarious, in part because of the restriction. Menstruation is often lumped into this category—but the menstrual taboo is a product of societal injustice.

If people react negatively when you discuss periods, this is a sign that your work is *needed*. Use that negative energy to *fuel* you. The Menstrual Movement exists because there is something worth fighting for: equality. Any pushback you receive is evidence that equality doesn't yet exist.

Your work as a Period Warrior and advocate really does start simply by *talking about periods*. Every person you are able to encourage to talk about periods, or even join you in the Menstrual Movement, is worth each uncomfortable conversation. If anything, when someone is adamantly against you, that just makes your job of convincing them that much more exciting—and makes the success of recruiting them into the Menstrual Movement that much more rewarding.

Cultures that celebrate menstruation do exist. Dr. Alma Gottlieb, an anthropologist and the co-editor of *Blood Magic*, told me about the Yurok tribe in California, which performs rituals around periods as a heightened spiritual experience. The women strive to sync their menstrual cycles, and anyone who is out of sync sits in the moonlight during a full moon for several hours so that her menstrual blood becomes synchronized with others. For ten days of each month, the Yurok women bleed together and "isolate themselves from men to engage in purification rituals that would heighten their powers and get them in touch with spiritual forces that they said empowered them." The men in the tribe engage in parallel purification rituals, also isolated from women.[17]

There is a concept I love called "menstrual transaction" that I was introduced to by David Linton (a board member of the Society for Menstrual Cycle Research). The concept recognizes that *yes*, there is this social phenomenon that surrounds menstruation that we all participate in. But we also very much have the power to change what that means. Both men and women—or anyone else, regardless of how they identify—play a part in "making up meaning" around how everyone relates and reacts to periods.[18] Whether we like it or not, as members of society we participate in carrying the taboo forward. It's up to us to break it, so let's do it!

CHAPTER THREE

•

PERIOD PRODUCTS

For all you menstruators out there, I'm sure that you're familiar with the experience of rushing to the bathroom while hiding your period product under a sleeve, or clutching it closely in a fist as if you were hiding a top secret product that would reveal something dirty to the world. I admit, I have many memories from middle school of my heart beating rapidly as I tried to hide a tampon under my shirt or in a sleeve, so that it would not be seen in a crowded hallway as I rushed to the bathroom.

Getting your period can clearly be nerve-racking, but fortunately, the taboo isn't so intrinsic that no one *ever* talks about periods. In fact, there is an entire industry dedicated to soaking up menstrual blood, with items that are often called hygiene products. Though some people in the Menstrual Movement take issue with the word "hygiene," I am not personally against using it when referring to period management. For too many menstruators, periods are not a safe or hygienic experience (which we'll explore a little later). Wanting to feel clean while menstruating does not mean that periods are inherently dirty, but it does mean that there are steps that one needs to take in order to not feel the wetness or smell the odor of one's period, and in order to avoid infection.

It was not until relatively recently (the beginning of the twentieth century) that today's more common period products were invented—and the story of how they came to be is also one of taboo and stigma. Menstrual pads have their source all the way back in "the 10th century in Ancient Greece, where a woman is said to have thrown one of her used menstrual rags at an admirer in an attempt to get rid of him." When disposable pads were not yet available, most menstruators used cotton rags, and even sheep wool or rabbit fur, to absorb their menstrual blood.[1] Fortunately, period product innovation has continued to today, and we are seeing more ecologically viable and inclusive products hit the market.

As Period Warriors in training, it's important to know what products are available—especially when it comes to access and affordability.

• THE PAD •

The pad is the most easy to use period product. It doesn't require the same level of comfort with your vagina that a tampon or menstrual cup does, because there's no insertion necessary. It is literally an absorbent pad (available in both disposable and reusable options) that is worn during menstruation. Pads are sometimes called "sanitary napkins," but most companies have begun (as much as possible) to shift away from language that implies that menstruation is inherently dirty. I choose to use the term "pad" because that's what it is—an absorbent pad.

There are several different types of disposable period pads that come in various shapes and levels of absorbency. Absorbency levels—which usually correspond to the thickness of the pad—range from ultra-thin to overnight, and all the way up to maternity-size (which are more like straight up pillows rather than period pads). There are also different shapes of pads to best accommodate the personalized needs of the menstrual experience. There are thong-shaped panty liners that are quite short and shaped like a triangle rather than a long oval. There are also very long pads that stretch from the vagina to what feels like the top of your butt—these are often helpful for sleeping hours when you're spending more time lying down.

One of the benefits of using pads rather than tampons is that there is no real hour limit for using one. There is no extreme health risk, like toxic shock syndrome (TSS) with tampons, so you can just change the pad when you feel it's necessary. You will most likely want to change your pad when it's no longer able to absorb any more menstrual blood and starts to feel wet and uncomfortable. And you'll *know* when you know. It *is* important to change pads regularly, especially when they're filled with blood, because pads can put you at risk for infections that might cause a rash, for urinary tract infections (UTIs), or for other vaginal bacterial infections. Another benefit of using pads rather than tampons is that there's a smaller chance of menstrual blood staining your underwear.

Disposable pads act like stickers to your underwear. To use them, simply find a clean area where you can pull down your pants, remove the paper from the pad's adhesive backing, and stick the pad to whatever underwear you're wearing, in a place where it will best absorb the menstrual blood coming from your vaginal opening. Oftentimes there are two adhesive "wings" in the middle of the pad, one on each side. When you fold these wings over the sides of your underwear, that better secures the pad.

Cloth menstrual pads are the reusable option. These act just like disposable pads and are even shaped similarly, with two absorbent wings on the side. In the long-term these are the more sustainable and afford-able pad option. The wings of a reusable pad can usu-ally snap together around the underwear so that the pad doesn't move around.

When you're ready to change your pad, whether disposable or reusable, simply remove it from your underwear and replace it with another one. If you're using disposable pads, roll up the used one and throw it away in the trash. DO NOT FLUSH. Most public bathrooms will have a small trash can in each stall. If you regularly use a bathroom that doesn't have a trash can in each stall, then make it happen. Be fear-less and talk to whoever is in charge about making sure there is access to a receptacle available to dis-pose of your period products.

If you're using reusable pads, then remove the pad from your underwear and wash. At home you can either hand-wash the pad and hang it up to dry or throw it into the washing and drying machines. If you're washing the reusable pad in a load of laundry, an easy trick to make sure that no menstrual blood gets on other clothes is to hand-wash the reusable pad in cold water first. Of course, there are going to be times when you feel like you need to change your pad but you aren't anywhere close to a bathroom to do so; for this reason I suggest finding cloth pads that have a plastic lining on the bottom, to prevent blood from soaking through and staining your clothes.

It is very normal for stains to occur on reusable pads. To prevent these stains from becoming more permanent, just soak your pad in cold water immediately after use. (This also works for bloodstained clothing from leaks!) You can always choose cloth pads made with darker fabric as well, so that bloodstains don't show up.

•TEAM TAMPON •

The word "tampon" is defined as a "plug of soft material inserted into the vagina to absorb menstrual blood." The word derives from the French word "*tampon*," which means "plug" or "stopper." In the nineteenth century, "tampons," as these wads of fabric were called in French, were used by soldiers to plug bullet wounds.[2] So, quite literally, a tampon is meant to act as a sort of vagina cork to absorb the blood from the uterus so that it does not leak out during menstruation.

The attraction of using tampons rather than pads is that you have the freedom to swim without leaks and move without always feeling something between your legs, and you don't have to worry about a bulge. Though, I say, "Own that pad bulge if you have it!"

And just like with pads, tampons vary in absorbency levels, from light to ultra-heavy.

A plastic or cardboard applicator can be used to insert the tampon. The cardboard applicator is more earth-friendly but doesn't have the rounded tip that allows for easier and more comfortable insertion. However, as ecological awareness increases and we see more of a desire to minimize personal trash, the use of plastic and even cardboard applicators has decreased in favor of digital tampons (as in, insertion using your finger). These tampons do require that the menstruator be a bit more comfortable with touching themselves.

In every box of tampons, instructions will be included. But here are some standard directions for inserting a tampon.

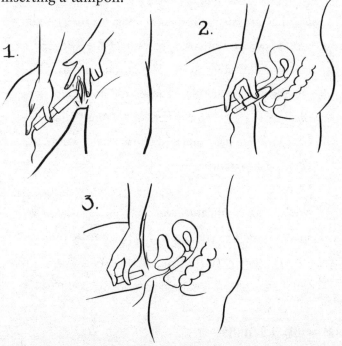

Prepare

Wash your hands. Grab a tampon, take it out of the wrapper, don't drop it on the floor, and hold it in your dominant hand.

Position yourself

Sit or stand in a position where you feel comfortable. I prefer to sit on the toilet, but you might find it more comfortable to stand with a slight bend in your legs. Every menstrual experience is different, so explore what position feels right for you.

Position the tampon

With an applicator tampon

Hold the tampon with the string end facing away from you. You may notice places on the applicator that are meant for your fingers, usually right around where the larger section of the applicator meets the smaller tube. Have your pointer finger resting on the very end of the applicator farthest away from you, where the string is hanging out. Your pointer finger will eventually guide the tampon into your vagina.

With a non-applicator tampon

Hold the end of the tampon, and aim the tip of it toward your vaginal opening. The string should be pointing away. Some directions for non-applicator tampons may specify that you use the string to expand the cotton into an umbrella-like shape so that you can place your pointer finger directly inside the tampon to push it into your vagina. But regardless, your finger becomes the applicator.

Spread the labia—we're almost there!

Using your nondominant hand—the hand that is not holding the tampon—spread the labia (the folds of skin on the two sides of your vaginal opening). Keep breathing. Touch the end of the tampon to the vaginal opening.

Push it in!

We're almost done! Keep breathing, and slowly insert the tip of the tampon into the vaginal canal. If you are using a tampon with an applicator, once you have inserted the applicator as far as it will comfortably go (the fingers of your dominant hand, which should be at the end of the large section of the applicator, will actually touch the labia), use your pointer finger to push the smaller part of the applicator (the thin tube) into the larger one. When this happens, the thin tube pushes the tampon out through the tip of the large section of the applicator and into you. Once the tampon is pushed in, you should be able to remove the applicator and throw it away.

If you are using a non-applicator tampon, push

the tampon up into the vaginal canal with your finger. Once the entire tampon is inside you and just the string sticks out, then the job is done.

Check the string

Whether or not the tampon you are using has an applicator, make sure that the string is hanging out when you're done. This is important for removing it.

Wash your hands and enjoy the day!

Go about your life and enjoy it. Feel confident and capable; act upon your potential.

Removing and changing your tampon

Change your tampon after eight hours maximum, sooner if you feel like you need to (like if it becomes uncomfortable or you begin to see leaks). To remove the tampon, just pull it out using the string. You may experience a feeling of pressure when you first start pulling on the string. If you still need a tampon, just repeat the process! You got this!

Avoid flushing the tampon down the toilet. Instead put your used tampon into the trash. It's important not to flush it because these products are specifically designed *not* to break down in water and instead to absorb and hold liquid. So flushing a tampon will ruin the plumbing.

Don't be discouraged if your first time trying to use a tampon doesn't work. It takes some practice. But don't worry. Soon enough your muscle memory will take over, and it will feel like second nature. It's also totally fine to prefer not to use tampons.

Here are some tips and tricks if it's your first time using a tampon:

Breathe

Yes, it can be nerve-racking! That is totally understandable! After all, you're trying to put a frickin' cotton ball inside you—it is a bit odd. Just breathe. As you relax, this will open up your vaginal canal a bit more so that the tampon can slide in more easily.

Tampon lube?!

Sort of. If it feels too dry around your vaginal opening and you're having a hard time pushing the tampon or applicator inside you, try using some vaginal lubricant (the best-known brand is K-Y Jelly, which can be found at any grocery store) to help make the process (literally) glide more smoothly.[3]

Look at your vag

Don't be afraid. Some people find it very helpful to use a mirror the first few times using a tampon. Menstruators have three holes in the genital area, and yes, it can be confusing if you have never explored.

If needed, find a handheld mirror, and actually look at what you're doing and adjust where you're aiming the tampon to start.

If the tampon is inserted properly, the menstruator should not feel it in any way once it's there. You may feel the string at first, but your body will likely adjust to it quickly. And there should be only minimal chafing, if any, from the string. The only times you have to change a tampon are when you hit the eight-hour mark for the recommended maximum time of absorption or when you feel it's full. If you have a heavy flow, you'll have to use a tampon that's more absorbent, or you'll have to change more frequently. Seeing blood on toilet paper after you wipe yourself is a sign that the tampon has absorbed quite a bit of blood and is ready to be changed.

You do *not* have to change your tampon when you go to the bathroom, because urine does not come out of your vagina—there's a whole separate hole for that, called the urethra. And I think you already know that the same goes for poop—that comes out somewhere else too.

The major risk associated with using tampons is that if they're left in for too long, bacteria may grow and lead to toxic shock syndrome (TSS). Some symptoms of TSS are muscle aches, headache, redness of throat, sudden high fever, dizziness, vomiting, red eyes, sunburn-like rash, and diarrhea, all of which can easily be mistaken for general symptoms of the flu. If TSS is not diagnosed early enough, the syndrome can progress extremely quickly. And if it goes on long enough, the infection can spread into other parts of your body and may cause the loss of limbs to amputation, and in the worst cases TSS can even cause death. It is advised that if you have these symptoms of TSS—headache, sudden fever, dizziness, and so on—remove the tampon immediately, and contact your doctor.[4]

I know that TSS can sound very scary, and you should talk to your doctor if you have any concerns. But bear in mind that tampons alone do not cause TSS. It's the improper use of tampons (mostly leaving them in too long) and the development of bacteria that can lead to TSS. There are very easy ways to lessen the chances of ever developing TSS, such as:

Clean tampon insertion
Make sure to wash your hands before inserting your tampon! It may sometimes be a pain, but those extra few seconds to wash your hands can really make

a difference. If you want to be extra careful, you can also make sure that your nails aren't too sharp and that you don't cut any of the skin in or around your vagina, which might increase susceptibility to bacterial development.

Change your tampon!

This is one of the main reasons I do not personally use tampons. There is a *strict* time limit to how long you can leave a tampon in. And PLEASE promise me (and yourself, for your own well-being) that you will not leave your tampon in for longer than advised. Most manufacturers recommend changing your tampon every four to eight hours.

Here's a tip: don't go overboard! When I first got my period, right after I inserted my first tampon, my mother told me the story of how her friend lost a limb and almost died from a bad case of TSS. (Thanks, Mom. Great timing.) So for my first few cycles, I changed my tampon *at least* every four hours—and that was way too much for my body. I started to chafe from applicators and tampons being pushed into and pulled out of me so frequently.

Use a pad, not a tampon, when sleeping

This doesn't pertain to everyone—some people really prefer to use a tampon instead of a pad when sleeping, for purposes of comfort. Most doctors and health educators, however, advise people to alternate between using tampons and pads, and to use only pads during sleeping hours. Even if you're pretty sure that you won't be sleeping more than eight hours (the time limit for keeping a tampon in), developing TSS is not something you want to risk.

Do *not* use a tampon if you're *not* menstruating

I'm not sure why you would think to use a tampon if you weren't menstruating, but just don't do it.

• THE MENSTRUAL CUP •

Ah. The menstrual cup. If you ever want to distract me from what I'm saying, just mention the menstrual cup, and I will instantly go on and on about my love for mine. So, since you asked:

Getting my first period was a big moment for me. I was so excited to finally "become a woman," I started using cardboard applicator tampons that first night. As a newly menstruating woman who was terrified of contracting TSS, I changed my period products much more often than necessary, and this was exacerbated by the fact that I hated doing laundry, so I often doubled up on pads at sleep time to avoid staining my underwear or bedsheets. Within days of my first period, I became so frustrated with myself by how quickly I'd filled our bathroom trash can with those colorful wrappers from the many pads and tampons I had used. After my first cycle, I was hungry for a more earth-friendly option.

Before I got my second period, I spoke with my mom about other, more earth-friendly options for period products. She told me about a silicone cup that she stuck inside her vagina during her period. The cup diminishes TSS risk (because it collects instead of absorbs period blood) and has no additional wrapping, and she could easily rinse it in the bathroom sink.

When my mom told me about this magical period cup, I was confused. I was excited about the prospects of having a more relaxing period experience because I wouldn't have to worry about TSS or my environmental impact—but I was mostly confused. When my mom had said "cup," I'd imagined a foldable coffee mug that she expected me to roll up and fit into my vagina. At the time even the cardboard applicator felt like a stretch—both for my body parts and for my emotional readiness to stick anything inside me.

I trusted my mom, though, and as soon as she warned me that I might not be able to use the cup because I wasn't very experienced with my body or period yet, the insecure and overly competitive little girl (who is still with me today) was motivated to become an avid cup user. The next day was grocery day, and my second period had just begun.

When my mom got home from shopping, I met her at the car. She said she would give me the cup once all the groceries were in the kitchen. That was the fastest I had ever carried the grocery bags up to our third-floor apartment. My mom proudly handed me the pink-and-purple box of my very first DivaCup, and for the next hour I repeatedly read the instructions, trying different folds of the cup until I got it successfully positioned to prevent leaks. With great pride I washed my hands and strutted up to my mom to tell her of my great feat. I did not take that DivaCup out for the next few days, because I was so excited that there was little risk for TSS . . . and because it hurt very badly every time I tried to pull it out. It wouldn't be until a few periods later that I finally got the hang of emptying out my cup every few hours, as you are supposed to do.

Since that first day of using my menstrual cup, I haven't used anything else. It wouldn't be until November 18, 2017, during the very first PERIOD CON (the world's first youth activism conference on menstruation, hosted by PERIOD), that the co-creator of the DivaCup, Carinne Chambers, would offer to replace my original when I oddly boasted to her about how much I loved the product and how I had used the exact same one for almost seven years straight. While it is possible to continue using the very same menstrual cup for as long as a decade, most manufacturers recommend changing it every two to four years because of the unattractive discoloration of the cup.

I assure you that when you meet women who normally use menstrual cups, you will feel from them an overwhelming passion for the product. The feeling when you make the switch from a disposable product (that you have to pay for monthly, and that creates waste) is absolutely glorious. Still, today surveys have found that almost 98 percent of women in the United States use a combination of disposable period products, while only "2 to 3 percent opt for reusable products."[5]

Menstrual cups are one of the most sustainable, affordable, convenient, and comfortable options for menstrual hygiene. Using disposable period products for an entire menstrual career can cost thousands of dollars, for upward of "17,000 tampons and pads," and create tons of waste. Meanwhile, a single menstrual cup costs around $20 or $40 and doesn't often need to be replaced.[6] A 2011 study by Canadian physicians revealed that more than 90 percent of women who tried menstrual cups liked them so much that they would recommend them to fellow menstruators.[7]

When you first look at a menstrual cup, it's

intimidating—but once you get past the initial fear, the long-term comfort and ease is so worth the effort. You will find your own way of inserting the cup that is perfect for you.

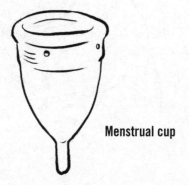

Menstrual cup

So how do you use this magical cup? It's a simple four-step process, similar to the insertion of a tampon:

Fold the cup

There are a few different folding options; I tend to use the C-shaped fold.

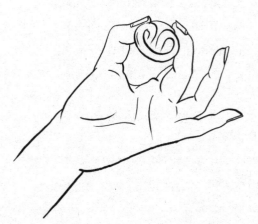

Hold it with the cup part facing toward the vaginal opening.

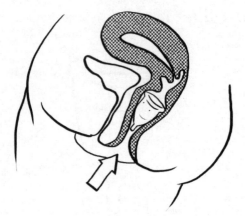

Insert

After the cup is inserted, wait for a suction sort of feeling before removing your fingers.

Remove

To remove the cup, reach inside your vagina (you will immediately feel it), and pull on the stem until you reach the base of the cup. Give the base a pinch to break the suction. Then pull the cup all the way out. Empty the menstrual blood into the toilet.

Wash, rinse, repeat!

To wash your menstrual cup, you can use fragrance-free soap and water. For a deeper cleaning before storage, you can boil your menstrual cup.[8]

• SO WHAT DID PEOPLE USE BEFORE THESE MODERN PRODUCTS WERE INVENTED? •

It's only recently in history that these products have actually existed. For menstruators in our grand-mothers' (and even mothers') generation, their first period product was most likely the belt. The sanitary belt was patented in 1956 by Mary Beatrice Davidson Kenner, who filed more patents than any other African American woman in history. Because of her race, though, Kenner has become a "forgotten black woman inventor," despite her contribution to revolutionizing period products in her time.[9]

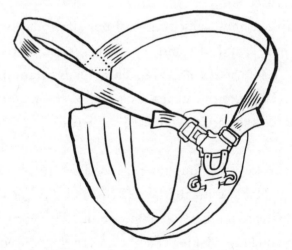

The belt-and-pad model was the mainstream solution until the 1970s. Even though modern tampons and stand-alone disposable pads became available in the 1920s, "catalogs and stores of the time, and until the early 1970s, sold dozens of models"[10] of belts. These were essentially jock straps with a pad-like wad near the vaginal area to absorb the menstrual blood. The belt itself was a thong-like elastic that sat on one's hips, and the cloth or disposable pads had tabs at each end that were attached to this belt.[11] The emergence of the disposable pad with adhesives to stick the pad to underwear is what eventually killed the belt-and-pad market, but it still took a while. Any talk about period product alternatives such as tampons was considered sexually improper, and so tampons couldn't be heavily marketed.[12] The taboo kept belts successful.

Kotex pads, which are still popular today, were the first brand of sanitary napkins to hit stores in the United States in 1920. These pads were made from Cellucotton, which was one of the materials used to take care of wounded soldiers during World War I.[13]

The kind of tampons that we have today were not available until the late 1920s and did not gain mainstream market acceptance until 1936, when the Tampax brand launched. They were introduced to the market under many brand names, all hoping to make it big in the blossoming period product industry. Some of the tampons that appeared were called "Fax,

Fibs, Holly-Pax, Moderne Women, Nappons, Nunap, Slim-pax, and Wix. Some claim Fax was the first."[14]

• SO WHOSE IDEA WAS THE TAMPON WE'RE FAMILIAR WITH TODAY? •

A dude! A dude came up with the first tampon! In the early 1920s John Williamson, then working at Kimberly-Clark, used a condom to make what would become a tampon. He poked some holes in the condom, took some Cellucotton (the material that was used in the Kotex pads at the time), and put it inside the condom. Williamson's father also worked for Kimberly-Clark,[15] and the young Williamson pitched his idea of this condom-based tampon to his father as a potential solution for periods. Legend has it that John's father refused to even consider his son's idea, saying he would never think to put "any such strange article inside a woman!"[16] John ended the experiment after his father warned him that if he were to mention the idea to anyone, he would be "so loaded with legal problems that [he'd] never get out of court."[17]

The elder Williamson's concern about sticking something into a woman's vagina was widespread at the time. People thought, *What do you mean you can't feel it when it's inside you? What does that mean for a girl's purity? Will it break her hymen?*

The version of the tampon that John Williamson created didn't have an applicator, and that was perhaps another reason for its short-lived career—it required an implied familiarity that was uncomfortable for the company.

The first cardboard tampon applicator, invented by Earle Haas, appeared in 1931.[18] Haas's motivation to create a method of menstrual hygiene that could be used intra-vaginally came from the challenges he had witnessed his wife struggle with as a ballerina trying to hide the bulky pads that were used at the time. Haas independently came up with the idea for creating the first tampon after a female friend told him that she had been using a small sponge inside her vagina to absorb her menstrual blood.[19] The addition of the applicator to the tampon lessened the "moral and hygienic concerns surrounding their use."[20]

The version of the tampon that he created was made with compressed cotton, and the applicator was constructed for easy insertion, without the need to actually touch or reach inside the vagina. This applicator was made from "telescoping paper tubes," the same as they are now.[21]

Haas earned the patent for his creation in 1933. "Combining the terms 'tampon' and 'vaginal packs,' he called his product Tampax."[22] Haas sold both the patent and the trademark to Gertrude Tenderich for just thirty-two thousand dollars.[23] She then grew the brand and business of Tampax from her own home,

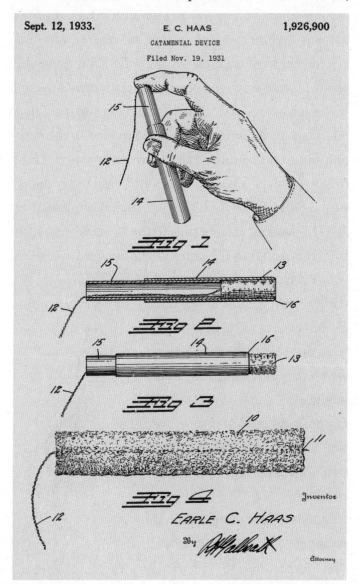

Sept. 12, 1933.

E. C. HAAS

1,926,900

CATAMENIAL DEVICE

Filed Nov. 19, 1931

Fig 1

Fig 2

Fig 3

Fig 4

Inventor

EARLE C. HAAS

By

Attorney

hand making all the tampons using Haas's compression machine and her own sewing machine.[24]

Tampax hit stores in the mid-1930s and became an immediate success. The demand for such a product was high because of women's increased physical activity during and after World War II. Boxes of the product were delivered by mail to customers directly, with each box priced at thirty-five cents and including ten tampons.[25] Tampax continued to lead in the tampon industry even as other larger corporations tried to get into the market with very similar products, such as Kimberly-Clark's Fibs (a digital tampon).[26,27]

The leading pad brand at the time, Kotex, also tried to break into the tampon market with a version of a tampon that was inserted with a stick. This was supposed to be easier to use than the telescoping cardboard inserter, which they described as a "bulky applicator." Their version of the tampon, called Kotams, looked like a sort of lollipop, with two strings attached for easy removal.[28,29]

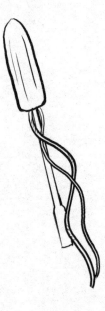

One of the selling points for tampons at the time was that they were able to completely hide that a woman was menstruating—a magical concealment of any period signs. This also led to the creation of other products for concealment, such as deodorant for the vaginal area and deodorant tampons. However, deodorant tampons, which are still available for sale today, sparked concern from physicians because of allergic reactions.[30]

The plastic applicator that we know of today, with the dome-shaped top for easier insertion, was introduced to mainstream markets by Playtex in 1973.[31]

• BUT WHAT ABOUT THE MENSTRUAL CUP? •

Though it may seem like menstrual cups are the newer alternative to pads and tampons, the first menstrual cup, called the "Menstrual Receptacle," was patented all the way back in 1884 by Hiram Farr. And for anyone who menstruates, it seems obvious that this was invented by a man. I mean, it was designed to hold *multiple cups* of menstrual blood. The upper section labeled with a lowercase *a* (see diagram following) was to be inserted into the vagina. The blood would go through the tube (labeled B in the diagram) and would then be held in the wider chamber (labeled A), worn outside the vagina. When it was time to empty it, the cap (labeled e) was unscrewed so that the menstrual blood could be poured out without having to remove the main device from the vagina. What is remarkable about the Menstrual Receptacle is how much more involved and comfortable it demands the user to be with one's vagina—especially considering this was patented in the 1880s.[32]

H. G. FARR.

MENSTRUAL RECEPTACLE.

No. 300,770.   Patented June 24, 1884.

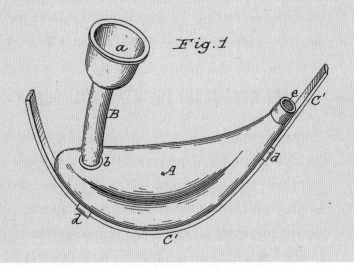

The modern menstrual cup as we know it was patented in 1935 by Leona Watson Chalmers, an actress and inventor in the United States—only two years after the modern applicator tampon was patented by Haas. She called her device the "catamenial appliance."[33] The word "catamenial" means "of or relating to menstruation"; "catamenia" refers to menses. Chalmers was inspired to invent the cup because she herself was searching for a more convenient and less time-consuming product. As an actress she was constantly working a busy schedule and touring—often as a member of the Harold Square Opera Company—so she needed a period product that did not demand that she rush to private spaces consistently throughout the day to make sure it was still in place under her garments. This was especially the case during performances in which she played the lead character; she could not have her period cause her to miss any cues to go onstage.[34]

In 1909 Chalmers landed the "lead role of Adelina in the upcoming Broadway premiere of *The Climax*." This role had her in a delicate white dress, which wouldn't be able to cover the "bulky straps, suspenders, and girdles" that were needed to keep pads strategically placed to absorb menstrual blood. As a solution she and other menstruating actresses in her touring group made "something akin to homemade tampons" by "rolling up scraps of fabric and manually inserting them."[35]

Decades after Chalmers's touring days as a lead actress, she referenced such experiences as the core inspiration for her invention of the first modern menstrual cup. In her book *The Intimate Side of a Woman's Life*, published in 1937, she wrote "it eliminates belts, pins, napkins, and inconvenience," and "the device does not have to be removed in answering a call of nature. It is truly a Godsend to professional and business women."[36]

Other menstrual cups had been available before this one, but Chalmers was the first person to both market and sell the product to the public. What made her product more successful than all others was that hers was made of softer material: vulcanized rubber.[37] The cup that Chalmers made also came with illustrated instructions that look almost identical to the ones we see today.[38]

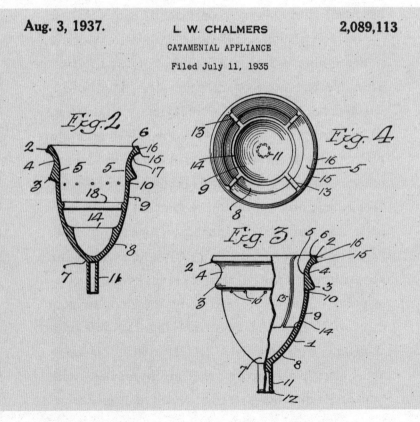

Aug. 3, 1937. L. W. CHALMERS 2,089,113
CATAMENIAL APPLIANCE
Filed July 11, 1935

Back then (and even now) menstrual cups were not an appealing option for women who were hesitant to interact with their own vaginas and menstrual blood, and who saw disposable products as much more attractive. For a while during World War II, menstrual cups were not being produced, because of a rubber shortage.[40] But in the late 1950s, Chalmers partnered with Robert Oreck, the president and founder of Tassette, Inc., for the restart of menstrual cup production.[40] "*Tasse*" is a French word for "cup," and the "-ette" was added to describe the product as a "little cup" for one's period.[41]

The reintroduction of these menstrual cups with more widespread advertising was not successful, and without making a profit, Tassette dissolved in 1963.[42] However, Tassette's attempt to sell the menstrual cup did expand boundaries for the industry of menstrual hygiene. It is said that in 1961 they displayed the first "outdoor ad devoted to a feminine personal hygiene item." The thirty-by-forty-foot billboard promoting Tassette was displayed prominently on the corner of Broadway and Forty-Sixth Street in Times Square.[43] During a time when it was still extremely taboo to talk about periods and period products in public, this was a major step for the fight against the stigma.

It wasn't until 1987—when another menstrual cup called the Keeper, a latex version of the menstrual cup, came out—that the market for menstrual cups started to be profitable. But even then the cup was not very successful, because it wasn't very durable, nor was it hypoallergenic.[44]

The most well-known brand of menstrual cups now is the DivaCup, founded in 2001 by a mother-daughter duo. Francine Chambers (the mom—president and cofounder) had been dreaming about founding her own menstrual cup company since she was fourteen years old. When she thought of the idea, she didn't know that menstrual cups already existed, but when she found out that they were available, she went to work for the Keeper for almost ten years, even selling them out of her local jewelry store. At that time Francine even made her own packaging to make them appeal more to consumers. When her daughter Carinne graduated from school, Francine and Carinne teamed up to modernize the cup to make a silicone version, and had a mission to make it more attractive to the mainstream consumer.

The DivaCup story is another testament to how product innovation and its commodification pushed against taboo and stigma. After finalizing the design for the DivaCup, Carinne and Francine started to travel around to various trade shows, trying to sell their product to retailers and potential consumers. Carinne says that for a while "people were mostly shocked," and "most people ran away from our booth, totally freaked out and thought it was the grossest thing ever. Interestingly enough, most of the men were more receptive to our idea than the women." She thinks that this is "because men understand that it's like a gadget for your period," so they treat it like a lifestyle tool— rather than women, who have to think about the personal experience of using one.[45]

At that time, it was challenging for many women to get over the "ick factor" of "touching themselves or getting that close to their vaginas." Carinne says that the taboo around talking about periods openly was why it was such a long road to start selling in their first chain store. It took them eleven years—but it was *so* worth it![46] And I, as a loyal cup user, am more than grateful.

I would be upset with myself if I didn't give a shout-out to other menstrual cup brands that are tackling the taboos and stigmas of menstruation, so here are a few:

LUNETTE

Founded in 2005 by Heli Kurjanen, the Lunette cup is made from 100 percent medical-grade silicone (approved by the US Food and Drug Administration). The inside of the Lunette cup is completely smooth (no ridges), which is supposed to make it easier to clean, and the stem of the Lunette cup is flat, so no period gunk can gather there and foster a haven for bacteria.[47]

KEELA CUP

According to the founder, Jane Adamé, the "Keela Cup is the only cup in the world that has a pull string stem that breaks the seal, making it as easy to remove as a tampon. This makes it accessible to more users, such as those who have mobility or dexterity challenges or dysphoria with reaching inside of their bodies." The design of this cup has "eliminated the process of wrestling with it to get it out, or having to overexert your pelvic floor muscles to push the cup down."[48]

SAALT CUP

The Saalt Cup launched in early 2018 and was founded by two couples with seven daughters in total, driven by their shared passion for the "inseparable connection between menstrual hygiene and education."[49]

XO FLO BY GLADRAGS

This cup has a longer and more flexible stem than most cups, and GladRags CEO Tracy Puhl says that the XO Flo can hold more menstrual blood than usual because it has a rounder shape. The support rings to keep the cup in place are on the inside of the cup, not the outside—so there are no ridges that touch the walls of the uterus to cause any discomfort.[50]

FLEX

The Flex Company offers a menstrual disc called Flex that offers a "disposable tampon alternative"— somewhat similar to a menstrual cup. It claims to be the "most comfortable period product in the market" because it sits at the base of your cervix and molds to fit your body. The company says that you can wear the disc for up to twelve hours, and it has not been linked to TSS. Lauren Schulte founded the Flex Company after she was getting yeast infections every single month for more than a decade, starting with her first period. With this product she was solving her own problem.[51]

• WHAT ABOUT UNDERWEAR? •

Period underwear is a much newer approach to menstrual hygiene. It is quite simply underwear with more absorbency around the crotch area, which acts like a cloth pad. The leading brand of period underwear right now is Thinx, started in 2011 and founded in 2014. The company made headlines for their take on stylish period underwear that was meant to be so comfortable that the user would forget that they were menstruating in the first place. From boy shorts and thongs to regular panties, Thinx offers a range of products with patented technology to absorb varying amounts of menstrual blood. Each pair of Thinx underwear is meant to "absorb up to 2 tampons' worth of blood, yet they look and feel like a regular pair of underwear."[52]

• PERIOD PRODUCT INNOVATION •

It is exciting (and in some ways angering) to realize that we have really just scraped the surface in terms of what period products can offer. From moving toward products that are more sustainable to finding new ways to engineer devices that can maximize the potential of what menstrual blood has to offer, there is so much more to explore when it comes to period product innovation. I see a bright future. Maybe a reusable pad that doesn't need to be cleaned constantly with water and instead uses high-tech fabric technology? A sanitary pad that can test for pregnancy or sexually transmitted infections from menstrual blood alone? A tampon that collects blood to be donated for medical purposes, such as experiments and basic health tests? There are so many possibilities.

One of the most interesting period product innovations that I have heard of is a high-tech tampon that collects menstrual blood as a blood sample either to donate or to help detect diseases and track a woman's health. In 2014 Ridhi Tariyal, an engineer at Harvard, found a way to collect menstrual blood as a medical sample after she realized that there was so much useful blood that was literally being flushed away. Tariyal and her business partner, Stephen Gire, had at one point thought "about putting diagnostic chips inside tampons to give women real-time updates about their health," but the idea of having "chips and transmitters" inside your vagina elicited too many "heebie-jeebies" for them to move forward with that idea. The product that they ended up patenting is a device that provides an easy and efficient way for a menstruator to test their sexual and reproductive health.[53] One of the most challenging parts of starting a business like this, according to Gire, is that when "you say that you're going to build a company around menstrual blood, people think you're joking."[54] (That persisting stigma!)

There are a lot of new tampon alternatives and accessories as well—many of them more earth-friendly and made with chemical-free materials. For example, the first reusable tampon applicator was recently launched by UK-based company DAME.

The product is made with cleaning technology built right into it, with Antimicrobial Sanipolymers to help keep the reusable applicator clean.[55] Thinx, the well-known period underwear company, is also developing a reusable tampon applicator. They say that "20 billion menstrual products end up in landfills every year" and "tampon applicators alone account for 7 billion" of those products.[56]

As the conversation about periods becomes more empowering, more period product companies are appearing that focus on convenience and on supporting the success of women. There are a number of companies—such as Lola and Cora—that sell kits of period products that are delivered monthly to your doorstep. And now there are companies, like Aunt Flow, that sell directly to businesses and schools so that they can provide free period products in those locations.

There are other natural alternatives to tampons, such as sea sponge products, which are quite literally sponges that grow in the sea that people wear intra-vaginally as a sort of tampon to absorb menstrual blood. The attraction to using sea sponges as a menstrual product is that they're rather comfortable, are earth-friendly, and are a pretty affordable option. To use the sponge, you make it damp, squeeze it tightly, and compress it to be small enough to stick into the vaginal canal. They are meant to be rinsed and changed as often as every three hours, to avoid TSS. Perhaps the most attractive thing about the sea sponge is that it's totally biodegradable.[57]

As taboos about periods break down, it seems that the obstacles to period product innovation also shatter. But there is so much more that we can be doing to break down persisting stigmas to maximize the potential of our menstrual experience, like what periods can tell us about our health, how menstrual blood might be able to have other functions, and how we can make periods less disruptive for all menstruators.

•

CHAPTER FOUR

THE HISTORY OF THE PERIOD STIGMA (IN THE US)

In 1981 (not so long ago) Tampax conducted a national study on how people thought about periods. The company asked 1,034 men and women questions about menstruation and hygiene. It seems that the study was prompted by a sudden interest in menstrual hygiene after the "advent of TSS," a "rare disease associated with tampons." Here are some of the study's findings:

- 22% of Americans believed that the side effects of menstruation are psychological and not physical
- 87% of Americans thought that women are irregularly emotional while on their period
- 35% of Americans believed that menstruation negatively affects women's thinking ability
- 81% of women thought that they can function just as well at work while menstruating as not

- 66% of men thought that women can function just as well at work while menstruating as not
- 68% of Americans believed that women should conceal menstruation
- 26% of Americans believed that women cannot function as well on their periods as not
- 52% of Americans believed that you can conceive while menstruating
- 33% of Americans thought that it is socially acceptable to talk about periods in general
- 67% of Americans thought that periods should not be discussed at work or in social circles
- 35% of Americans thought that it is acceptable to talk about periods at work
- 74% of Americans thought that it is okay to talk about periods at home
- 91% of Americans thought that menstrual health should be taught in school[1]

Reading these results in 2018, I wasn't surprised; instead I read through them nodding my head because, unfortunately, they totally made sense to me in today's environment, decades later. People continue to not want to talk about periods, and even worse, the belief persists that menstruators are limited, emotional, and less capable when on their period.

When I arrived at Harvard a few years ago, I was

super excited about having access to one of the largest libraries dedicated to women, gender, and society—the Arthur and Elizabeth Schlesinger Library on the History of Women in America. This library quickly became my second home. There is something empowering about being surrounded by books and other documents written by feminist leaders who fought for my right, as a young woman of color, to attend an institution like Harvard—and also fought for my right to advocate for periods so publicly. It was in the Schlesinger Library that I found a cache of menstruation education pamphlets.[2]

When period products hit the market in the twentieth century, companies needed to advertise them to the public.[3] And one way companies did that was by producing menstruation education pamphlets that were mailed to homes and also served as educational materials in schools. The majority were published between the 1940s and the 1960s, hectic and pivotal decades for the United States. It's important to understand the context in which these pamphlets were introduced, in order to fully grasp the significance of their language and to account for their BLATANT sexism. As the rights and opportunities of women expanded (and sometimes decreased), the language around menstruation changed as well. Over the course of the twentieth century, menstruators started (*very* slowly, but surely) "regarding menstruation as normal, continuing regular activities" during their periods—but, of course, staying quiet about it. These pamphlets *did* help lay the groundwork for broader acceptance of the fact that menstruation is a "thoroughly natural and normal thing and nothing to worry about for a minute,"[4] even if we are still today fighting some of the negative messaging from the pamphlets, such as what activities menstruators are prohibited from engaging in while menstruating.

• A QUICK HISTORY LESSON •

The publication of period pamphlets increased after the Great Depression, which ended in 1939, when the entrance of the US into World War II in 1941 increased the demand for labor. As men went off to fight, more women than ever before entered the workforce. During and immediately after the war, with the economy getting stronger and stronger, consumption was also on the rise, so women needed to be on the move for work.[5,6]

The end of WWII in 1945 marked the beginning of the baby boomer years (between 1946 and 1964, peaking in the 1950s), named for the surge in the birthrate in the US.[7] With so many men returning from the war and reentering the labor force, many women were pushed out of their wartime jobs and back into the traditional gender roles of wife and mother in the home. The 1950s was a time of widespread social conformity, and women were expected to stay in their lane.[8] (UGH, I know. . . .) Not all women wished to return to their solitary work in the home, though: women still composed about one third of the labor force after World War II.[9]

With the baby boom, the mass production of cars, and the strong economy in the late 1940s, America began to build suburbs, and soon many husbands were commuting from bedroom communities to city jobs.[10] Although women were increasingly pushed to stay home as housewives, some of them started wanting *more*. Simone de Beauvoir's iconic 1949 book *The Second Sex,* which questioned and fought strict gender roles, gained influence throughout these years.[11] However, it is important to acknowledge that we women of color probably wouldn't have had this exact experience, because the "ideal of domesticity was primarily aimed at middle-class white women." Women of color, especially African American women and those of low socioeconomic status, were forced to work outside the home because of economic need.[12]

Women's desire for liberation and social equality came to a boil as America entered the 1960s. In 1960 the US Food and Drug Administration finally approved the first commercially produced birth control pill—which didn't make it readily available, but at least it was entering the market and heading toward the mainstream. In 1965 the United States Supreme Court "struck down a law that prohibited birth control" at the state level.[13,14] By the end of the 1960s "more than 80 percent of wives of childbearing age were using contraception," which allowed them "more choices, and freedom, in their personal lives."[15]

Also in the 1960s second-wave feminism was born in response to women's lack of access to education and employment. Betty Friedan's groundbreaking 1963 book *The Feminine Mystique* revealed the crushing malaise many women experienced from living within their assigned roles; they wanted to do more than just raise kids and clean the house. That same year the Equal Pay Act was passed, declaring it unjust for women and men to be paid differently for the same job.[16] (Though you probably know that nonetheless, almost sixty years later, equal pay has still not been accomplished.) Again, women of color were "underrepresented in both the racial and gender movements," and still today the "wider feminist movement" continues to struggle with incorporating equal representation in terms of race.[17]

Gender inequality was by no means the only

social injustice being challenged. During these same years the civil rights movement saw African Americans using "sit-ins, freedom rides, and protest marches to fight segregation, poverty, and unemployment." In 1963 Martin Luther King Jr. delivered his famous "I Have a Dream" speech, and in 1964 and 1965 respectively, the Civil Rights Act and the Voting Rights Act (prohibiting racial discrimination in voting) were passed.[18]

It was largely thanks to all this cultural upheaval that cracks began to appear in the period stigma. People didn't just wake up out of the blue and say, *Let's talk periods*. It happened *because* these conversations about social justice were happening. Meanwhile, throughout this entire era, period pamphlets were being provided in schools and distributed en masse. By 1964 *The Story of Menstruation* (produced in 1946 by Kimberly-Clark, which partnered with Disney to make this movie!) had reportedly been shown to more than forty-seven *million* people, and as of 1984 that number was more than one hundred million. Two accompanying pamphlets "had together been distributed to about 31 million girls" by 1964 as well. It's kind of astonishing that one corporation could reach so many people. Kimberly-Clark's educational materials were shown to about 20 percent of American girls.[19]

• PERIOD PAMPHLETS AND OTHER MATERIALS •

But what *exactly* was this distributed information telling girls and women for all those years? The film *The Story of Menstruation* spent ten minutes giving school-age girls "health and hygiene advice" via "cartoon illustrations of the menstrual cycle."[20] There were "Disney animated ovaries, cute little eggs, and wiggly sperm that looked like tadpoles."[21] It also followed a young "pubescent girl's happy day-dreams" of dating, getting married, and becoming a mom—yes, every girl's biggest and only dream. At the time THOSE WERE THE ONLY CULTURALLY APPROVED OPTIONS.[22] *The Story of Menstruation* also lists activities (such as bathing and strenuous exercises) to avoid while menstruating. Similar educational videos advised that if girls "really are laid low with this menstruation business," they should consult a doctor because "he'll try to help you feel a little happier about being a woman."[23] EXCUSE ME?! *He* will help women enjoy being women?

Infuriatingly, this kind of messaging is a common thread throughout these educational materials. Apparently if you do not smile and exhibit lots of "pep" during your period, then you must hate being a woman. This expectation that women be perpetually cheerful was very much thanks to the fact that society viewed it as a woman's top priority and most significant responsibility to alleviate the stress of the men around her (especially her husband) and to be totally happy about it. Of course, at that time there was absolutely no mainstream understanding or acknowledgment of anything outside the strict gender binary.

The menstruation film "fit comfortably within a 1950s culture" that stressed the "containment" of sexual desire in support of serving the "stability of the nuclear family and the suburban household." The film thus embodied the "glorified and idealized" scenario of white motherhood. As a twenty-first-century feminist looking back at the movie, it's hard not to get angry about these accepted limitations. And I hope that the women's movement in the United States has progressed enough that our dreams have expanded to include changing the world, becoming leaders, and extending our voices beyond the home.[24]

As a twenty-first-century political progressive, it's very easy to criticize everything that a large corporation like Kimberly-Clark has done, especially in the educational sector. That said, since I've studied how the women's movement and the Menstrual Movement have progressed over the last century, it's glaringly obvious to me that the cracks in the silence around menstruation were also a result of corporate marketing—in the form of period pamphlets.

Throughout the brewing social discontent of the 1950s and the momentous transformations of the 1960s, pamphlets with titles such as "Marjorie May's Twelfth Birthday" (published by Kotex) were distributed liberally at schools and libraries, in shops, and in most publications aimed at women and teen girls. Because the manufacturers got them to as many people as possible in order to sell more product, these period pamphlets became "revolutionary in extending the reach of rudimentary sex education for girls."[25] Even though they seem hopelessly out-of-date today, at the time they were showing girls and women that it was okay to talk about periods—as long as it was out of the public eye and only with other females.

Many of the period pamphlets I reviewed were geared toward moms and daughters—the people that periods were most acceptably discussed between. I found pamphlets with strategic titles such as "Now You Are 10" and "Very Personally Yours," so that even the word "period" didn't appear on the covers of booklets about . . . periods. Many have titles such as "How Shall I Tell My Daughter?" because the prospect of having to discuss genitalia, and then answer questions about why menstruation happens, seemed *scary*, partly because of mothers' own shame around menstruation and the taboo against openly discussing it.[26] The "period talk" can also be intimidating for parents because periods bring the possibility of pregnancy—and lots of parents probably prefer not to face the fact that their teenage daughters might have sex. Having a resource that allowed mothers to distance themselves from "the talk" was a perfect in for the companies. The pamphlets seemed to say, *HAVE NO FEAR, women of the twentieth century! PERIOD PAMPHLETS ARE HERE, brought to you by corporations and health departments ready to instruct you on what products to buy and what to do or not do while you're menstruating.*

In my efforts to understand the stigma around periods, I started tracking when ideas around menstruation changed over time. Here's what I learned about how periods were discussed in educational settings in the beginning and middle of the twentieth century:

#SHHPERIOD

The message was, *Don't talk about your period with other people, and try extra hard to hide it from men. If you feel you absolutely have to talk to someone—if you have questions or are freaked out about it—you should talk about it ONLY with your mother, never in social spaces, not even with friends.*

#PERIODSHAME

Period deodorant was an actual product, and a popular one. According to one ad, "Napkin odor is an offense that no one can discuss or forgive. Smart women know this. That's why they choose Quest, the Kotex napkin-deodorant powder—to guard against offending. . . . Protect your daintiness with Quest." A similar message was used to sell tampons, the "daintier method of protection," because pads might show through clothing.[27]

#PERIODRULES

There were rules for what you could and could not do on your period—with charts and illustrations! Included on the "do not" list? Strenuous activity, swimming in cold water, jumping, hiking, and even getting your feet wet. (Several pamphlets advised readers to "change your shoes and stockings if you've been walking in the rain.") In many of the pamphlets' illustrations and photographs, skinny young white girls get advice from white male doctors in lab coats.

A lot of the literature, especially from the early decades of the twentieth century, warned, *Whatever you do,* do not take a bath *while you are on your period, for fear of sitting in your own discharge.*[28] And again, there was an emphasis on girls' fragility or daintiness, and the need to protect it. God forbid you even *think* about going to "tumble about in the snow!" And if that seems extreme, I found one pamphlet from 1902 warning girls that if they were exposed to chilly temperatures, they would face a "future of invalidism."[29]

#PRETTYPERIOD

"Every girl wants to be as attractive and pretty as possible."[30] Apparently, when on your period this is an especially difficult task, and the things that make girls feel pretty are makeup, cleanliness, exercise, sleep, good posture, and healthy food.

Feeling cramps? Feeling sad for yourself because you're menstruating? Well, apparently the best fix is some makeup, a smile, a pretty dress, and a stiff spine.

As a Kimberly-Clark pamphlet from 1961 advised: "Pull in your stomach, hold your head high and your chin in, and you'll find yourself not only looking better, but feeling better, too. Good posture—whether you're standing, walking, or sitting—gives you more room inside for the organs to function properly."[31]

And again: "Just think of the pretty clothes and parties and high school later on. You'll look even prettier in your party dress for your body will take on soft, girlish curves."[32]

And then there are the illustrations, which make it clear that feeling pretty isn't just to feel better for yourself—it's for men. In many of the images tall white men hold in their arms, gaze longingly at, or otherwise objectify young, skinny white girls. (SUPER PROBLEMATIC MESSAGING ON VARIOUS LEVELS!) First of all, the (almost certainly white) people who created these pamphlets clearly equated prettiness with whiteness and the social expectations of their middle-class suburban lifestyle. The pamphlets don't even seem to address non-white girls. Second, at the time the most relatable dream or goal for a young girl was . . . to find some hottie to hold you and marry him. And all in the guise of menstrual health and buying period products!

As funny as these pamphlets can seem, I have to say that reading them sort of makes my blood boil. They are clearly *mansplanations* of periods and instructions for how to stay charming even when Aunt Flow comes to town. They suggest that no matter how low you might feel, or how debilitated you are by cramps, or how sore your boobs are, *just smile* and "give special attention to your hair and nails," and it will pass.[33] Clearly these pamphlets were written by someone who'd never menstruated. A Kotex ad asked viewers, "Do you ever wonder why some girls always seem to keep smiling no matter what time of the month it is?" Spoiler alert: it's a Kotex product. Above all else, the ad suggested that "an ounce of confidence is worth a pound of makeup."[34]

CHAPTER V

How To Take Those Days In Your Stride

SMILE — when you get these advance tips!

Most girls wouldn't have any idea when their menstrual period was due unless they checked it off, very carefully, on a calendar.

And others have "advance notice." For some, there are a few signs which come a few days before they start to menstruate.

Those signs are nothing serious in themselves. You may never have any of them—and you certainly won't have them all. Here they are:

THE "BLUES": Little problems are apt to assume gigantic proportions just before menstruation. Remember your woeful feelings are only temporary.

FEELING FAT: You feel as if you'd gained *pounds*, all around the middle! You haven't—it's the same business as the backache. Forget it.

NO PEP: Don't be surprised if you don't feel like climbing Pike's Peak. Lots of people *never* do!

CRAMPS: Sometimes they can be rather severe without being serious. If they are annoying enough to really bother you, relax, take things easier.

BACKACHE: This isn't an ache, but a sort of heaviness in the lower regions. It'll vanish. So don't brood about it.

SWELLING UP: Is this *your* bosom? Don't let a very slight swelling or tenderness get you down—it goes away, fast.

[10]

#PERIODSUPERSTITION

"Can unmarried girls use Tampax?"

For a while Tampax sales were hindered by the public's fear that tampons would break young girls' hymens. No doubt this concern was fueled by the popular view that men preferred to marry virgins.

The company strived to convince consumers that, after observing the use of tampons in 110 nurses, it was clear that yes, unmarried women could use tampons, and Tampax had the vaginal canal measurements to back up their assertion![36]

#PERIODPERSONALITY

In 1905 Dr. Emma Walker wrote a book called *Beauty through Hygiene: Common Sense Ways to Health for Girls*. Though not a pamphlet, it was one of the first guides for girls that talked about what she called "the periodic illness." Among other things, she advised girls to avoid making any "serious decisions" during what she called the "menstrual week"[37] and to "keep a tighter grasp on self-control and try to appreciate the fact that you are not quite your best self."[38]

Similarly, in 1949 the manufacturer Modess published a pamphlet that advised girls to "go out of your way not to be a 'sour-puss.'" Kimberly-Clark's pamphlet from 1952, called "You're a Young Lady Now," instructed girls to never "use menstruation as an excuse for being rude or mean" and to acknowledge that their period was a time when they would "cry easily, lose their tempers over nothing."[39] God forbid they show any sort of overt emotion on their cycle.

EXCUSE ME, but if I am menstruating, I hope that I can CRY and COMPLAIN, because menstruation can be a painful process, and my hormones are going to naturally shift how I am feeling, and I have no control over that. *However*, this does not render me incompetent or unstable! Crying is often considered a sign of weakness or instability, and being emotional is seen as a bad thing. Whereas it's much more socially acceptable for men to lose their tempers (which is what they often do instead of crying), and they are rarely labeled "emotional" or considered unfit when they do so (even though anger is an emotion too).

So, I am glad that we live in a society that is getting closer to acknowledging that it's totally A-OK to just be you and let your feelings flow, especially when your menstrual blood is also *flowing*.

In the pamphlets it's expected that periods will cause "some distress and discomfort," but there is no reason to worry—none of the period experience has to be "unpleasant when the woman has learned to take care of herself both physically and emotionally." Many of these pamphlets suggest that it does take resilience to even go through a period, because it will be the time when "way down deep you may be resenting being a girl or you may be rebelling against getting grown up and this is what makes you so miserable." Most menstruators would acknowledge that getting your period can sometimes be a hassle, and yes, when menstrual hygiene is not accessible, your period really can be something you come to resent. Nevertheless, periods should be celebrated because they mean that your body is healthy.[40]

It's worth noting that some menstrual literature from the beginning and middle of the twentieth century talked about menarche positively, emphasizing the excitement girls should feel in anticipation of getting their first period. The thing is, the positivity generally centered on the idea that periods are a "part of the wonderful process of changing from a child into a woman," and that will lead to falling in love, getting married, and having children. . . . Not exactly a feminist message! But hey, at least they wanted girls to feel happy about their periods; that's something we can celebrate.[41] Baby steps are still steps forward!

But some historians and menstrual activists point out that even these more positive period pamphlets were detrimental to the Menstrual Movement's efforts to redefine the menstrual experience for the better. Why? Because at the end of the day, the companies that published period literature had to convince consumers that they *needed* to buy the company's products if they wanted to be more capable and confident. The company had to reinforce the stigma in order to make a profit. In general, these pamphlets portrayed menarche as "a hygienic crisis solvable through the purchase of the right hygiene products."[42] These products were sold as a way to buy capability and, in a sense, freedom. That same theme lives on in menstrual marketing today. One of the most popular and well-recognized brands of pads right now is Stayfree, and it was originally called New Freedom.[43]

The most important thing we can learn from these period pamphlets is how the stigma about periods was promoted and cemented during the previous century, whether for a company's profit or to uphold social practices and codes. Though brands today continue pushing past the period stigma, especially with the growing market of more sustainable and progressive products, we still experience the stigma in other facets of life: in schools, in the workplace, and elsewhere.

In 1978, long after the introduction of period pamphlets, Gloria Steinem published her satire piece "If Men Could Menstruate" in *Ms.* magazine. In it she describes how if men—cis men—menstruated, periods would suddenly become "an enviable, boast-worthy, masculine event: Men would brag about how long and how much." If men menstruated, suddenly "men-struation" would be used as a justification for their more pronounced power in politics, religion, and even the military.[44] In the event that "male liberals and radicals, however, would insist that women are equal" but they didn't get their period, then there would be some sort of process to undergo just to be considered equal—women would have to "recognize the primacy of menstrual rights" or even "self-inflict a major wound every month" to symbolize the giving of blood as a substitute. If men could menstruate, it would be talked about openly and in an empowering way in mainstream media. Even decades later these stigmas still persist, and the more we talk about them in daily life and in the media, the more we can facilitate a shift toward equality.

CHAPTER FIVE

●

PERIOD POVERTY

> For those who can afford it, periods are simply a necessary nuisance—and tampons an obligatory monthly expense. But for low-income women and girls, and especially those who are homeless, lack of ability to access feminine hygiene products can compromise their health and well-being. Just imagine the sheer difficulty of spending a full day in public, attending work or school, without enough tampons on hand.
>
> —Jennifer Weiss-Wolf, *New York Daily News*[1]

Period poverty is the state of being unable to afford period products (or necessary items to feel clean) while menstruating. It's a term more popularly used in the UK, beginning in 2017. In the United States period poverty is still a problem, to the surprise of many. Megan White Mukuria, the founder of ZanaAfrica Foundation, says that "in the US, people are just realizing that homeless people need sanitary pads. The US is super behind the curve on reproductive rights, and it is only getting worse in this era of Trump."[2]

Periods are expensive, and they really shouldn't be. The Huffington Post estimates that the "total cost of your period over your lifetime" comes to $18,171. This is based on the calculation that "on average, a woman has her period from three to seven days and the average woman menstruates from age 13 until age 51. That means the average woman endures some 456 total periods over 38 years, or roughly 6.25 years of her *life*." The $18,171 takes into consideration what is needed to cope with the pain and hassle of menstruation—so it includes, among other things, heating pads, acne medication, period products, pain relievers, and birth control.[3] Tampons and pads are "a $718 million dollar market." (This doesn't even include menstrual cups or other alternative products for menstruation.) It's estimated that the average menstruator uses "about 17,000 pads or tampons during her entire menstruation lifetime." So period products are a big, profitable industry, where the demand does not stop, because—big surprise—menstruation across a population continues regardless of cost.[4]

When my family experienced housing instability, I met many homeless women and talked to them about periods at the bus stop in Old Town, where I transferred lines. I took notice of their stories about using toilet paper, socks, and even brown paper grocery bags and cardboard to absorb their menstrual blood. I never had to worry about where I would get my period products, because I had a progressive mom who bought me a menstrual cup early on; so even when my family faced a time of housing and financial instability, my period was taken care of. To all the menstruators who are reading this: take a moment to imagine what it would be like if you got your period and had no period products on hand, and no bathroom or shower of your own, but had the same pressure to go about your day and function as if you were not on your period.

After I decided to do something about this unaddressed natural need for period products for homeless women, I started researching to find a way to channel my efforts and newfound passion into something productive. The first step I took was visiting a church I knew of in which many members of the congregation were homeless, to ask about available tampons and pads there and at the neighboring shelters. The majority of the places I visited did not have any period products available.

"It's too expensive."

"No one ever asks for them."

"Most of the people that we serve probably don't get their period."

"People don't like to donate tampons and pads."

These were usually the reasons given when I asked why period products weren't available in shelters. "Sheltering" refers to when homeless people hop between homeless shelters and various other services to provide for their basic needs—as opposed to "squatting," the actual experience of living on the streets. Most homeless services assume that the majority of their clients will be men, so menstruation, commonly assumed to be a "woman's issue," is ignored. When the majority of the demographic that is served doesn't experience their period, organizers don't see the obvious need for period products, and thus they think that menstrual hygiene is not in high demand.

We are also conditioned to not talk about periods openly, so period products become an invisible need. Even if the need is understood, it can be embarrassing to walk into a shelter to donate period products, knowing it may initiate a conversation that the person donating or the person accepting products may not want to have. In fact, U by Kotex commissioned a national survey that found that even though menstrual products are often listed on the donation wish lists of many organizations, only "a mere 6 percent of respondents had ever donated period products to homeless shelters. Three times as many said they had donated other toiletries." So even when people are collecting toiletries or hygiene items to donate, period products are often forgotten. [5]

And organizations don't usually prioritize spending money on period products or ensuring that they have these items readily available, because homeless women similarly don't feel comfortable going up to the authorities of these shelters (which are usually run by men) to declare, *Hello! I'm on my period! I need a pad [or tampon]!* The stigma is a double-edged sword that prevents organizations from receiving period products and from understanding that these products are needed in the first place. When organizations do have the resources to have a limited supply of period products on hand, they are often kept behind counters and distributed only to people who come up and ask for them—but, again, the stigma makes this "ask" a difficult one.

• WHAT IS IT LIKE WHEN YOU ARE HOMELESS AND MENSTRUATING? •

On October 18, 2016, a short video titled *How Do Homeless Women Cope with Their Periods?* was released by Bustle as "the first installment of Bustle's new documentary series, NSFWomen." For every share up to 250 shares, Bustle promised to "donate a pair of THINX underwear to homeless women in need via Distributing Dignity."[6] The video went viral. By early 2018 it had garnered more than 136,500 shares and 37 million views on Facebook, and more than 9.7 million views on YouTube.[7,8]

The video tells the stories of multiple women currently experiencing homelessness and includes an interview with Julissa Ferreras-Copeland, a New York City council member. The main star of the video is twenty-seven-year-old Kailah, who hasn't had a home since she was a ten-year-old and is spending her eighth consecutive winter on the streets. As she puts it, "Period times are not good for us," because it's not only a hassle to clean yourself, but menstruating without products is very uncomfortable. The video follows her daily routine as she finds public restrooms, usually around parks, to wash herself— her best option for cleaning her vagina is to use a big cup to splash water onto herself. Kailah shows how she makes her own tampons out of menstrual pads by ripping them apart and twisting the pieces to form a tampon shape. Other interviewees mention paper towels, toilet paper, plastic bags, towels, cotton balls, makeup pads, socks, and ripped-up tank tops as other options for maintaining menstrual hygiene as much as possible. An older woman recalls how when she menstruated while homeless, it was easier to "sit still until we came up with something."[9]

I think that this video in particular (which is one of many about the issue of homelessness and periods) went viral because it did a fantastic job of igniting empathy in viewers by framing period products in the context of hunger and access to food—another very basic human right that is undeniable. Victoria, one of the women interviewed, said that "you can't eat if you buy tampons." Alexa, another woman, points to a Walgreens and says that in the store the cheapest box of tampons is a little more than seven dollars, which is more than she and her boyfriend spend on a meal together. It's a hard decision, though, because she'd "rather be clean than be full."[10] Often the choice isn't a choice at all, and women have to find alternatives to safe and clean period products.

One night when I was sitting at my bus stop in downtown Portland, a homeless woman I had seen quite regularly sat next to me, holding cotton balls. I watched her out of the corner of my eye as she stretched about five of them apart—picking at them from different directions, slowly forming loosely fitted clouds in her hand. After a little while she caught my gaze and bluntly said, "What you looking at?" Curious, I smiled and innocently asked, "What are you making?"

After letting out a laugh, she leaned over to me

and whispered, "A pad," and we giggled together. She then proceeded to explain to me that for years her method of menstrual health management—when she didn't have access to the rare tampons and pads made available by local shelters—was to take cotton balls from bathrooms or the "hygiene kits" she received and pull them apart. Then she'd squeeze the cotton together to shape either a thicker, wider, and flatter pad or a twisted tampon that she could insert into her vagina. (Toxic shock syndrome warning!) What really sticks with me today, many years later, is that she told me that if she was lucky, sometimes she could rinse it out or simply squeeze the menstrual blood out enough that she could reuse the cotton balls—and she would do this until the cotton either wouldn't hold together anymore or smelled so bad that she couldn't stand it.

Another time a homeless woman showed me her strategy. I watched with wide-open eyes, shock, and awe at her resilience as she tore off a piece of the cardboard she was sitting on and demonstrated how she used the inside of it for a pad. She stripped off the outer layers to get at the ridged middle, because the inside of the cardboard was a bit softer and more flexible. Cardboard, as she told me, was what she'd learned to like using the most for period management, because she could find it in so many places—especially in recycling bins behind businesses. Also some shelters would give out cardboard boxes when requested.

Opinions about using the word "hygiene," for some in the activist community, are similar to the debates around the word "sanitary" that we discussed earlier. Some people (who, for the most part, all live in more developed countries) strongly believe that saying the word "hygiene" is offensive because it directly implies that periods are dirty, that periods are something that need to be cleaned up, like a bacterial infection. I personally feel okay using the word "hygiene" because, to be completely honest, for too many people, menstruating is an experience that feels messy and unclean, because they're forced to use trash as period products. This is not right. We should live in a society where no one feels unclean or less capable because of such a natural need. But, unfortunately, that society doesn't exist yet. So I say, let's own up to it and acknowledge that for some people (especially those who can't afford period products), having one's period is not a very clean experience.

Homeless women's stories of makeshift period management barely scratch the surface of the problem—and those stories sparked a fiery curiosity within me, a drive to ask questions, seek answers, and then take action. Perhaps you will feel similarly when reading on and learning more about the detrimental effects that a lack of menstrual hygiene can have for homeless women.

So what are the different ways in which period poverty is an issue for homeless women?

LIMITED SUPPLY

Organizations usually don't have period products readily available to meet the full demand, because period products are expensive. To provide for as many people as possible, institutions often have to put a limit on the number of period products that one person can take. This creates a never-ending cycle of need, because if homeless women have a hard time getting period products, when the products are available, those women want to stock up on as many as possible (knowing that their next period could come unexpectedly, and having an additional pad or tampon makes a big difference). The organization's staff then think that individuals are taking too much of the available supply, and so the staff put a limit in place. Usually the limit is such a small number that what's provided is not enough to cover one full menstrual cycle.

LACK OF MOBILITY

Menstruation is a time when one is caring for one's vagina much more than usual, needing to find time to wipe and wash it and replace period products when they're available. I have heard homeless women say that it's easier to just sit in one place and wait their periods out, rather than move around and cause more discomfort or flow. On their periods, homeless women may also change their daily routines and travel plans so that they can stay near public restrooms to wash any clothes they might bleed onto, wash their genital area and the insides of their thighs, change their period products, or use toilet paper to create makeshift pads.

IMPROMPTU SOLUTIONS

Too many people have to turn to unconventional menstrual hygiene management methods that are not very clean or comfortable. Worse, these methods can actually carry a number of dangerous health risks—most notably a higher risk for cervical cancer, TSS, and other infections—especially when homeless women have nowhere to turn but to items that have been thrown away. While some of these health consequences may be easily treatable, most homeless women do not have access to health care or even clinics, and symptoms worsen quickly without treatment.

Toilet paper and paper towels

In 2015 *Cosmopolitan* interviewed four homeless women about their experience menstruating. Megan, a twenty-five-year-old who spoke with them, said that in her experience there were tampons and pads readily available at services in California, but it was a totally different game on the East Coast. When she wasn't in California, her usual solution was to use the "raw, brown, hand-drying paper towels from the bathroom that's thicker than toilet paper." When Megan couldn't find paper towels, she would "roll toilet paper over my hand like five or six times and use that."[11]

Any cloth
Many of the homeless women that I've talked to through PERIOD's services have told me they use any sort of cloth that they can find for an impromptu pad: socks, pillowcases snagged from shelters, and old T-shirts.

Cotton balls
The standard hygiene kits given out to homeless people often contain a bar of soap, travel bottles of shampoo and conditioner, a toothbrush and toothpaste, a packet of tissues, and cotton balls. In early 2016, two years into working on PERIOD, I started to read more articles that profiled homeless women talking about their periods, and I was surprised to see that cotton balls came up multiple times as a period hygiene solution.[12]

Grocery bags

Homeless menstruators often find a temporary solution in both plastic and paper grocery bags. They are an easy find: readily available at stores and carelessly disposed of. The most common solution that I heard of in Portland was to use either the Fred Meyer or Trader Joe's brown paper grocery bags. Women would fold them up to make their own version of a pad. Bundled-up plastic bags can also be used; although plastic doesn't absorb, the ridges of the twisted plastic hold blood. The problem with both of these bag options? They are extremely unsanitary and uncomfortable, they don't stay in place, and they often smell bad.

Cardboard

Over the last few years, I learned of another way to use cardboard for makeshift pads. Instead of using just the middle layer, some people roll the whole piece of cardboard until it's really soft and flexible. It isn't a very absorbent solution at all, but it does block the blood from flowing onto any clothing or underwear—and *that* is especially important when clean pants and underwear are not readily available.

STARK CONTRASTS

Menstruation happens regardless of whether or not you have a home. Most homeless people were not homeless when they were younger, and perhaps they had access to period products when they first started menstruating. For many homeless menstruators, getting their period can remind them of just how different their lives are now compared to a (possibly) more stable and secure past life that they feel too distant from.

The touching moments that stick with me most when on service trips with PERIOD are when simply handing a care package (filled with enough period products for an entire menstrual cycle) to someone brings them to tears because of the reaffirmation that they deserve (just like everyone else) to feel confident, clean, and capable while menstruating. The stark contrast of these clean period products highlights that they, for too long, have been using trash to take care of a basic human need.

• SO, HOW BIG IS THE PROBLEM OF PERIOD POVERTY? •

Unlike toilet paper, which is provided for free in school restrooms, students are typically on their own to access menstrual supplies. Yet in order to be fully engaged in the classroom, these are as much of a necessity as pencils and paper. This is especially true for younger teens who are more likely to be caught off guard by the arrival of their period and without budgets of their own to buy emergency tampons or pads.

—Jennifer Weiss-Wolf, author of *Periods Gone Public*[13]

The most obvious population of menstruators affected by period poverty is homeless women, who struggle to afford any basic necessity, including shelter. And as we just discussed, period poverty for homeless women can be dangerous and detrimental to their health. What too many people don't realize is that the lack of access to period products affects many more people—not just homeless women but also menstruators who simply cannot comfortably spend the money on period products. These people may go to school or have a home or a job, but those extra four to seven dollars are just too much to spare and can make the difference between having a couple of meals or going without. The demographic experiencing period poverty is growing rapidly, and there's no sign that the number of people affected will decrease anytime soon.

What consequences occur when low-income menstruators can't afford the period products they need?

In 2008 it was reported that "over half of the 37 million Americans living in poverty today are women."[14] According to 2014 statistics from the Shriver Report, in the US approximately "42 million women live in or close to poverty."[15] And US women are "35 percent more likely to live in poverty than men."[16] In 2015 more than one in eight women—totaling more than 16.9 million women—lived in poverty, and "more than 2 in 5 (45.7 percent) of these women lived in extreme poverty, defined as income at or below 50 percent of the federal poverty level."[17] The disparity between men and women when it comes to financial stability is worse in America than in many other countries. In fact, the Center for American Progress states that "the gap in poverty rates between men and women is wider in America than anywhere else in the Western world."[18]

It is much more expensive to be a woman than a man in many ways—from how dry cleaners "often charge women three times as much to clean shirts," even when the shirts seem identical to men's dress shirts; to haircuts and toiletries that cost more (because of what, the pink packaging?); to higher interest on home loans and cars; and even to health care.[19] The term "pink tax" refers to the extra cost tacked on to "products and services targeted at women."[20] Studies such as one conducted in 2010 by *Consumer Reports* found that "personal hygiene products can be up to 50% more expensive for women [than] they are for men,"[21] and one study conducted recently by the University of Central Florida showed that products such as deodorant can cost around "30 cents more per ounce than men's, even when the only difference between the products was the smell."[22] By greatly gendering the marketing of products that are basically the same—to somehow create a "women's" and a "men's" version of anything, from soap and shaving cream to razors—these large corporations are working to convince us all "that men and women are so biologically different that we need completely different products, as though we are different species."[23]

Some economists might not agree that discrimination is always the reason why women spend much more money on general living costs. Another economic theory is that the disparity results from women being less likely to prioritize cost comparisons when deciding which products to purchase, and instead relying more on "word of mouth recommendations when choosing." Women are also less likely to haggle and ask for discounts.[24] This is an excellent opportunity for me to remind you to know your worth, claim your worth, and demand it. This disparity in spending is linked backed to period products, because periods are an additional cost that menstruators *alone* must carry.

So, how can the simple distribution of tampons and pads make a difference? You may be surprised to learn that periods and poverty in America are directly related to each other. Poverty rates between men and women are relatively the same throughout childhood, but an "increase for women during their childbearing years and again in old age"[25] has been documented. And what are childbearing years? Answer: when a woman is menstruating.[26] For people who are living penny to penny and dollar to dollar, period products, which can cost more than seventy dollars a year, are a next-to-impossible investment.[27]

Women living in poverty are also much more often single parents than men are—so it is common that an impoverished woman also has children to support. More than 50 percent of all poor children live in families with single mothers.[28] In 2015 "more than 1 in 3 single-mother families lived in poverty," which adds up to "about 525,000 single women with children" who also had full-time jobs and were still poor. Single-mother households are much more likely to experience poverty than households headed by men or by a married couple. When the single mother is a woman of color, the chances of experiencing poverty are even higher.[29] This problem can both be explained by and exacerbated by the wage gap between men and women. Even in 2016, women who were working full-time jobs in the United States were on average paid 80 percent of what their male counterparts were paid, a 20 percent gap![30] The pay gap for women varies among racial groups, with Hispanic women experiencing the largest gap. Hispanic women made only

54 percent of what their white male counterparts were compensated in 2016.[31]

Of course, breaking the cycle of poverty (and the disparity in poverty rates between men and women) requires more than addressing periods—but having free period products supplied in the workplace or in homeless centers is a great start, to take some of the pressure off these women. We also have to fight for equal pay for equal work, make upward economic mobility possible for women through more employment opportunities and mentorships, ensure access to quality affordable childcare and to maternity leave, and continue fighting violence against women.[32] When we think of gender equality, and women and men having the same opportunities for economic and social mobility, menstruation as it is now perceived and handled in our society is an obstacle for women (physically, emotionally, and economically) that men do not even have to think about.

When menstruators cannot afford period products, they often feel anxious at work and feel held back in their productivity (or in their ability, if the work is physical and does not allow for more frequent bathroom breaks). The same goes for menstruators who are still in school. When a student menstruates and has no access to period products, whether they left them at home or in a locker, or cannot afford them, the stress and embarrassment around free bleeding in school can diminish confidence and hinder participation.

• IMPACT ON EDUCATION •

It is an all too real experience for many menstruators around the world (including in the United States) to feel limited because of their periods. From a psychological perspective on its own, if a person's family can't afford tampons or pads, it is hard to stay engaged in school when all you can think about is the risk of bleeding through your pants and everyone seeing it when you stand up. Of course, some may say, "Own it," and, "Don't be ashamed of that period stain," but I understand the concern. The same sort of anxiety can be triggered by the worry that you might bleed through the improvised toilet paper or piece of cloth, or it might start to smell or show as a misshapen bulge through your clothes. These worries alone can cause young menstruators to avoid classroom spaces, sometimes altogether.

The British Broadcasting Corporation (BBC) interviewed two teenagers in the UK about the negative effects on performance in schools caused by a lack of access to period products. One told her story about not being able to afford period products because she had a single mother who had "five mouths to feed," so instead the girl resorted to wrapping socks or whole rolls of toilet paper around her underwear, or would take "a few days off school every month." The other said, "When I went on my period I started taking time off school, because I didn't know what was actually going on with my body. That made my attendance really low and I was getting in trouble." It took her teachers visiting her house to inquire after her absence and travel with her to actually bring her back to school.[33]

Even when period products are made available at schools, they may not be readily accessible. Menstruators might have to travel to a certain bathroom with a dispenser, or talk to multiple administrators in order to get a tampon or pad. Meanwhile, a male counterpart is in the classroom getting a head start on the material or on an exam.

Hannah, a period activist based in the UK, shared her story with Broadly in the summer of 2017. When she was growing up, her family couldn't afford to buy tampons or pads, and so she regularly used "wadded-up toilet roll" or sacrificed public transportation and food to save up for tampons or pads. Hannah says that even when she was "given lunch money," she "would put a little bit aside and eat slightly less." She describes not being able to afford period products in school as a "really lonely and horrible experience." Through her work distributing period products to schoolgirls in the UK, she discovered that girls were being sent home because they had bled through their school uniforms. The Broadly video feature on Hannah's group, Fourth Wave, ends with another member explaining how, because of a lack of access to period products, "Kids are missing a week of school every month," and she makes the point that it's important to invest in menstrual equity because "in the long run it is better for the economy that people are in school."[34]

• MEDICAL RISK •

When faced with a limited supply of period products (coupled with not enough education about the best practices for how to manage your period), many will use tampons and pads for as long as possible, and there can be serious consequences when period products are used for long stretches of time, such as a higher risk for cervical cancer, TSS, and other infections.[35] Even if not homeless, low-income menstruators who are living in extreme poverty are also forced to turn to unclean methods of maintaining menstrual hygiene. A nineteen-year-old from Tulare County in California shared her story with the public through the local daily newspaper, *The Fresno Bee*, and recalled using newspaper when her family was out of toilet paper. She grew up "very poor" and said that "it was a burden to bleed," because her family didn't have money to afford period products and she "was charged 75 cents" for them at her middle school. The hardest part about hearing stories like this is to realize that they are not uncommon, especially in poor school districts.[36]

• WHAT DO WOMEN IN PRISON DO ABOUT PERIODS? •

Simple supplies like pads and tampons can become bargaining chips, used to maintain control by correction officers, or traded among incarcerated women, according to former inmates and advocates on the issue.
—Zoe Greenberg, *The New York Times*, "In Jail, Pads and Tampons as Bargaining Chips" [37]

By 2017 women comprised "13 percent of the country's local jail population, and though policies change from state to state, horror stories about menstruating inmates abound—regardless of location."[38] Since women are living in such close quarters while in prison, menstrual cycles easily synchronize, and with so many female inmates menstruating simultaneously, shortages in period products and heightened "discomfort and smell" are common.[39] Without access to period products, inmates are faced with having to use disposable pads and tampons for longer than is healthy, and again, some turn to "molding tampons and pads out of toilet paper."[40]

When there is an extreme shortage of period products, tampons and pads can become bargaining chips that emphasize the powerlessness of inmates. In an article published in the *New York Times* in 2017, a twenty-four-year-old inmate named Tara Oldfield-Parker remembers having to ask for a pad from the officers supervising her in a holding cell. She had to wait for more than an hour before they returned with "the kind of rectangular gauze used to bandage an arm, with no adhesive."[41] This story pointed out that the problem isn't always a lack of stock. In fact, "the facilities have enough supplies, but they are not available equally to all the women who need them."[42] It is usually left up to the officers to determine how pads and tampons are distributed, so "there is an easy opportunity for mishandling."[43]

One former inmate of the Rose M. Singer Center on Rikers Island recalled that "you had to be sort of chum-my-chummy"[44] with officers to have a chance of receiving any tampons, which were much harder to obtain than pads. The *New York Times* piece features memories of women being called "disgusting" for having menstrual blood dripping down their legs because no pads were available, and of correction officers throwing tampons into the air and watching as inmates dove "to the ground to retrieve them, because they didn't know when they would next be able to get tampons."[45] Currently the New York City Department of Correction "provides 144-count boxes of thin, non-adhesive pads per 50 inmates, per week" (only about 2.9 per inmate per week) at this Rikers Island jail, where name-brand period products can alternatively be purchased at the commissary for up to $7.65.[46]

In 2016 the American Civil Liberties Union (ACLU) published a report called "Reproductive Health Behind Bars in California" that documented some of experiences of menstruating while incarcerated. One woman named Halle, an inmate in a California county jail, said that "pads are not dispensed as they are supposed to be. We are forced to reuse them, we are forced to beg for what we need, and if an officer is in a bad mood they are allowed to take what we have and say we are hoarding."[47] According to Halle, it is even worse for inmates in solitary confinement, who "are not given sanitary products at all," which forces them to "bleed on the floor that already has urine and feces on it." By law, jails are required to "provide women with the personal hygiene supplies they need to manage their menstrual cycle." However, "reports from incarcerated women" all around the country still show how jails "fail to meet this obligation."[48]

The ACLU collected other stories from women behind bars who don't have access to period products when they need them. The products may not be "immediately available, are available only on certain days or in set amounts that are insufficient, are selectively doled out by trustees, or are hoarded by other women because they are in short supply."[49] There are also stories of women "being forced to continue wearing soiled uniforms" after not having enough pads or bleeding through their pads, and "guards withholding supplies as a way to humiliate women." In Washington state one incarcerated woman said, "Most people in here describe having your period in prison as one of the worst things about being locked up. It creates stress and uncertainty due to the conditions that we have to deal with."[50]

Similarly, the Correctional Association of New York released a report in 2015 titled *Reproductive Injustice: The State of Reproductive Health Care for Women in New York State Prisons* and recognized "insufficient sanitary napkin supplies" as a problem for women in the Department of Corrections and Community Supervision (DOCCS). While a monthly supply of pads might be given out, the majority of women still report not having enough to meet their needs. DOCCS "distributes 24 sanitary napkins to women in general population each month," but many find this amount inadequate. Some found the pads to be of such low quality that they had to wear up to four at a time so that the pads would absorb enough.

The only way to get more pads is to receive a "special permit from the medical department." The report explained that DOCCS wants a woman to prove that she has a more serious condition if she needs more pads, because DOCCS wants to "treat the underlying problem, not the symptom." *Excuse me* . . . but some menstruators have a heavier flow and might need more products, and it isn't because of any sort of serious health condition.[51] It seems safe to assume that the reason why the people making decisions about prison resources don't understand the menstrual experience is because they tend to be men—and may not be educated about menstruation.

At Bayview Correctional Facility, a women's prison formerly located in Manhattan and now closed, women had to prove that they needed more period products by providing evidence in the form of "a bag of used sanitary napkins to show that she actually has used them and needs more" because the prison was often understocked. This is an issue for at least two reasons: "correction officers should not have authority to deny women extra supplies" and "asking officers for pads can be an uncomfortable situation for women, especially if the officer is male."[52]

The hesitation to provide more pads to women in prison comes from the concern over the price and also the belief that "women run out of supplies because they use pads for other purposes, for example, to quiet squeaky doors, steady uneven tables and chairs, and clean their housing area." Hey, DOCCS, PROVIDE SOME OTHER SUPPLIES for them to use for broken furniture and cleaning, *and* stop denying women enough pads.[53]

Additional period products can be obtained from prison commissaries, but this puts women who do not have excess "financial resources and outside support" at a great disadvantage. As mentioned in this same report on prisons in New York state, in 2015 each tampon cost between twelve and twenty-four cents, and each pad cost twenty-one or twenty-two cents. Although this doesn't sound expensive for many of us, this is very expensive for inmates, considering that the usual prison wage is around seventeen cents per *hour*. The report says that at these rates a woman "would have to spend her entire week's earnings to buy a single 20-pack box of tampons or pads." Women in prison are also not allowed to receive pads or tampons by mail from any family support outside of prison.[54] A 2015 study conducted by the Prison Policy Initiative found that prior to their incarceration, inmates had an income that was "41% less than non-incarcerated people of similar ages."[55] So these inmates would likely not already have the money for period products, either.

In the summer of 2016 a court video from Kentucky went viral and garnered almost three million views on YouTube in just over a year.[56] In the video a female inmate is brought into court wearing no pants. The woman's lawyer explains to Judge Amber Wolf that "her client had not received hygiene products or been given pants since she arrived in jail three days previously." Judge Wolf reacts with anger and disbelief, just like the millions of viewers did when watching. "This is outrageous," she says in the video. "Is this for real? Am I in the twilight zone?"[57] At one point in the court video, Judge Wolf is angrily on the phone with a jail administrator. "I have a defendant who has been in you all's jail for three days who is standing in front of me completely pants-less," she says. "And she has also been denied feminine hygiene products. What the hell is going on?"[58]

In 2015 Chandra Bozelko, who spent six years at York Correctional Institution in Connecticut, wrote a piece for the *Guardian* titled "Prisons That Withhold Menstrual Pads Humiliate Women and Violate Basic

Rights." At York two female cellmates were given only five pads per week to split. Bozelko says, "I'm not sure what they expect us to do with the fifth but this comes out to 10 total for each woman [per month], allowing for only one change a day in an average five-day monthly cycle."[59] Even if inmates were to save all the pads that they received on a weekly basis, that would leave them having to "wear a single pad for multiple days." Chandra would avoid this by "fashioning a diaper with six pads quilted together after purchasing extras from the commissary."[60] While in prison, Chandra was able to purchase additional pads from the commissary, but she stated that "80% of inmates are indigent and cannot afford to pay the $2.63 the maxi pads cost per package of 24, as most earn 75 cents a day and need to buy other necessities." Even when she did have the funds, sometimes the commissary would run out of pads because they kept such a short supply.[61]

What is especially powerful about Chandra's op-ed is that she provides a look into the psychological experience of not having access to period products while in prison. Not having enough pads and having menstrual blood seep through underwear and clothes, leaving stains, "serve as an indelible reminder of one's powerlessness in prison. Asking for something you need crystallizes the power differential between inmates and guards; the officer can either meet your need or he can refuse you, and there's little you can do to influence his choice." Asking for a tampon is even harder "when a guard complains that his tax dollars shouldn't have to pay for your supplies . . . but you say nothing because you want that maxi pad."[62]

In December 2014 eight female inmates represented by the ACLU of Michigan sued Muskegon County in federal court for "deplorable jail conditions." They cited incidents of male guards who would watch the women change clothes, bathe themselves, and use the bathroom—and regular incidents of being denied changes of clothes and period products. One of the plaintiffs, a former inmate named Londora Kitchens, said that when she was menstruating, a guard denied her pads and "warned her that she'd better not 'bleed on the floor.'"[63]

Miriam Aukerman, a staff attorney at the ACLU of Michigan, said that "Muskegon County has abdicated its constitutional duty to ensure conditions of confinement at the jail just and consistent with health, safety, and human dignity."[64] There have been multiple court cases in the past that have ruled "that failing to provide or denying access to sanitary items violates the Eighth Amendment, which enshrines a prisoner's right to a 'basic human need' . . . in its Cruel and Unusual Punishments Clause."[65] I mean, I would say that, like toilet paper (which is adequately rationed out to inmates), menstrual products address a *very* basic human need. But unfortunately the judge in the Muskegon County case ruled against the female prisoners on this issue.[68]

I hope that as you read through this chapter, there were moments when you gasped, or sighed and shook your head at how unacceptable it is that period poverty is such a serious yet underprioritized issue. I also hope that when that happened, you felt some emotion that energized you and made you ready to say, *This needs to change. This ends now. PERIOD.* When we have the freedom and the platform (social media or otherwise) to ask questions, challenge systems, and speak out, we have a responsibility to do so—because so many in this world, including in our own communities, as we learned from this chapter, may still feel silenced about certain issues, such as a lack of access to period products.

The incredible thing about the fight to address period poverty, though, is that there are very tangible ways to contribute and take action. Collect period products and donate them to those who need them?

Easy! Start conversations to break the stigma and raise awareness about period poverty? We can do it! Work on long-term solutions to ensure that supplies of period products are available to all, regardless of living situation or socioeconomic status? Policy makers, here we come!

•

CHAPTER SIX

PERIOD POLICY

When it comes to social movements, I believe that there are really two realms in which we can achieve meaningful success: social change (changing people's hearts and minds) and systemic change (addressing all the different pieces—laws, institutional practices and attitudes, built-in biases, etc.—that make up the system that's perpetuating an injustice). Eventually, to make long-term systemic change, different ways of doing things need to be written into policy for local, state, and federal governments. And in order to do that, you have to first transform culture and public opinion. In this chapter we will explore period policy, which is just as important to the Menstrual Movement as providing immediate relief to those who cannot afford period products, and policy change is much trickier.

For example, as we saw in the last chapter, even

with the *obvious* need for and right to have access to period products, especially for women living in poverty, "most American programs designed to help low-income families" still don't count menstrual products as essentials. Programs such as Medicaid, the Supplemental Nutrition Assistance Program (SNAP—i.e., food stamps), and the Special Supplemental Nutrition Program for Women, Infants, and Children (WIC) don't consider period products a basic necessity, "even though the FDA considers them 'medical products.'" UGH. In her book *Periods Gone Public*, Jennifer Weiss-Wolf discusses at length how "SNAP and WIC classify pads and tampons alongside 'luxuries' like pet food, cigarettes, and alcohol."[1]

The Menstruation Movement is still a relatively small community of Period Warriors, as periods have been a mainstream topic for only a couple of years now. In fact, the first articles from advocates calling for more equitable access to period products started to appear in the mainstream press only a few years ago. One of the very first, in 2014, was by Jessica Valenti, a columnist for the *Guardian,* titled "The Case for Free Tampons." In her column Valenti pointed out that even "in the United States, access to tampons and pads for low-income women is a real problem." As things still stand, in 2018, "food stamps don't cover feminine hygiene products, so some women resort to selling their food stamps in order to pay for 'luxuries' like tampons." The main message of the article? *Menstrual hygiene products should be free for all, all the time.*[2]

Valenti goes on to explain that the United Nations and Human Rights Watch have declared that menstrual hygiene is a key factor in ensuring human rights on an international scale. Jyoti Sanghera, chief of the UN Human Rights Office on Economic and Social Issues, has referred to the intense cultural pressure not to discuss menstrual hygiene itself as "a violation of several human rights, most importantly of the right to human dignity." And yet the shame and disgust around menstruation remain in place, and period products continue to be "inaccessible and unaffordable" for many people who menstruate. "Breast pumps, vasectomies and artificial teeth are sales tax-exempt," just like Rogaine and Viagra, but "tampons are not even exempted from sales tax" in most states.[3]

In 2015 Jennifer Weiss-Wolf wrote one of her first major pieces on the subject of menstrual equity, "Helping Women and Girls. Period," published in the *New York Times* through Nicholas Kristof's blog, *On the Ground*. Weiss-Wolf spoke out about the burden that a lack of access to period products causes for women and girls all over the world who cannot afford tampons and pads. This op-ed raised awareness and inspired many around the country to get involved in collecting period products to donate to those in need. It ends with her call to action for "tampon drives" as a "remarkably easy but infinitely meaningful way to help women take charge, and take care, of their bodies and their lives."[4]

And it's true. Nongovernmental organizations and individuals are working to make sure that tampons and pads are free and accessible in school and workplace bathrooms, even without legislative requirements or support. As more young menstruators come forward with stories of not having period products when they needed them, and stating the need for greater access, more schools devote resources and staffing to make menstrual products readily available. In 2015 a mother of two in Dublin, Ohio, named Jenn Bajec lobbied local elementary and middle schools to put free tampons and pads in bathrooms, after learning that her sixth-grade daughter couldn't make it to class in time when she needed a menstrual product because they were kept almost hidden in the nurse's office.[5] Similarly, Nancy Kramer, a school parent in Columbus, Ohio, created the campaign Free the Tampons[6] to provide free period products in schools.

These interventions by community members pushing school administrations to provide free period products in restrooms are amazing *short-term* solutions. However, this is not a dependable kind of change because it relies on an administrator overseeing the provision of period products, with no budgets or procedures in place to ensure that the practice continues.[7]

In order to effectively advocate for policy change, it is not enough to only raise awareness. We need to have data on the need for, and potential impact of, proposed policy changes. This presents a large obstacle for period policy, since there is next to no hard data on the harmful effects that menstruators experience when they don't have access to period products. We're able to make anecdote-based claims, for instance, about how period-related pain and lack of access to tampons and pads constitute the leading cause of absenteeism for girls in school in the United States, but we don't have the hard numbers behind it because people have yet to realize that this is such a drastic issue.[8] Which brings us back to the point about needing social change to make systemic change, and vice versa—and it all begins with raising your voice.

• COMBATING PERIOD POVERTY THROUGH YOUR LOCAL GOVERNMENT •

"In a city where we hand out free condoms, we should be making tampons more affordable and accessible. It's a matter of avoiding health risks, affordability and women's equality. . . . We should make them available in school bathrooms. It can take away from the shame, the taboo."

—Julissa Ferreras-Copeland[9]

In 2016 the New York City Council made headlines by introducing a bill that would be our country's most progressive policy on menstrual equity to date.[10] Passed in July 2016, the new law made period products free and accessible in correctional facilities, public schools, and homeless shelters, addressing the three major areas of need we discussed in the last chapter.[11] This was a monumental bill package that required more than three different pieces of legislation, working across the Departments of Education, Correction, and Homeless Services.[12] After the New York City Council passed the bills, Mayor Bill de Blasio signed them, noting that "tampons and pads aren't luxuries—they're necessities."[13]

Council Member Julissa Ferreras-Copeland launched her journey toward passing this bill package after holding a roundtable in June 2015, which was actually inspired by Jennifer Weiss-Wolf's "Helping Women and Girls. Period." The roundtable consisted of more than twenty women representing different groups—such as Planned Parenthood, the Women's Prison Association, the

Legal Aid Society, and the Food Bank for New York—discussing issues they were facing.[14,15] This meeting motivated Ferreras-Copeland to take immediate action,[16] especially since long before this bill passed, public schools in New York City were giving out condoms for free. As Copeland said, "If we were able to remove the taboo from condoms . . . then we should be able to do this. Just like the schools order toilet paper, they should be ordering these supplies."[17]

And so, beginning in fall 2016, in all NYC school buildings housing sixth through twelfth graders, tampons and pads have been free for students.[18,19] This covers the needs of most menstruating students in public schools between the ages of eleven and eighteen. Though some schools were already handing out products, as Council Member Ferreras-Copeland said, "a young girl should not have to tell her teacher, to then tell her counselor, to then be sent to the nurse's office, to then be given a pad to then go back to the bathroom while a boy is already taking his exam in his classroom."[20] Thanks to the new law, the period products are provided in schools through a dispenser installed in each restroom that has a "timing mechanism so you can't just push the lever again and again and clean it out."[21]

This bill package was also great news for New

York City's menstruating inmates. As we discussed in the last chapter, female inmates in prisons across the country are provided with vastly insufficient period products. At the time the bill became law, the Department of Correction was distributing fewer than three pads per inmate per week. Furthermore, because these period products were so desperately needed, they became tools of power—regularly held just out of reach, forcing women to stain their clothes, for which they were often period-shamed. The New York legislation was historic because it demanded change to address how the access to pads for female inmates in New York City was inadequate.[22]

The powerful 2015 report on reproductive injustice that was published by the Correctional Association of New York, discussed in the previous chapter, surely helped Ferreras-Copeland's bills get passed. The report's foreword was written by a woman named Judith Clark, who has been incarcerated since 1983. She wrote that for women who have been incarcerated for decades, the "quality of medical care available to us is a matter of life and death." Regardless of whether a person is in prison or not, "health care is a human right that should not be diminished by incarceration."[23] The report was a call to action for new policy to be codified and implemented, and for all involved parties (including all inmates, officers, and medical staff) to be educated about what protections the policy ensures. In keeping with those goals, New York City's bill requires the city's Department of Correction "to provide all female inmates" with the period products they need "as soon as practicable upon request."[24,25] No more using period products as tools of power!

It's important to point out that New York City isn't the only place where change is happening on a local level. In late 2015 (even before the NYC bill) the Dane County government in Wisconsin passed a resolution to "provide menstrual products in public restrooms of county buildings."[26] Beginning in 2016 period products had to be made available in eight county buildings, including the correctional facility, through coin-free dispensers. Before the resolution was passed, pads were free in prison but given out only upon request[27]—so once again inmates had to ask for a period product from what would most likely be a male guard.

One of the biggest criticisms of working in policy is that GOVERNMENT IS SLOW. Achieving policy change requires constant campaigning, hard-fought approvals each step of the way, wading through the bureaucracy and its forms, and getting through the ample red tape. To be fair, there is a good reason for this lack of real speed: the legislation has to be written, lobbied for, renegotiated, and approved. Some of the red tape is legitimate checks and balances that prevent ridiculous laws from getting passed haphazardly, and some of the red tape is unnecessary and frustrating. But it's still very slow, when it's hard to be patient for necessary change.

Another hard and frustrating thing about policy is that even once it's passed, it always comes with limitations. It's never exactly what you want it to be. For instance, while the NYC law might ensure that there is funding or enough product out there, it doesn't address the culture around period products or how menstruation is discussed (or not discussed) in the first place—and the bill can always lose funding if public opinion turns against it. There's also limited enforcement legislation. How is the NYC government going to make sure that these products are readily available upon request in every school, prison, and shelter, and that prison guards are not withholding pads from inmates?

Because changing government policy through lawmaking can be so difficult, in the past people have sometimes argued that there is protection under existing laws, and they've tried to increase enforcement of the menstrual health protections that are already in place. For example, a number of court cases have fought for adequate access to period products in prisons by using the Eighth Amendment's prohibition against "cruel and unusual punishments." These cases insist upon the constitutional right to basic cleanliness.

A recent case was *Atkins v. County of Orange* in 2005, in which one of the plaintiffs told her story of being "denied sanitary food and basic hygiene items such as toilet paper, toothbrush and sanitary napkins." She sat in her cell "with 'blood all over legs' because she was not provided with sanitary napkins," and when she "begged and pleaded to her jailers to give her some water," she was denied. The court ruled in favor of the inmates on this issue, who came forward with their stories of injustice, declaring that "the failure to regularly provide prisoners with . . . toilet articles including soap, razors, combs, toothpaste, toilet paper, access to a mirror and sanitary napkins for female prisoners constitutes a denial of personal hygiene and sanitary living conditions." As had been argued, the denial of access to period products "violated basic standards of decency" and subjected the inmates to "cruel and unusual punishment in violation of the Eighth Amendment."[28]

Over the last few years more and more municipalities have started to fight for access to period products. The NYC Council legislation in the summer of 2016 was one of the more highly publicized instances of progress for period policy, but similar bill packages have been making headway in cities all around the United States. Citizens and politicians are really starting to change things in their own immediate communities. We still have work to do, but progress is happening! LFG!

• STATE LEGISLATION •

So, cities and counties are making things happen—but what about at higher levels of government? We are just beginning to see period policy passing into law at the *state* level. But with a larger constituency to please, it's harder to pass a blanket law like the New York City bill package. State advocates have to be more select in what they try to do and how they try to do it.

One goal is the provision of free period products in schools. Recently, on October 12, 2017, California Governor Jerry Brown signed Assembly Bill Number 10 (AB10).[29,30] AB10 was spearheaded by Assemblywoman Cristina Garcia, who said, "Menstrual products are medical necessities, and it is important we recognize that not having access to these products impacts a young girl's education." The bill was passed together with other measures, including one about the provision of a diaper assistance benefit for low-income families. The overall bill package was designed to "make a positive difference for women, children and families across the state."[31]

Prior to the law's being passed, every public and private school in California was required to have bathrooms open during all school hours, and each one was required to be "maintained and cleaned regularly, fully operational, and stocked with soap and paper supplies." AB10 added that all public schools with students between sixth and twelfth grade "where at least 40 percent of students meet federal poverty standards" must provide free period products in at least 50 percent of the bathrooms.[32,33] Because the bill would mandate changes statewide throughout the state, AB10 is a strong example of the power of continuing efforts on a local level.[34]

AB10 is an expensive legislative initiative. It's estimated that it will cost millions of dollars to install tampon dispensers at all of California's eligible schools, and hundreds of thousands of dollars each year to stock them, but it is a *worthwhile and needed investment* to ensure equality in schools between menstruators and non-menstruators.[35] Nevertheless, since expensive programs are funded by the state's budget, anything else the state provides based on the taxes it collects is affected.

In addition to getting free period products into California schools, Assemblywoman Garcia has been a vocal advocate for repealing the state's sales tax on period products, often referred to as the tampon tax, which she argues "punishes women for their biology."[36] Repealing the sales tax levied on tampons and pads is about more than just saving a menstruator several cents per dollar. It's about fighting the fact that government (at every level) considers menstrual hygiene a *privilege* and not a *right*. As Jessica Valenti put it, fighting things like the tampon tax is "less an issue of costliness than it is of principle: menstrual care is health care, and should be treated as such."[37] In the middle of 2015, arguments against the tampon tax began reaching mainstream media and raising public awareness. In October of that year, Prachi Gupta wrote an article for *Cosmopolitan* called "Why the Hell Are Tampons Still Taxed? It's Time for the Government to Stop Fining Women for Having Ovaries."[38] YASSS. YAS, Prachi, YAS.

At the time when Gupta's article was published, only five US states chose to specifically not tax period products: Maryland, Massachusetts, Pennsylvania, Minnesota, and New Jersey. The forty-five other states either had no sales tax at all or didn't count menstrual products as a necessity.[39] In 2015 *fifteen* states (three times as many—ugh) treated candy as a necessity, counting it as a tax-exempt grocery. Ten of these states didn't tax soda or candy but *did* tax tampons.[40] Now, in 2018, "nine states have exempted menstrual products from their sales tax, and seven have introduced legislation aimed at doing the same"—this is not including the five states that don't have any sales tax at all. [41]

California was one of the first states "where a bill was introduced to slash taxes for menstrual products." Assemblywoman Garcia, who led the fight,[42] became known for carrying around her Tampon Barbies, which were Barbie dolls holding tampons. She used a blond one and a brunette one to "illustrate her campaign to end the California sales tax on tampons."[43]

Sadly, in September 2016, Governor Brown vetoed the legislation, even though "both the diaper and tampon sales tax repeals unanimously passed the legislature" the month before. Governor Brown acknowledged the cost of such tax breaks as the major obstacle. He said, "tax breaks are the same as new spending," meaning that not gathering revenue from taxes is effectively the same as spending money on new programs. Assemblywoman Garcia tweeted her reaction to his veto, saying, "@JerryBrownGov please #mansplain why it's ok to balance the budget on women's backs? The unfair #tampontax continues."[44]

California makes a *lot* of money (about $20 million a year) by making menstruators pay this luxury tax on menstrual products—and the brilliant strategy of the California legislators to move forward on the bill was to find a more appropriate place to earn that revenue.

In March 2017 Assemblywomen Cristina Garcia and Lorena Gonzalez Fletcher[45] proposed "getting rid of the tax on tampons and making up the budget short-fall by raising a tax on hard alcohol." The legislation would have had no effect on beer or wine. Garcia said the tax would barely have made a noticeable difference for consumers, "just two more cents per cocktail," and it would have yielded about "$72 million in new revenue for the state."[46] Unlike MENSTRUATING, which is very much not a luxury, DRINKING ALCOHOL is a choice. "There is no happy hour for menstruation," said Assemblywoman Garcia. "Our tax code needs to reflect the fact that it's not ok to tax women for being born women." It's bad enough that women are "already being underpaid, undervalued and under-appreciated," and no one should have to pay more just because of the body they're born into.[47]

SO COOL, RIGHT?! And at least for me personally, it makes total sense. Unfortunately, this bill also failed. Its opponents had argued that the state should *not* favor necessities for women and children over alcohol. Large alcohol corporations, including "Bacardi and Diageo lobbied against the bill, as did groups representing restaurants and alcohol distributors," and the alcohol industry was powerful enough to shoot the proposition down. Representatives from the industry argued that "the tax hike would cost

$170 million in retail sales and 2,400 jobs,"[48] even though the California tax on hard liquor is relatively low compared to that of other states.

While the initial fight to repeal the sales tax on period products in California failed, it paved the way for legislators to propose similar bills in other states—including Illinois, New York, and Connecticut.[49] Throughout the various campaigns for providing free period products, one of the cleverest tactics has been to compare tampons and pads to toilet paper. Toilet paper, more than tampons and pads, is considered a necessity that all people should have access to, and it's also taxed. In 2015 legislators in New York fought against the tax on toilet paper. One of the more vocal advocates for eliminating the tax was Republican State Senator Phil Boyle from Long Island, who said, "It's a crazy thing to tax toilet paper. It's a necessity of life—like food. . . . Everyone, whether rich or poor, has to use toilet paper." At the time, only seven states didn't tax toilet paper.[50] Senator Boyle proposed legislation to do away with the tax.[51] The *New York Post* reported that "the typical American family buys 119 rolls of toilet paper a year, and each person flushes 50 pounds of paper down the toilet, according to industry estimates."[52]

A Democratic assemblyman, David Weprin of Queens, came out in support of repealing the sales tax on toilet paper and also spoke out about the importance of repealing the sales tax on period products, saying, "Toilet paper shouldn't be taxed. Tampons shouldn't be taxed. This is about more than dollars and cents. . . . This is a quality-of-life issue. We have to buy toilet paper. Women have to use feminine hygiene products."[53] The legislation concerning toilet paper is still making its way through the state congress.

But in July of 2016 New York became the eleventh state to eliminate the luxury tax on menstrual products.[54] Governor Cuomo signed a bill (A.7555-A/S.7838) approving the exemption of such products from the "state's 4 percent sales tax, as well as local taxes."[55,56,57] Cuomo explained that the tampon tax is "a regressive tax on essential products that women have had to pay for far too long and lifting it is a matter of social and economic justice." The tampon tax in New York had been in effect since 1965, and when repealed "fifty-one years later, people in New York state are now projected to save $10 million a year when buying menstrual products."[58] This progress has an impact on so many, especially considering that "more than 10 million women of childbearing age live in New York."[59]

This measure was co-sponsored by Senator Sue Serino (R-Dutchess County) and Assemblywoman Linda Rosenthal (D-Manhattan).[60] Rosenthal had introduced a similar bill one year earlier, in May 2015, but the idea didn't get any traction until a bigger, national conversation began. For Rosenthal the 1965 implementation of the tampon tax was representative of a time "when women were not part of government and the decision-making process."[61] Once the bill passed, she announced the victory in a short and sweet tweet: "Good riddance to sexist tax."[62] Senator Serino viewed the signing of the bill as "a monumental step forward in reforming our out-of-touch tax laws and we are sending a strong message to New York's women that they are being heard."[63]

Within a few months after the legislation passed, it became apparent that not all retailers of period products were aware of the change. In fact, especially for the smaller stores, many hadn't even been aware that the sales tax had existed. The big chains like Duane Reade and Walgreens had quickly adapted to applying the tax when it was established, but not to removing it when the tax was repealed. According to Jennifer Weiss-Wolf, all sellers of period products in New York were sent a letter on August 1, 2016, notifying them of the new law—but that didn't mean that all retailers received, read, or appropriately reacted to it. Weiss-Wolf noted that it's "fairly easy for a notice like this to get lost in the shuffle," but there was still more that the state could do to "make sure sellers are aware of this high-profile update." In response to this lack of implementation, on September 1, 2016, Weiss-Wolf "organized a social media campaign called #TweetTheReceipt, aimed at seeing which stores were cutting the tax from day one." Governor Cuomo later implemented a way for people to submit receipts online through the Department of Taxation and Finance to receive reimbursements.[64]

There were a lot of efforts in 2016 to repeal the tampon tax. In just the first half of the year, fifteen states "introduced legislation or initiated legislative debate to eliminate the tampon tax."[65] And these efforts have started to bear fruit: In August 2016 legislation sponsored by State Senator Melinda Bush was signed into law in Illinois—to take effect on January 1, 2017—with the state's Department of Revenue Regulations declaring that tampons, menstrual pads, and menstrual cups were now "exempt from the Retailers' Occupation Tax."[66] Before then, "menstrual and incontinence products" had cost consumers "$14.7 million annually."[67]

• PERIOD POLICY AT THE NATIONAL LEVEL •

If the bulk of decisions about women's health remains in the hands of state governments in this country, what can we do at a national level? US

Representative Grace Meng of Queens, New York, the *Ultimate Period Warrior*, had a great idea. In 2016 Congresswoman Meng "persuaded the Federal Emergency Management Agency [FEMA] to allow homeless shelters to buy feminine hygiene products with federal grant funds."[68] She did this by sending a powerful letter to Homeland Security Secretary Jeh Johnson, who oversaw FEMA. Before that, homeless assistance providers had been able to spend the money that they received from the agency's Emergency Food and Shelter National Board Program on "personal necessities" such as blankets, toilet paper, soap, toothpaste, and underwear, but as usual, period products had not been considered eligible items. Congresswoman Meng also sent letters to the secretary of Health and Human Services (HHS) and the secretary of Housing and Urban Development (HUD) to ask that homeless assistance providers also be allowed to purchase period products with grants from those agencies.[69] Plus, she worked to make sure that women can buy menstrual products with their flexible spending accounts.[70]

It's difficult to make changes on a national level when many policies are decided state by state. But in 2015 and 2016 period policy came into the national spotlight for a variety of reasons. Access to affordable health care for women and children was a core pillar of Hillary Clinton's campaign, and people across the country used the slogan "Women's rights are human rights." In 2016, when the Supreme Court was faced with the question of whether employers could be exempted from the Affordable Care Act's mandate that they offer employees insurance coverage for birth control, the court essentially sent the issue back to federal appeals courts to decide. And as a general reaction to health care changes, lots of people joked (angrily) that being a woman was basically considered a preexisting condition when it came to seeking insurance coverage.

Donald Trump himself catapulted menstruation into mainstream media coverage when he "accused Fox News moderator Megyn Kelly of having 'blood coming out of her wherever.'"[71] And after Mike Pence joined Trump's campaign as vice presidential candidate, Pence came under attack for signing a law saddling Indiana with some of the "country's most restrictive" antiabortion rules.[72] Women all across the country began to engage in #PeriodsforPence, "tweeting at Republican vice presidential hopeful Mike Pence with details about their menstrual cycles."[73,74] The Twitter campaign went *viral*.

The #PeriodsforPence social media crusade began in March 2016 as a Twitter account run by an anonymous woman, who encouraged "women to call Pence's office to talk about their periods," saying, "Let's make our bodies Mike's business for real, if this is how he wants it." She started to regularly share examples of conversation transcripts of how to (in a fun but powerful way) share very personal information about one's menstrual cycle with Pence's office.[75] The content of these tweets ranged from women inviting Governor Pence to their gynecology appointments, to keeping him updated on their menstrual cramps or their experiences of various menstrual products.

The #PeriodsforPence campaign was a way for menstruators all over the country to use humor and factual language about their bodies and health to stir up pushback against Pence's legislation—which the "Indiana branches of Planned Parenthood and the American Civil Liberties Union" were also fighting, with a federal lawsuit.[76] Though the campaign started in response to state legislation, the outrage was nationwide, in no small part because people were facing the prospect of Pence's extreme antichoice beliefs reaching the White House and possibly the Supreme Court—which is exactly what happened.

• PUSHBACK—THE IMPORTANCE OF VOICE •

It is true that people successfully fought the tampon tax before this decade—which raises the question,

Why hasn't that happened more often? In 1989 "a group of women in Chicago won a class action lawsuit" that challenged the city sales tax on period products.[77] They argued that "tampons and sanitary napkins were medical necessities of life."[78] At the state level, Illinois "had a sales tax exemption for 'medical appliances,' and considered tampons and sanitary napkins within that category."[79] However, the City of Chicago did not see period products as medical appliances because they "were only used for hygienic purposes." The city sales tax was eventually struck down because the Illinois Supreme Court ruled that the innovation of period products "created a reliance on these products," which did make them essential medical appliances. The court compared their invention to that "of the telephone and electricity"—things that, once they entered the market, people became reliant upon for very real reasons.[80]

Unfortunately, this tax exemption for tampons and pads was short-lived because eventually they returned to no longer being considered "medically necessary items" and were slipped back under the category of "grooming and hygiene products." As of October 2015, they continued to be taxed at the "6.25 percent rate by the state," in the same grouping as deodorants, moisturizers, breath spray, condoms, and foot powders.[81,82]

Most of the time social change and institutional change have to happen hand in hand, spurring each other on. A failed 2015 bill in Wisconsin shows just how much systemic change depends on public mind-set. When State Representative Melissa Sargent introduced Assembly Bill 555 to provide "feminine hygiene products in state buildings and school buildings," the bill failed to pass the state legislature because Wisconsin lawmakers weren't yet ready to view access to menstrual products as a right.[83] You need to change some people's minds in order to enact new policy, which then, hopefully, will change still more minds.

It's important to let legislatures and politicians know our discontent, because our voices have the power to make a real difference. In her *Cosmopolitan* article about abolishing the tampon tax, Prachi Gupta recalled key times when energized and vocal public opinion against government-imposed sales tax made a difference in changing legislation. For example, politicians in California realized they "ate candy with cake, indiscriminately" in 1971 and decided that candy should have "the same tax-exempt benefits as other grocery items" like cake. Another example was when people got pissed off because the state of Iowa in 2006 was attempting to "impose its 5 percent sales tax on pumpkins sold as jack-o'-lanterns." In response the "then-Iowa Gov. Chet Culver called on the Department of Revenue" to "suspend collection of this tax and offer refunds to consumers or retailers" who were affected. Since then, "pumpkins have been exempt from the sales tax," but *tampons* have not been.[84]

Jennifer Weiss-Wolf has said about the Menstrual Movement, "It's important that it's not just one woman trying to do it, it's about women as a collective working for this issue." She knows that period policy advocacy is no new thing. Female legislators started bringing it up decades ago, but they never made headway, simply because before now people were less open to even discussing menstruation, not to mention changing the laws.[85]

Periods are tricky when it comes to policy. In order to talk on a political level about periods and the need for menstrual equity, and to convince rooms full of legislators (usually mostly men), we need a *cultural shift* toward acknowledging that menstrual hygiene is a *right* and *not a privilege*. As we've seen, we need influencers, celebrities, and leading politicians to speak out in support of the Menstrual Movement.

On November 2, 2015, Michelle Obama wrote a piece for the *Atlantic* titled "Let Girls Learn: Addressing the Global Crisis in Girls' Education Requires Not Just Investment, but Challenging Cultural Beliefs and Practices." "Let Girls Learn" is also the name of the initiative she and President

Obama started to "fund community girls' education projects . . . educate girls in conflict zones; and address poverty, HIV, and other issues that keep girls out of school." The article is about how pressing global issues such as equality in schools are often thought of "as a matter of resources," with people thinking that we have to invest more in school fees, uniforms, transportation, and bathrooms so that more menstruators can stay in school. Michelle Obama says that a true solution must go beyond policy and resource change—there has to be a cultural shift. "Scholarships, bathrooms, and safe transportation will only go so far if societies still view menstruation as shameful and shun menstruating girls."[86]

While this article mostly focuses on the problem of periods in other countries, it's true here in the United States too—we have to prompt a major shift in the way we perceive and talk about menstruation and growing human bodies. Again, policy and social change go hand in hand. We can't change policy without public opinion becoming more progressive on issues such as menstrual equity, and we won't have effective policy implementation unless people understand why it's important and needed. And to do that, those pushing for change need to raise their voices.

• THE ROBIN DANIELSON ACT •

An excellent example of policy shift coming as a result of activism involves the issue of ingredients in period products and their link to toxic shock syndrome.

Three big companies control much of the period product market: Procter & Gamble (Tampax), Energizer Holdings (Playtex), and Kimberly-Clark (U by Kotex). Together they "control 85 percent of the tampon market."[87] The products sold by these large companies (the name brands we are probably all very familiar with) are often criticized as being "mass-produced, heavily marketed, and cheaply made—out of bleached rayon and plastics."[88]

The Food and Drug Administration (FDA) does "not require companies to disclose the ingredients in their pads and tampons."[89] The most controversial ingredient in generic tampons and pads is also the "#1 ingredient" in them: rayon. Rayon is made by taking cellulose (a natural fiber) and transforming it through a process that involves "chemicals such as carbon disulphide, sulfuric acid, chlorine and caustic soda." To get the bright white color of most of our period products, the materials for tampons and pads are bleached with chlorine, "which results in the production of dioxin, a chemical linked to breast cancer, endometriosis, immune system suppression, and various other ailments."[90]

In 2012 Lauren Wasser was living in Los Angeles and modeling professionally. One day she woke up "feeling a bit off but attributed it to be the beginning of flu season." She was on her period at the time and "ran out of tampons and headed to the grocery store" to restock. She was supposed to go to a birthday party later that evening, but as the day progressed, she started to feel worse and worse. She barely had the energy to push herself out of bed and take a shower before joining her friends for dinner. By the time she reached the party, she "felt like a truck had hit [her]" and only stayed for a "few minutes before heading home" and going straight to bed with a high fever.

Lauren and her mom are very close—they talk every day, often more than once—so when Lauren didn't respond to her mom's messages, her mom knew something was wrong. She "called the police asking for a welfare check" to make sure she was okay, and a police officer woke Lauren up from her bed to check on her, and said, "You're really sick. You need to call your mom because she's worried about you," and then left. Lauren called her mom and let her know that she did not think she needed an ambulance, and then she asked her mom to "check on me in the morning." She doesn't remember anything after that.

She was later told that the police eventually returned to check on her and "this time found [her] face down on the floor. [She] was unresponsive, had a fever of 108, and was covered in [her] own feces and vomit." She was rushed to the hospital, where she encountered doctors who were confused by her symptoms. An infectious disease doctor had to be called in, who decided to send her tampon to the lab for testing. "Three days later the results came back with signs of TSS-1." Lauren said later, "I was placed into a medically induced coma, all of my organs were shutting down, my blood pressure was unstable, I suffered a heart attack, my fever was out of control, and I was on life support."[91]

Lauren woke up from the coma "a week and a half later," with the constant feeling of her feet being on fire. She was transferred to "UCLA for Hyperbaric treatments. (That's where you're put into a chamber made up of increased oxygen to help the blood flow.)" And the "fight was on to save [her] legs." Both legs developed gangrene that "was moving quickly," and her left leg had a "50/50 chance of surviving." The heel on her left leg, and all five of her toes on that foot were "severely damaged."[92] Lauren's surgeons recommended removing both of her legs at the time, but she "chose to fight to save her left leg, opting only to have her toes amputated." Her right leg was "removed completely, in a below-the-knee amputation."[93]

Two years before Lauren had her initial battle with TSS, a twenty-year-old woman named Amy lost her life to TSS.[94] Amy was healthy and had very mild symptoms, but less than a week before her death, on a Wednesday afternoon, "she developed a fever and began vomiting." Like Lauren, she assumed that she had the flu, and her symptoms seemed to go away after she took some ibuprofen. A couple of days later she "woke up very weak with a sore throat and sore muscles." She was admitted to the hospital later that day, and her blood work showed that "her kidneys were at 25% function." The next day, on Saturday, only three days after she'd first started experiencing noticeable symptoms, Amy "had become septic," and "she developed fluid in her lungs, was sedated and put on a ventilator." She passed away the next day.

Hearing stories like Amy's was what pushed Lauren to realize that she was lucky "to have gotten out alive because so many victims don't." Through the website You ARE Loved, where Amy's mom shared her daughter's story and tried to "educate women and young girls about the dangers tampons can have," Lauren was able to connect "with survivors all over the country," and that helped her realize that she wasn't alone. The other women who shared their stories were anywhere between fifteen and thirty-three years old—all of them fighting "through numerous surgeries, some losing physical parts of themselves, others struggling with kidney and heart failure."[95]

In her article in *InStyle* in November 2017, Lauren shared the news that she would have to have her other leg amputated. For the previous five years, while she'd been fighting to save her left leg, Lauren had lived with "an open ulcer, no heel, and no toes."[96] Now twenty-nine years old, Lauren Wasser posted the news on Instagram in early January 2018 that she had "had successful surgery on the removal of her left leg." Her partner, Jennifer, "kept fans updated on social media throughout the surgery," garnering thousands of likes and "hundreds of positive comments."[97]

Lauren is now an avid activist working to raise awareness about the dangers of TSS and ways to prevent it. She says, "TSS has been killing and harming women for more than 30 years: let that sink in. How many lives is it going to take for something to change?" Over the last few years she has been working with legislators to "pass the Robin Danielson Act, named after a woman who lost her life to TSS in 1998." If passed, the bill would require period product companies "to disclose exactly what is going into these products and what their long-term health effects are. Shockingly the bill has been rejected 10 times."[98]

The Robin Danielson Act, originally titled the

Tampon Safety and Research Act, was first introduced in 1997 by Congresswoman Carolyn Maloney
from New York. The research component of the bill
required "the National Institutes of Health to research
the health risks associated with menstrual hygiene
products."[99] An act like this is needed, to prevent more
menstruators from contracting TSS, especially since
the syndrome "affects nearly 8,000 people nationwide
annually and as many as 1 in 700 women will acquire
tampon-related TSS in their lifetime."[100]

Besides the fight to pass legislation such as the
Robin Danielson Act, activists are also pushing for
more research on what exactly the health consequences are of using period products that may contain "residue from chemical herbicides . . . because
we are not testing for [these herbicides] in relation to
tampons." We do not have "reliable data that tells us"
whether or not the potentially harmful ingredients in
period products are safe or not, even though "the
average woman has a tampon inside her vagina for
more than 100,000 hours over her lifetime," according to *Newsweek*.[101]

I just want to quickly mention that my organization, PERIOD, has chosen to work with the large
companies that make period products (along with
smaller providers and manufacturers), because our
main goal is to get products to people who need

them. The products must be used as instructed—carefully managing the time during which tampons are kept in, and regularly changing pads. We make sure that anyone distributing product on our behalf has a strong understanding of the risks of each product and knows how to use (and teach people how to use) them in the right way. YES, we are not 100 percent sure tampons are safe, but do people still use them? Do people still want them? Do people still benefit from them? Yes.

• REPRESENTATION •

You may have noticed that when it comes to menstrual equity, most of the people who are speaking out for change and are initiating it in the government are women. Well, representation matters.

In January 2016 "Barack Obama likely became the first president to comment on menstruation," in a video interview with Ingrid Nilsen, YouTube star and lifestyle guru.[102] During the interview Ingrid asked President Obama about the sales tax on period products as luxury items. His response to the question, which then went viral, was, "I suspect it's because men were making the laws when those taxes were passed."[103] EXACTLY: Representative democracy is essential for meeting the needs of *all* Americans. Women make up more than half of our country's population, but only 20 percent of the congressional seats are held by women.[104] If the remaining 80 percent of those positions are held by men, many of whom are made squeamish by the mention of tampons or pads—God forbid we talk about menstruation in Congress—then we will continue to have legislation such as a sales tax that considers menstrual hygiene a *luxury*.

The United States is *not* great at *all* about representative democracy when it comes to having women in office, and over time we have gotten progressively worse about it. In 2017 data from a study conducted by the Inter-Parliamentary Union revealed that the US sank "from 52nd in the world for women's representation to 104th" over the last two decades. From just 2016 to 2017 the US dropped from 95th to 104th place in the rankings of more than 190 countries.[105] A 2011 American University report titled "Men Rule: The Continued Under-Representation of Women in U.S. Politics" showed that in the worldwide rankings of women in the national legislature, top countries such as Rwanda and Andorra had women in more than 50 percent of national legislative roles, while the US had women in only 19.3 percent, putting it in 90th place.[106] *No wonder* we in the US have such a difficult time making more institutional change toward menstrual equity. We can bring about a huge cultural shift in the perception and treatment of menstruation if we do two things: (1) get *more* women into office and (2) elect *more* men who are ready to talk about menstruation matter-of-factly, to acknowledge the importance of menstrual equity, and to empathize with the importance of having access to period products.

We have to work to encourage women to embrace political ambition, and we have to encourage voters to support women candidates. We also want women to run for higher positions! The American University study revealed that women tend to run for *lower* positions in public office, but in general more than twice as many men as women run for office. Women have much less confidence about having the qualifications to run, whereas men are less likely to think they are underqualified when they are. And men are more likely to consider themselves very qualified when they aren't. When men look in the mirror and see someone who they do not think is qualified to run for office, 55 percent of them will still consider running. Meanwhile, if women doubt their own qualifications, only 39 percent of them will still consider running for office.[107]

When I ran for office, I learned in the many candidate training sessions I attended that *confidence is everything*. Political campaigns are *expensive* and require resources and people power. You have to ask for money, and with each potential donor you are challenged with the task of convincing them you're qualified on a professional and personal level. (And I know that this is *so hard*, especially when you're socially trained to have this hidden insecure voice inside you questioning your own abilities and qualifications.) As a candidate you are fighting for every donor, volunteer, and voter to support your ideas and believe in your capabilities and potential as a public servant. When negative campaigning and vocal haters jump into the picture, those private voices of insecurity are suddenly made *public*, adding a whole new level of scrutiny you have to be prepared for.

It's scary to run as a young woman, and as a woman of color, and that's also why it is SO NEEDED, because it shouldn't be that way. We need more women to run, and we need to support women running, because without true representative democracy, we end up with legislation that is not in line with the real-life needs of all members of constituencies. This includes access to period products and other reproductive rights, as well as affordable quality childcare and parental leave for families (another factor that the American University report points out as an obstacle that prevents more women from running for office).[108]

Do I think that the dearth of women in public office is linked to menstruation? Um. YES. At around the age of thirteen, when kids start going through puberty, boys feel more manly as their voices drop in tone, their bodies become more aligned with societal views of masculinity, and society pats them on the back for becoming men. Girls, on the other hand, get their periods—and the strongly embedded stigma within our society tells them that this onset of menstruation makes them less capable and less reasonable. They are taught to feel anxious and ashamed about their periods, that menstruation is something they have to invest in financially, physically, and emotionally, just to be able to compete at the same level as their male counterparts. Postpuberty men are encouraged to puff out their chests, own their manhood, stand tall, and proclaim their power—whereas menstruating women are faced with something that they have probably learned to keep hidden.

Around the time that puberty sets in, students are most likely at the tail end of middle school or entering high school. During these formative years, kids are pushed to proclaim their passions in and out of school, to embrace and pursue their academic interests. Athletics are taken much more seriously, especially going into high school, when there will probably be a sudden distinction between varsity and junior varsity, and boys' sports are almost universally given more attention and funding than girls' sports. These are also the years when early teens often begin to compare their own bodies to others', including in the media, and teens more deeply explore sexuality and even dating. So . . . taking into consideration the pervasive and powerful societal constructs of what it means to be a man or woman, and recognizing that these constructs have direct and long-lasting effects on how teenagers form professional and personal dreams—I see an undeniable correlation between the stigmas around menstruation and female bodies, and the lack of women in positions of power, as well as in STEM (science, technology, engineering, and math) professions.

I don't think this situation is permanent. (If I thought it were unchangeable, I wouldn't be writing this book.) One of the most important things we can do immediately is ACKNOWLEDGE the problem. We need to reach a place of comfort in order to have honest and serious discussions about how we can reshape the experience of puberty for all people. And we need to discuss how such changes will be supported in school, at home, and from a bodily health perspective in a way that fosters equality and the empowerment of women, girls, and those who don't identify within the constraints of the gender binary. We need to work in all these areas so that young people can go on to hold positions of power and enact real legislative change, which will lead to further equality for all genders.

CHAPTER SEVEN

•

MENSTRUATION IN THE MEDIA

Throughout history, ads, TV shows, movies, news, and product packaging have often sent the message that periods make people less capable. It is common for TV shows to have episodes that feature women "going crazy" while they're on their period. Jokes like these send the message to men (and women) that women who are on their period are out of control, emotional, and irrational. In Lauren Rosenwarn's book *Periods in Pop Culture: Menstruation in Film and Television*, published in 2012, she argues that when periods do actually come up in pop culture, they are portrayed as awful for everyone. Her argument is described, "they are often depicted as the source of women's bad moods, mediocre sex lives, and hassles for men."[1]

There is also the problem of the lack of conversation around menstruation. In the ten years of airtime for the hit sitcom *Friends*, "only *once* did producers see fit to mention periods—when Chandler and Monica are figuring out the best time to have sex to get pregnant ('The One Where Rachel Has a Baby')." This is despite the fact that the "series existed for 3,650 days and 840 of those days would have involved at least one of them being on their period," referring to the three main female characters, Monica, Rachel, and Phoebe. This lack of acknowledgment of menstruation as a very natural and routine part of life, in a show that is about candid friendships and everyday experiences, is problematic (or at least very telling) because it advances the taboo, encouraging people to stay silent about menstruation.[2]

I certainly received lots of negative pop-culture messages about periods as a kid. Like most of my classmates, I grew up watching *Family Guy*, which often treated periods like they're shameful to have. For example, in one episode "Stewie reads a book about menstruation and calls it 'the most disgusting thing I've seen in my entire life!'"[3]

Since men are not often expected to learn anything about menstruation in school, jokes about periods in ads and TV can be the only information they get about it. This means that men may take misrepresentations of periods in the media and news to be true, and they may start to believe that people who are on their periods cannot be trusted with decision-making.

As you can imagine, the ripple effects of this are huge!

The good news is that in just the last few years we have seen a wave of media redefine the period experience. Changing media portrayals of menstruators is a crucial aspect of changing public opinion and making menstruation an open conversation, so that menstruators aren't held back from reaching their full potential. There is no question that menstruation (on a universal and global level) is taboo as a subject of conversation right now—and so the first step toward making progress is to just get people talking about periods. Say the word "period" instead of one of the thousands of euphemisms people use to avoid saying the actual word, and talk about menstrual equity, period poverty, and perhaps even the broader topic of how periods fit into the world of reproductive rights and women's health.

Elizabeth Yuko, a writer and bioethicist, and the health and sex editor of SheKnows Media, says that pop culture is a powerful "entry point to discussion" and thus a very powerful tool for changing the way we think and talk about periods. Yuko also teaches a class at Fordham University called Ethics and Pop Culture, where she makes it a point to devote a few sessions to talking about menstruation in the media. She says the topic always makes some male students visibly uncomfortable.[4] To ease the discomfort, Elizabeth says, the best way for periods to be presented is in a lighthearted fashion and "injected with a bit of humor."[5]

It is only very recently, though, that media has even been able to mention, much less discuss, menstruation. In an article for SheKnows Media, Yuko declared that "2017 Was a Big Year for Periods on TV," and it's true—from Netflix's *Anne of Green Gables* adaptation, where Anne questions having to skip school because of her period, to Netflix's *GLOW* episode where two of the main characters engage in period sex, and the man holds that up as proof that he really likes the woman.[6] Also in *GLOW*, the women wrestlers "swap tampons and maxi pads and talk about how ridiculous the diaper-like pads are" when they're all in the locker room together.[7] The topic of period sex got some notable airtime in the musical TV show *Crazy Ex-Girlfriend*, where an entire musical number was dedicated to "Period Sex."

ABC's hit show *Black-ish* also has a strong period moment, when young "Diane gets her first period at school and all the women in her family try—in their own unique ways—to help her." In reality Diane "knows what she's doing" and doesn't really need any help at all.[8] Her mom, Rainbow, tells Diane her own period story of being kept home from school by her mom when she got her period "because it meant she was 'dirty.'" This is a powerful portrayal of how ideas around menstruation and the female body are changing, and changing fast.[9]

That episode of *Black-ish* was broadcast "almost 27 years, to the date" after the character "Rudy Huxtable got her first period in an episode of *The Cosby Show*."[10] Similar to the *Black-ish* story, Rudy gets her first period, and "Clair [her mom] wants to have a traditional women's only day to celebrate her woman-hood. Rudy wants no part of it and says she under-stands everything and needs nothing from her mother," because she trusts the information she's already gotten from her friends. Just like *Black-ish* does, this episode of *The Cosby Show* highlights the progress society has already made in terms of girls talking about their periods. Clair recounts that when she was growing up, menstruation was treated as "the horror." Both shows note "that this milestone means something beautiful," that these young women "can someday have [their] own children." Unique to *Black-ish,* though, is that the portrayal of menarche "hints at how this rite of pas-sage can become a gateway to female empowerment," since the male characters notice that postmenarche, Diane has become "even more fiery than usual," with a sort of heightened power.[11]

Menarche also got airtime in mainstream media on Netflix's animated series *Big Mouth* in 2017. The show works to stay close to "the gender-inclusive vision laid out by co-creators . . . who decided that periods and penises deserved equal time on their half-hour comedy." The second episode featured the character "Jessi getting her first period inside the Statue of Liberty."[12,13] While hiding in the bathroom because of the bloodstain on her white shorts, Jessi "turns to an animate Statue of Liberty, who moans, 'Periods are nothing but pain and misery.'" On the bus ride home, Jessi "imagines a tampon who sounds remarkably similar to Michael Stipe, singing a song called 'Everybody Bleeds' that sounds a lot like R.E.M.'s 'Everybody Hurts.'"[14] As Refinery29 points out, this storyline is a representation of "the female side of puberty humor, comedy real estate that's sparsely populated. For every ten jokes about balls dropping and voices cracking, we hear maybe one about the terrors of becoming a woman during adolescence."[15]

In the same episode Jessi makes a "new invisible best friend, the Hormone Monstress (Maya Rudolph), who informs Jessi that, as a young woman, it's now her duty to listen to Lana Del Rey on repeat, cut up all her T-shirts, and 'scream at your mother and then laugh at her tears.'" This episode of *Big Mouth* is a towering example of how we're at a pivotal moment in the overall Menstrual Movement. For the first time in mainstream media, we are seeing periods presented as an experience that can really suck but that can also be a source of great power and emotion. This episode also comments on the injustice of the period stigma. Jessi's mom acknowledges this when she says, "You know, if men got their period, it'd be an Olympic sport. They'd give out medals for the heaviest flow."[16] The comment is reminiscent of Gloria Steinem's 1978 satirical piece in *Ms.* magazine, "If Men Could Menstruate."

Elizabeth Yuko calls Comedy Central's *Broad City* another great example of a TV show that introduces its audience to much-needed conversations about periods. The two "inspired comic minds" behind the show, Abbi Jacobson and Ilana Glazer, who play imaginary versions of themselves, brilliantly represent the hilarity and absurdity that can come with menstruation, while at the same time pointing out the very real problems of the period stigma—from highlighting how the media dramatizes menstruating women, to the injustice of considering period products a luxury in our society.[17]

In season three Ilana uses her "period pants"—a pair of jeans with a comically large bloodstain on the crotch—"to sneak weed through airport security."[18] She explains to Abbi that "she wore the pants to prevent further questioning from TSA officials so she could successfully smuggle weed to their vacation destination, stored snugly in her vagina." And it works. While the TSA dog does start to sniff around her vagina, the officer has the dog back off immediately after he sees the large bloodstain.[19] The scene was relatable, eye-opening, and super funny—all at the same time. I laughed while I watched it, both from the comedy of the scene and also in recalling how I used to do something similar (along with all my friends in middle school). We would get out of gym class every day by telling our older male teacher that we were menstruating—and he never questioned the idea that we were on our periods 24/7 (all of us, at the same time, all the time). He just accepted that it made us unable to participate in physical activity. We totally took advantage of it—which, if anything, accelerates the idea that periods make menstruators less capable. It is angering that the stigma around menstruation is so strong that women can in some instances operate within the taboo to our advantage, and men often will not even engage in conversation, because they're uncomfortable.[20]

In the final episode of season three, "Jews on a Plane," Abbi "gets her period unexpectedly on an international flight to Israel" and has to enlist Ilana's help in searching for a tampon, since hers are all locked away in her checked bag. Their blunt "female-driven, female-centric comedy" is refreshing, especially when they talk about their periods, saying things like "I'm currently sitting in a pool of my own uterine lining." Period poverty also makes a debut in this episode. At one point Ilana says, "This is what homeless women must feel like. You have money: do you buy food or tampons?" and her friend replies, "Tampons should be free, all sizes." To which Ilana responds, "The only reason they aren't free is because the government hates women."

When you watch the show, you find yourself laughing—and then you realize . . . everything they're saying is very accurate, as we learned with the persistent tampon tax in the majority of states. While "Abbi and Ilana went around asking all of the passengers for an elusive tampon," the audience is shown that there is a pristine pack of tampons sitting right in plain sight in first class—a clear message of how menstrual hygiene is made so much more available to those who can afford it, as though it's the sort of luxury that our society makes it out to be.[21]

When Abbi asks an older-looking woman for a tampon, the woman says she no longer experiences menstruation. Abbi tells her that "she often forgets about menopause," to which the older woman responds, "Menopause isn't represented in mainstream media, like no one wants to talk about it." META TRUTH. People don't want to talk about menstruation, much less *menopause,* in the media, and what is amazing about this episode is that it both talks about periods and menopause and also calls out the fact that it's much too rare for these topics to be mentioned in the media.[22] Ilana and Abbi's desperate search comes to an abrupt end when members of the flight crew hear them saying that unless they find a pad or tampon soon, there might be "blood everywhere" from an "explosion"—which prompts the flight attendants to mistake the women for terrorists and take them both down.[23]

All of these period-positive TV depictions come a decade after menarche appeared in the movie *Superbad,* starring Michael Cera and Jonah Hill. In the movie "Seth (Jonah Hill) dances with a girl at a party. He's pleased with this achievement—until she leaves, and Seth discovers a small period blood stain on his jeans. He's disgusted. . . . In laughing at the joke, we sympathize with Seth, who's grossed out. We should really be empathizing with the girl, though. After all, the joke is at the expense of her exploring her sexuality at a party when her period ruins the whole encounter. It hinges on shame."[24] There's a stark contrast between the female-led period comedies and this earlier depiction, in a film released only a decade earlier.

So, in ten years we have made tremendous progress in redefining the first period experience as something that young women feel prepared for (often to the surprise of their close family members) and something that centers less on shame and more on candor, empathy, humor, and celebration. Of course, away from males and out of the public eye, women and girls have always laughed about menstruation with their friends—because sometimes it's really funny! It's fantastic that, finally, this kind of menstrual humor, as opposed to the shaming kind, is making it into the public sphere.

Just as humor can serve as a conversation starter, so can dramatic television. *Orange Is the New Black* (OITNB) has been breaking down boundaries around talking about periods and the need for menstrual equity in prisons, and it's been an amazing cultural conversation starter. Yuko talks about how in the first episode of season five, "Gina smears menstrual blood on her face to convince one of the prison guards she is injured so he will let her into the electrical room. He does, and she proceeds to stop the alarm as well as cutting power to all of Litchfield [the prison]."[25] In earlier seasons the show featured scenes where inmates wait in long lines for period products, "only to be turned away because the prison is completely out of maxi pads." When asked for an explanation, a prison worker says, "There's a hundred new inmates, but the same budget for inessentials. You can buy tampons at commissary."[26] That episode follows the inmates' developing anger at "MCC, the corporation that runs Litchfield," which decides not to increase the number of free period products available, "even though the number of inmates has practically doubled."[27] As the prison starts to completely run out of tampons and pads, the women talk about how to deal with it, with one of them saying, "I've got a wad of toilet paper so far up my hoo-hoo, I'm not sure it's ever gonna to come out."[28]

As mentioned before, one of the concerns that correctional facilities have about possibly distributing more period products than they currently do is that the products are not always used to collect menstrual blood. Prisoners sometimes use period products to do things such as clean cells, hold doors open, and, as OITNB shows, make shower shoes. During the first season "Piper Chapman emerged from the shower" wearing some slippers made out of maxi pads.[29] What OITNB also shows, though, is that while period products might sometimes be used for non-menstruation matters, they are still being used for menstrual hygiene, and the need for period products does not go away.

So why are female-led episodes about periods now making it to TV comedies and dramas? Again, representation matters. Women now hold positions as writers, directors, and producers in television to make it happen. The comedian, writer, and actress Tina Fey has said that her "proudest moment as one of the head writers of 'SNL'" was the 2011 Kotex Classic sketch, written by another female *Saturday Night Live* (SNL) staffer.[30,31] The sketch was modeled after the popular Coke Classic campaign of the time, which sold products through "nostalgia sales pitches." David Linton of the Society for Menstrual Cycle Research (SMCR) described the sketch: "It features women proudly flaunting their Kotex belts and bulging sanitary napkins, even in a swimming pool and while wearing low cut, tight evening wear. A man in the ad comments approvingly, 'Them girls are Old School!'" In the process of getting the script approved by the mostly male higher-ups, Fey learned that "they didn't know what a maxi pad belt was. It was the moment I realized that there was no 'institutional sexism' at that place. Sometimes they just literally didn't know what we were talking about." So, the Kotex Classic skit not only helped break the stigma around periods in a hilarious and liberating way, but it also educated the entire audience about historical period products.[32]

What is still largely missing in the media, though, is the menopause experience. Suzanne Moore wrote in the *Guardian* that in pop culture, aging is also taboo for women—and menopause is a biological testament to growing older. So if aging is not talked about much in the media, menopause becomes sort of invisible.[33]

It is exciting to see that in the last couple of years there have been more positive and empowering depictions of menstruation on TV. It's a definite sign of progress, and the generation of kids currently watching TV will grow up with a more open and nuanced perspective on periods.

• PERIODS IN ADS •

Although television ads were first aired in 1941,[34] it wasn't until 1975 that we saw one for a menstrual hygiene product,[35] and in 1985 Courteney Cox (best known as Monica Geller from the sitcom *Friends*) became the first person to ever use the word "period" during a commercial, for Tampax.[36] In it she's dressed exactly how I imagine people in the eighties dressed to work out—a casual shirt, purple tights, leg warmers, and a leotard. Looking into the camera, she starts her thirty-second pitch as two other girls stretch behind her: "Do you change your life for one week because of that time of the month? Still using pads? Then let me tell it to you straight. Tampax can change the way you feel about that time. Tampax tampons protect differently than a pad, so you feel cleaner, and feeling cleaner is more comfortable. Plus, more women use Tampax than any other tampon or pad. Now, that's something. Remember there's a feeling with Tampax. It can actually change the way you feel about your period."[37]

As recently as 2010, an ad for the tampon brand U by Kotex was banned by major US television networks because it mentioned the word "vagina." When U by Kotex replaced the word "vagina" with the phrase "down there," a couple of the networks still refused to run it. Even when talking about tampons, you're not supposed to talk about the PLACE WHERE THE TAMPON ACTUALLY GOES. Whereas there's never been a problem mentioning "erectile dysfunction" for ads on prime time for Viagra and Cialis.[38] Kotex was attempting to redefine how period products are sold in a pretty bold way—they wanted to talk about periods more straightforwardly and "ditch the euphemisms and ridiculous scenes of happy, dancing women in favor of real talk and some good old-fashioned self-mockery."[39]

"The first ad to ever feature menstrual blood" appeared in 2011, and it was "considered revolutionary" and "a historic moment." Can we just acknowledge that it's almost unbelievable that it took until 2011 to have an accurate depiction of a period product in an ad? Even then, the menstrual blood was depicted as a tiny red droplet. And it took until 2017 before we saw a TV ad for a period product that actually used red liquid (as opposed to the red dot mentioned above) to demonstrate absorbency. Although we (hopefully) know that menstrual blood is not blue, "for years, advertisements have demonstrated period blood stains on sanitary pads with a mysterious blue elixir."[40]

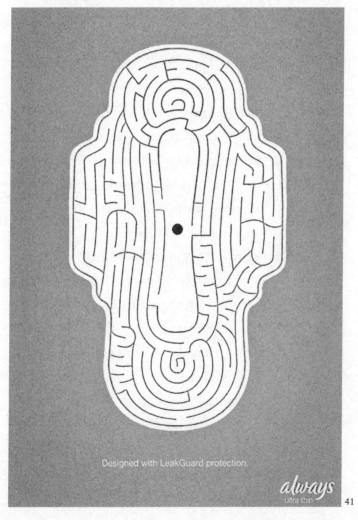

Designed with LeakGuard protection.

always
ultra thin

[41]

In October of 2017 Bodyform (a UK-based period product company) ran a twenty-second video ad showing a series of visuals, accompanied by electronic dance music. There's "a man unabashedly buying pads at a convenience store, a woman dressed as a giant pad arriving at a costume party, and blood rolling down a thigh in the shower." The video concludes with a red slide and the words "Periods are normal. Showing them should be too." It's part of a larger campaign that Bodyform is calling Blood Normal, aimed at breaking down the stigma around periods and presenting menstruation in a more realistic way. In a survey that the company conducted in ten different countries, they found that of respondents aged thirteen to fifty, about 75 percent "said they wanted periods to be presented more realistically in advertising."[42]

In 2016 Bodyform "claimed to be the first to show a pad being used as it would be in real life, with an ad featuring a trapeze artist putting one in her underwear." In another ad they made in 2016, a video titled "Blood," a montage of badass female athletes run, surf, play rugby, mountain bike, skateboard, rock climb, box, and dance ballet. There is quite a bit of blood in the video, but not menstrual blood—instead it's from the athletes' injuries as they get struck down during a boxing match, get hit during a rugby game, or fall while running, but they get back up and keep going. To be honest, I cried the first time I watched it—especially when it showed the bloody feet of a ballet dancer (an image I saw much too often as a young ballerina). My tears really came to a pinnacle at the very end, when the women triumph—celebrating the rugby game they just won, running faster than ever before, or landing a trick on a skateboard. At the end, text appears on-screen: "No blood should hold us back. . . . Don't let your period stop you."[43] It was as if I were watching the period product ad I had been waiting for all my life.

The "Blood" video is "part of the company's 2016 Red.Fit program meant to educate women about how the menstrual cycle affects health and fitness regimens. This is particularly important because existing research on exercise medicine and sports have left women largely underrepresented." In a statement released by Bodyform on Twitter on May 27, 2016 (the day before 2016's world Menstrual Hygiene Day), the company stated that the lack of information on women and fitness is "because women are perceived to be too complicated or variable to study, resulting in ambiguity and a lack of understanding." It's infuriating that the majority of companies prioritize research on male bodies because they find periods confounding. Bodyform believes that "this can and should change," especially since the "lack of knowledge can prevent women from being active and exercising during their menstrual cycle and can have a negative impact on the way they feel." Bodyform created "the Red.Fit hub, an online portal designed to provide valuable information about what happens during the menstrual cycle and how women and girls can work with their bodies to stay active."[44]

The education program for Red.Fit is split into four different sections, each representing "a stage our body goes through during our menstrual cycle." The stages are bleed, peak, burn, and fight. Because of our changing hormone levels throughout the menstrual cycle, "we feel different, mentally and physically, at different times." In partnership with local universities and health experts, "the hub offers tips for each stage, such as what exercises to do during 'bleed' to ease stomach cramps and what food to eat during 'burn' to keep yourself fueled for working out." The marketing director at Bodyform, Nicola Coronado, said, "Menstruation really is 'the last taboo' for women in sport, simply because we lack knowledge and understanding of this subject area."[45]

Another product company caused a stir with their ads—but this time on the New York subway. The Thinx (period underwear) ad campaign featured daring and subtly provocative images of grapefruit or egg yolks that were reminiscent of mucus-like period blood and vaginas. The campaign made waves in 2014, three years after the company was first founded in 2011. The Metropolitan Transportation Authority's advertising sales partner, Outfront Media, considered banning these simple yet powerful images because they contained the word "period" and might be a bit too provocative.[46,47] They said that the images of the women in underwear showed too much skin, and the grapefruit and egg imagery was "inappropriate."[48] Apparently, an ad selling period underwear broke the MTA's guideline that prohibits any marketing that depicts "sexual or excretory activities" or "sexually oriented business." COME ON. . . . There have been *so* many other subway ads that showed more skin. The only difference was that this ad was talking about periods, and not breast augmentation or sexy underwear that doesn't mention menstruation.[49]

UNDERWEAR FOR WOMEN WITH PERIODS — THINX hellothinx.com

50

Thankfully, the Thinx team fought for those ads to plaster the walls of NYC subways—and the ads were eventually approved, especially after the negative press coverage the MTA received for almost rejecting the proposals. It is this sort of resilience of brands that creates moments in press and social media to get people to talk about periods, and it is obvious why these images started conversations for subway users. According to founder Miki Agrawal, the subway scandal was the "third of its five viral moments to date—and in the process, had increased its revenue by a factor of 23."[51] So, obviously, it's also profitable for these for-profit brands to push boundaries to advance the Menstrual Movement.

The VP of brand Thinx, Siobhan Lonergan, says that the Thinx ads pair up simple photos of "grapefruits, papayas, eggs" or other everyday things that encourage conversation about female anatomy, with "naturally shot models wearing our underwear," both against solid backgrounds. The overarching goal is to make people *think* so that they start talking about periods—which are also why the tone and voice of Thinx's brand identity are very "approachable and casual, to create a level of openness to talk about periods the way you would talk to a girlfriend."[52]

The subway campaign was the brainchild of Veronica del Rosario, the young woman behind the

Thinx brand strategy, voice, and persona. At the age of twenty-two (*only* TWENTY-TWO and straight out of college), she developed the brand's "über in-your-face, bold and blunt, political, witty, millennial-girl height" voice. When she joined the team, Thinx was primarily using hashtags like #BreaktheTaboo in the context of the developing world, not necessarily here in the US. Veronica also quickly noted that even with the mission of starting conversations about periods, there was no mention of the word "period" in any of the branding. She knew that if Thinx was going to build itself into an engine to eradicate period shame, they had to demonstrate that they were shameless in their own presentation of periods. With the controversy surrounding the subway campaign and many campaigns thereafter, Veronica and her team of creatives were able to do just that.[53]

Another core team member who brought Thinx's brand to life is Chelsea Leibow. Leibow (then twenty-five) was the head of public relations, who would send out messages from the inbox of "Chelsea, high priestess of period PR" that were the kind of emails that made one giggle at random points throughout the day. As subscribers would recall the "beautiful, lightly deranged PR emails," they would forward them to their girlfriends to share the humor—thus sharing the Thinx brand to even more women.[54] GENIUS. Chelsea told me that when it comes to breaking the taboo on body-related topics, the "best way to approach it is from a really positive, light, humorous place." You can invite people to feel more comfortable by talking about bodies and periods in a conversational, not clinical way.[55]

Another company that has utilized humor to break the period stigma is HelloFlo—a media platform and e-commerce company that shares "content that will educate, inspire and entertain you" and offers "one-of-a-kind care packages to help women and girls through transitional times in their life."[56] Each care package contains tampons, panty liners, and some sugary treats. The tampons and pads are all "U by Kotex and Poise brand products."[57] So, no surprise that when HelloFlo launched their first two promotional videos, they BLEW UP on social media. The first time I watched these digital shorts, I was laughing, sending them around to family and friends—and I received the videos from so many people who wanted to make sure I saw them.

Both videos feature young girls telling their stories of getting or anticipating their first period—with the target audience being adults who might buy the HelloFlo Starter Kit to prepare a girl for and celebrate her first period. In its first six months the video titled "The Camp Gyno" amassed more than 12.5 million views on YouTube. In the video a charismatic young girl at summer camp complains about not being appreciated by the other kids at camp and feeling like "a big random loser." THEN, SUDDENLY, she gets her first period—or, as she calls it, "the red badge of courage." As the first one to get it, she becomes the "expert" on campus—a.k.a. the Camp Gyno—and basks in the life of a powerful and popular queen bee distributing tampons to others and educating them on menstruation. Her reign of power is strong among other girl campers, but she says, "as quickly as it began, it was over." Girls stopped coming to their "appointments" with the Camp Gyno, and it was all because they started receiving these "friggin' care packages in the mail . . . all perfectly timed to their cycles. It's like Santa for your vagina!"[58]

The second video, and my favorite one, is called "First Moon Party." It has me laughing for all 140 seconds of it, and it too has been watched millions of times. A young girl is expressing her frustration at seemingly being the last of all her friends to get her period. So, she fakes it! Taking a pad and sparkly nail polish, she paints a little blob of nail polish onto the pad and lies to her friends and mom about having started her period. Her friends, over FaceTime, welcome her to the "cherry slush club" and call themselves "blood sisters." Her mom, on the other hand? Calls BS, knowing that it's "Rubylicious nail polish."

To get back at her daughter for lying to her, she pretends to be excited about her daughter's first period and says they have to carry on "family tradition" and throw a "first moon party." Her mom enthusiastically welcomes grandparents, friends, her coworkers, and more to the house for a party that includes "pin the pad on the period," uterus piñatas, red chocolate fountains, and her dad embarrassingly popping out of a cake in a red unitard. Frustrated by how weird the party is, she admits to her mom that she faked her period, and her mom presents her with a HelloFlo Starter Kit, admitting that she threw the First Moon Party in place of grounding her daughter. "What'd she think, I wouldn't know? Periods don't have glitter in them," says the mom at the end of the video.[59]

• PERIODS ON SOCIAL MEDIA: INFLUENCERS AND INTERVIEWS•

With the rise of social media as an integrated part of everyday life—especially for our younger generation—and with the power of video in distributing information on these platforms, digital content has become increasingly powerful as a tool to start important inclusive conversations. Thanks to Snapchat, younger users have begun to both crave and expect fast-paced and even live-streamed content to document everything, even the seemingly mundane. With Instagram we are inundated with pictures that are cleverly captioned, designed to inspire and interest us. And Facebook has become a sort of overflowing source of news, longer content, and ways to engage and take action (whether via discussion, supporting causes, widely sharing content, or creating a community). The art of social media is a tricky one, but when it's mastered, social media can be unstoppable. Young people have a great advantage in this area, to the point where we now see "social media influencer" as a very realistic and profitable career option.

Videos of influencers talking about periods get viewers to connect more immediately and fully with the subject matter. The growing popularity of news outlets such as NowThis News and Mic shows that a powerful way to share content is to take longer interviews and shorten them to anywhere from thirty seconds to three minutes, highlighting the key takeaways. A strong example was social media and YouTube superstar Ingrid Nilsen's interview of President Obama. The original interview, released in July 2016, was more than sixteen minutes long and garnered almost 634,000 views on YouTube in two years.[60]

The interview, which we briefly discussed earlier, touches on terrorism, LGBTQ inclusivity, fighting cancer, and women's health. As we know, in response to her question about women's health, Obama admits that he has no idea why period products are taxed as nonessential items, and also that he didn't know of the tampon tax before Nilsen brought it up—but he offers the explanation that period products are taxed probably because men were the ones making those laws. (Mm-hmm.) He then goes on to explain how the Affordable Care Act is fighting to make sure that everybody has access to decent and protective health care, working from the very simple proposition that even if one does not have health insurance through their job, then they shouldn't be without coverage. He also mentions that the program could eliminate the possibility of women being charged more than men for the same type of coverage, that pregnancy should not be treated as an illness, and contraception is part of the standard health care package people receive.[61]

AJ+, a media outlet on Facebook, released a ninety-second clip from the interview that included his comment on the tampon tax and his response to Nilsen's statement that "we are being taxed for being women." In two years that video gathered more than 5.1 million views, forty-two thousand reactions, and fifty-one thousand shares—*much* more than the original interview.[62] It's easy to see that digital content is able to reach and entertain immensely large audiences, and social media can be used to amplify that distribution even further, especially when that content is reduced to shorter clips.

Of course, it's not just interviews of presidents discussing periods that go viral—there are endless ways to make your point about period justice. In March 2015 twenty-two-year-old Rupi Kaur (the popular young poet, author of *Milk and Honey*) posted a photo of herself with a bloodstain around the crotch area of her pants where her period blood had soaked through and made a small stain on the bedsheets.[63] The photo was part of a series Kaur had made for a school assignment.[64] Instagram quickly removed the photo, claiming that it was a violation of the "community guidelines." Kaur immediately reposted the photo, thanking Instagram "for providing me with the exact response my work was created to critique." In her caption of her reposted photo, Kaur pointed out that the photo in no way attacked a group, contained spam, or broke any sort of community guidelines.[65] Even after that powerful post, Instagram removed the photo . . . AGAIN.[66] #CriticalMistake

On Facebook and Tumblr, Kaur wrote longer posts that were shared more than eleven thousand times in the first day. Almost three years later that Facebook post had more than seventy-five thousand reactions and had been shared almost nineteen thousand times.[67] Instagram did eventually apologize, explaining that the removal of the photo was a mistake.[68] The bigger problem, though, is that people who saw this photo when it was initially posted decided to report it, and that alone "speaks to a deep-seated cultural fear of women's periods—the very issue Kaur's series addresses." She was motivated to focus her project on periods after reflecting how she herself puts effort into hiding from others the fact that she menstruates, and in acknowledging how some women are held back in their everyday lives because "they're considered dirty" on their period.[69]

Both Ingrid Nilsen and Rupi Kaur are examples of influencers who were able to amplify period talk to new heights, simply through social media distribution and the press and media coverage that supported its spread. Engaging influencers in talking about periods is powerful, especially when geared toward young people, who consume so much information from these digital platforms.

In the mainstream media, outlets such as BuzzFeed, *Cosmopolitan*, and *Glamour* have shared videos about periods and the stigma around menstruation and have been similarly effective. The period videos released by these corporate giants garner millions of views, and very quickly. For our young generation the people in groups like the Try Guys and other

BuzzFeed friends are becoming household names. Even our favorite magazines are becoming completely digital, like *Teen Vogue*, which is now turning to exclusively digital content, especially videos. When done well, these videos can be super effective at encouraging new topics of discussion in humorous and entertaining ways. Here are a few examples of some of my favorite period-related videos that have gone viral:

"WHY DO MEN ACCUSE WOMEN OF BEING ON THEIR PERIODS?"

On August 14, 2015, *Cosmopolitan* published a video called "Why Do Men Accuse Women of Being on Their Periods?" In it men on the street were asked what they think when a woman is grumpy or cranky. What do almost all of them say? "It's that time of the month." If women are acting "crazy"? "It's probably PMS." When asked why they jump to the conclusion that menstruation is the reason why women might be acting emotional or cranky, most of the guys responded that it was the safest bet because it made the men more understanding and forgiving, or let them know when to avoid the women in their lives.

The interviewer then asks the women sitting next to these men how the men's reactions made them feel. The women's answers are totally #RELATABLE. It can be upsetting to have someone accuse you of being on your period just because you're showing more passionate or amplified emotions, because it is INVALIDATING. A woman may actually be upset or angry about something, and for another person to turn to them and say, "Oh, you must be on your period," or "Oops. It's that time of the month," is essentially like saying, "I'm not taking you seriously, because I think your hormones are making you act this way, and I don't think your emotions are very real." One woman in the video describes it as "a disrespectful way of throwing a woman's emotions in her face and making a joke out of it."[70]

"GUYS EXPERIENCE PERIODS FOR THE FIRST TIME"

In 2016 three guys from BuzzFeed tried having a period "for the first time." A female colleague made the "menstrual rig" for each of them to have a steady drip of "blood" throughout their days. The rig was made out of a douche and a car siphon pump, and the blood was beet juice and cornstarch. The experiment was for the guys to wear the rig for three days, which turned into a week, using pads to absorb their menstrual blood. Within the first day they'd had enough of it—understanding the frustration of starting to bleed unexpectedly in public and not being able to find any period products, feeling the uncomfortable pad lodged between your legs nonstop, and, of course, having their "menstrual blood" soak through their underwear and pants. What was powerful about the guys' reactions was that they quickly gained empathy and were able to relate to some core goals of the Menstrual Movement: (1) people should not make fun of others for being on their period; it's difficult enough, and the menstruator has no control over it, (2) there should be period products everywhere for free because pads "should definitely be a right," and (3) everyone should be more understanding and knowledgeable about the period experience. Even these guys knew that they were having to deal with only one major symptom of menstruation. They didn't have to cope with hormones, cramps, or bloating.[71]

"GUYS TEST MAXI PADS"

A similar video, also by BuzzFeed, shows guys trying different types of pads (day vs. night, with wings and without). The guys had to wear the pads with a menstrual-blood-like formula (beet juice and cornstarch) on them, after it had been microwaved for ten seconds to simulate the actual warmth of menstrual blood. Their faces are shocked with disgust as they ask questions like, "Wow, that's a lot. Does it really look like that?" Yes, yes it does. "What are the chunks?" Shed uterine lining. The guys learn a lot in the short video, reading through guides about things such as how to best sleep with pads. They remain obviously grossed out, even as they slowly gain a real appreciation and respect for the period experience. As one guy puts it at the end of the video: "Women are incredible."[72]

"THIS IS YOUR PERIOD IN 2 MINUTES"

Glamour magazine also has a video, called "This Is Your Period in 2 Minutes," where an actress goes through the "science and symptoms of a woman's 28-day menstrual cycle," using theatrical facial expressions. From when you'll feel most fatigued or energetic, to the best times to exercise or take it easy because of cramps, to when to cut back on caffeine or to expect acne, to when you'll feel most productive and sexual (fertile), this video covers it.[73]

• PERIODS IN SPORTS MEDIA •

One of the pillars of period shame throughout history has been the assumption that menstruation makes women physically weaker. Or, as we learned from how period products were marketed in the beginning of the twentieth century, manufacturers promoted the idea that menstruators are less capable when menstruating. *Sooo*, over the last few years it has been a huge step that we are seeing more badass athletes talking about or even showing the fact that they do, indeed, menstruate—but still perform amazingly. It is astounding that in just a few decades we have pushed away from the narrative that menstruating women should not jump rope or skip around in puddles, to seeing women tell their own period stories. Because women are talking publicly about menstruation more than ever before, some of the recent stories of female athletes on their periods have blown up in the media.

Kiran Gandhi, an American musician ("former drummer for singer M.I.A."),[74] made headlines all around the world after running the 2015 London Marathon while free bleeding—"crossing the finish line with bloodstains prominently on display."[75] Here's an excerpt from Kiran's blog post "Going with the Flow: Blood & Sisterhood at the London Marathon," in which she relates her act to the greater need to talk about periods, including talking about period poverty around the world:

> I got my flow the morning of the London Marathon and it was extremely painful. It would be my first marathon and I remember already feeling so nervous for it. I had spent a full year enthusiastically training hard, but I had never actually practiced running on my period. . . .

If there's one person society can't eff with, it's a marathon runner. You can't tell a marathoner to clean themselves up, or to prioritize the comfort of others. On the marathon course, I could choose whether or not I wanted to participate in this norm of shaming.

I decided to just take some Midol, hope I wouldn't cramp, bleed freely and just run.[76]

In addition to making headlines in the press, Kiran's act of free bleeding brought international attention all over social media. The more supportive comments came from people who were in awe of Kiran's courage and awesomeness. Others who commented, even some who claimed to be feminists, just saw her decision as unhygienic.[77]

Periods also made headlines during the 2016 summer Olympic games, after "uninhibited Fu Yuanhui, the Chinese swimmer" discussed her period during a video interview after competing. According to a *New York Times* piece, the interview took place right "after the Chinese women's swimming team narrowly missed winning a medal in the 4x100-meter medley relay." While her teammates were being interviewed about the race, you could see Fu Yuanhui crouching in the background, seemingly in pain. She stood up for her interview, "grimacing in pain," and after the commentator guessed that she was "suffering from a stomachache," the swimmer turned to the reporter and quickly corrected her. "It's because I just got my period yesterday, so I'm still a bit weak and really tired. But this isn't an excuse for not swimming well."[78]

The comment went viral online. The comment sections of social media platforms blew up in response to Fu Yuanhui's candor about her period and how she thought that the pain might have affected her performance. Most wrote in support of her—comments such as "You are amazing. You are our pride," and "Only those who have gotten their periods know how deathly painful it can be. You are too awesome." Others made negative comments, only to be met with passionate responses that defended the swimmer. The many online discussions surrounding the interview brought to light the much larger issue of the persistent "silence surrounding menstruation in sports."[79]

It was also significant that the swimmer who made headlines for talking about her period with the media was *Chinese*. This is because "open discussion about menstruation has been more slow to catch on in China." Ads for period products are still banned from TV "during prime viewing times." China is one of the many countries where few women use tampons "because it is widely, and falsely, believed that they can rob a woman of her virginity."[80]

Seeing a Chinese woman talking publicly about her period gives me so much hope for women all over the world. All of us should learn from Fu Yuanhui—and from the women who responded to her in droves— that we can use the press and social media to amplify our message and expand the conversation about menstrual justice.

CHAPTER EIGHT

•

THE FIGHT FROM ALL SIDES

One of the beautiful things about periods is that they're a sort of equalizer across humankind. No matter where you live, what your background is, how much money or resources you have, what religion or culture you're from—if you are assigned female at birth, then you will most likely menstruate for forty years of your life on a monthly basis. Because menstruation is such a universal experience in this way, when discussing menstrual equity, it is so important that we're inclusive about the language that we use and the actions that we take—and it's also essential that we constantly push the discussions to be more diverse in terms of period experience and life experience. Menstruation is such a central and natural part of human life that it crosses many industries, topics, identities, cultures, and movements. I find that the Menstrual Movement is the embodiment of *intersectional feminism*.

The women's movement in the United States has been criticized since its founding stages for being exclusive in terms of race, class, gender identity, and sexuality—even from the suffragist movement in the early twentieth century, when white women were at the forefront of fighting for women's right to vote (with practically no emphasis on the right of women of color to vote).

Similarly, the basic goals of second-wave feminism in the 1960s were "equal pay for equal work, an end to domestic violence, curtailment of severe limits on women in managerial jobs, an end to sexual harassment, and sharing a responsibility of housework and child rearing"—mostly goals to help those same middle-class white women who had fought for their right to vote. In fact, much of the women's liberation movement was sparked by women's involvement in (and then forced isolation from) the civil rights movement. Women weren't allowed a voice in the fight for racial equality, so they broke off and fought for their own rights. And in doing so, white women gained access to the stage and, in turn, isolated their voice from women of color and from the LGBTQ community.

It is important to also acknowledge that while all women are penalized for being women, some still have privilege in other areas. For example, I identify as an Asian American woman, and I push myself to fight for representation for my own identity while also acknowledging that I am very privileged in many ways as a cisgender heterosexual individual.

For a person who feels stuck in what some call "white feminism" (a brand of feminism that forgets about or even excludes women of color), it's important to engage in some self-reflection about how you can be more inclusive. I think Emma Watson said this best in a letter to her own book club in early 2018. She wrote that when she heard criticisms of herself as a white feminist, she panicked, thinking people might be calling her racist—but she quickly realized that this was a learning opportunity to ask herself questions such as, "What are the ways I have benefited from being white? In what ways do I support and uphold a system that is structurally racist? How do my race, class and gender affect my perspective?"[1] As we gear up as Period Warriors and prepare to embark more boldly in the Menstrual Movement, it's imperative that we continue to ask ourselves similar questions as activists. How can we be more inclusive about different period experiences and engage with one another from sincere places of empathy?

• GENDER EQUALITY •

I believe it is undeniable that the Menstrual Movement is an integral part of achieving the overreaching goal of gender equality, as we've already seen from the negative societal narratives that still surround menstruation, the lack of equitable access to menstrual health, how something as natural as periods still significantly hold menstruators back from taking advantage of opportunities equally, all the way to how there is no guaranteed way for all young people to learn about the biology of periods . . . and I could KEEP GOING. Needless to say, WE HAVE WORK TO DO.

Leading activists and organizations such as the United Nations explain that in order for our global community to achieve gender equality, we need to meet goals that we can place into four distinct categories: (1) equal access to and opportunity in basic education, (2) opportunity in health care, (3) opportunity in employment and economic mobility, and (4) representation in politics and decision-making positions. SURPRISE. Addressing periods and advancing the Menstrual Movement is a key to moving the needle of success in all four of these areas.

We already discussed how a lack of menstrual hygiene can be a barrier to girls' education all over the world, and how addressing periods *is* a matter of reproductive and women's health. As far as the third category, the Menstrual Movement is all about fighting for the fundamental human right of economic mobility regardless of a natural need by providing period products to those who face a financial burden. And we've also talked about how the persisting culture around periods has demoralized and disempowered menstruators for far too long and kept them from achieving equal representation in politics and other high positions of power.

Gender Equality and Equity

Education   Health care   Employment and economic mobility   Representation in politics and decision-making

The Menstrual Movement

The fight for equitable access to menstrual hygiene and breaking the stigma around periods.

The fight for gender equality is a universal movement—one that is about breaking the cycle of poverty and demanding justice for our entire population.

Pushing toward these goals requires the attention and commitment of all involved, regardless of gender identity, which is why spreading awareness, tapping people in, and using inclusive language is so important.

• GENDER: NOT ALL WOMEN MENSTRUATE, AND NOT ALL MENSTRUATORS ARE WOMEN •

In the women's movement, we are seeing more inclusivity being stressed, in order to avoid whitewashed feminism, and there are conversations to be had in breaking down the gender binary as well. As we enter the community of fourth-wave feminism—that is more inclusive of those beyond the gender binary, of all races, and of all socioeconomic backgrounds—we have a responsibility to acknowledge how intersectional gender inequality is an issue, and push forward as a diverse and beautiful movement toward total gender equality.

When I started my work as a menstrual activist, I hadn't thought about the fact that there are people who menstruate and do not identify as women—which says something. If you think periods are stigmatized for women, imagine the taboo around periods for people who are not women but still menstruate. As soon as this topic was brought to my attention by someone my age who identified as nonbinary, I wanted to know more. I started googling and found a few activists who are transgender or genderqueer and talk about periods openly. Wanting to help spread the word about the need for gender inclusivity, I started to speak out about the intersectional issues of gender and menstruation. This was my first critical mistake, as I would learn very quickly to not speak on behalf of other's experiences—and I think it is a very easy mistake for other progressive and good-intentioned cisgender individuals to also make.

A leading trans activist and artist named Cass Bliss is the author of the coloring book *The Adventures of Toni the Tampon*. Toni the Tampon is a "trans little tampon" that has become a sort of mascot for the push for more gender inclusivity in the menstrual sphere.

On July 12, 2017, Cass posted a photo[2] of themselves sitting on a park bench on a sunny day, with their legs casually spread apart and a bloodstain at the crotch. In their right hand Cass held a notebook that read, "PERIODS ARE NOT JUST FOR WOMEN #BLEEDINGWHILETRANS."[3] That post ended up going viral internationally. Cass never anticipated the response, especially with media coverage—and there were, of course, plenty of haters along the way to keep the web traffic growing.

In addition to being an activist and artist, Cass is a

consultant—helping companies and organizations be more inclusive with their language, especially when it comes to marketing. Through their work Cass hopes to "push where there are safe spaces for people like me to exist. Places for people to discuss gender. It is a dangerous thing to push labels on people, and humans are complex and beautiful creatures. I would like a world where we have more space for people to be who they are. I want to live in a world where communities and organizations are actively representing trans people."

The #BleedingWhileTrans campaign continues, with the goal of raising awareness about the simple fact that TRANS PEOPLE MENSTRUATE TOO. Cass says that while they don't know if this will ever happen in their lifetime, they hope for a time when "it's not weird to see a guy going into the bathroom with a tampon, because people are aware." Sharing their own story is one of the many ways that Cass contributes to this vision. They say, "I like sharing my own personal story of being trans because there are people who are like me who are really scared. When I was going through that, I really looked up to people who were out, and I want to pay it back."

So, how can we be more gender-inclusive with our language? Here's a guide from Cass:

Rainbow Bleeding: A Guide to Making Your
(Period) Activism Gender-Inclusive
by Cass Bliss, a.k.a. the Period Prince

As a trans activist in the Menstrual Movement, I often get asked, "If you have a uterus and get periods, how can you say you're not a woman?" The simplified answer is that body parts do not equal gender.

Before we jump into this guide, let's go over a basic introduction of gender and sex. Though they are both too beautifully complicated to fit inside strict definitions, I'll give a brief breakdown of the differences between the two.

Gender is how you identify, feel, act, dress—it's made up of a bunch of different pieces that make you who you are. While most people understand gender as "boy/man" or "girl/woman," it can also include anything in between or up to and around those two arbitrary categories. (We'll get to that later.)

Sex is usually understood as your biology, though even that gets complicated, with variations of anatomy, chromosomes, and hormone levels that don't neatly fall into "male" or "female" camps. That being said, society at large tends to label sex based on what doctors say when they take their first look at your genitalia.

People who identify with the sex that they were assigned at birth (e.g., "It's a girl!") are cisgender, and people who don't identify with what they were assigned are covered by a variety of different names, including "transgender," "gender nonconforming," "nonbinary," and "agender." Like most man-made things, labels have their flaws, but what's critical to remember is that sex and gender are different, and they do not always match up.

However, when it comes to periods, society tries to make us believe exactly that. Menstruation is almost always tied to womanhood.

To illustrate the flaws in that logic, let's take a moment to think about the following questions:

If "periods = womanhood," does not having the ability to menstruate make you a man? And if menstruating is what makes you a woman, then are women who may not have periods, for a variety of health reasons, not real women? What about trans women? Are they not women because they do not have the capacity to menstruate? What about women who have entered menopause—have they lost some of their womanhood simply because an organ in their body has stopped shedding blood and tissue?

When I first got my period, it felt like the end of my freedom. Like most people, I had always been taught that menstruation was the entrance to the world of womanhood—a world that I desperately didn't want to enter. I thought that the arrival of my period meant I suddenly had to perform like all the girls my age and become someone I was not. Even now, years later, menstruation is a painful monthly reminder that society wants to shove me into a category that I don't belong in. The fact that my uterus squeezes out blood and tissue does not define who I am.

So, how can we make our period activism inclusive of people like me, who don't identify as women? Here are a few quick steps to get started:

Listen and Learn

Listen to the experiences of trans and nonbinary folks around you! Bleeding while trans comes with a lot of unique challenges that a cisgender person might not think about. For example, it can be difficult to know which bathroom is safe to use while menstruating, or to figure out how to smuggle a tampon into the men's room (and out of, since men's rooms don't have trash receptacles in the stalls) without being outed. We may experience swelling that makes our chests more noticeable, or we may feel forced to interact intimately with our vaginal openings. Both of these experiences can cause dysphoria (anxiety around our body not matching up with our identity).

Remember that there isn't a single universal trans or nonbinary menstrual experience, but it's helpful to take time to educate yourself about the unique challenges involved and to listen to people who deal with them on a regular (or irregular) basis.

Check Your Language!

When we constantly use "she" pronouns or the term "women" to refer to people who menstruate, we're leaving out an entire population of menstruators who are already marginalized. Start rethinking your language, and consider introducing a few more inclusive terms into your vocabulary.

Instead of "girls" or "women," try:

"people with periods"

"menstruators"

"girls, women, and trans or nonbinary folks who menstruate"

Instead of "feminine hygiene products," try:

"menstrual health products"

"period products"

Fight for Equal Access

Don't just stop at education and language. Commit to action by considering how your services, legislation, and campaigns provide equal access for menstruators of all genders.

Are you fighting for free tampons or disposal bins in public bathrooms? Don't forget to include men's restrooms and gender-neutral stalls!

Do you work with shelters or host period product donations? Make sure you're thinking about how you can create space for someone who may not *look* like they need period products to be able to access your services. Consider hosting a values clarification training on gender presentation for people working on the front lines.

Ensure Representation

Visibility and representation are important!

If you make or promote products (tracking apps, menstrual cups, etc.), widen color and style options to include a variety of choices for menstruators, regardless of whether they are trans or not!

If you post photos on social media or websites, try to include a diversity of gender presentations instead of being exclusive.

If you're organizing an event, ensure that your presenters are representative of the menstruator population. I'm not just talking about gender identity but also racial identity, socioeconomic background, ability, etc. Marginalized communities are too often left out of the conversation, even though we bring valuable and unique insights to the way society treats people with periods.

Though there are more than just these few ways to make your activism gender-inclusive, taking these first steps can make a huge difference in pushing the world to become a more accepting and affirming place for menstruators of all genders.

• CLIMATE CHANGE AND SUSTAINABILITY •

I've already mentioned the efforts to increase sustainability and reduce waste from disposable period products, but let's explore this topic a little more. It's estimated that a menstruator (if using only disposable tampons and pads) uses between ten thousand and sixteen thousand units in their lifetime. An estimated "12 billion pads and seven billion tampons end up in landfills yearly"[4] in the United States. The "average woman" disposes of between two hundred fifty and three hundred pounds of disposable period product waste in her lifetime.[5] At a global level more than "100 million women" use tampons, and even more use disposable pads.[6]

PLASTIC APPLICATORS

While most disposable period products are made primarily from cotton, both tampons and pads contain "plastic components"—the obvious one being the plastic tampon applicator (those that are not cardboard), and the "waterproof backing" and "the part that goes next to your skin" of most disposable pads.[7]

It takes CENTURIES longer for the plastic applicator of the tampon to decompose than the "lifespan of the woman who used it." That is a little morbid, but it's true, and it's helpful to put the reality into perspective. The trash from our periods is literally outliving us. . . . That's a problem![8]

Plastic pollution has negative effects on "wildlife habitat, wildlife, and humans by affecting lands, oceans, and waterways." Plastic pollution can also cause biological upsets with wildlife and marine animals that might consume plastic waste. Plastic pollution also negatively affects land, air, groundwater, and the greater ecosystem in the production and eventual disposal and decomposition of these products.[9]

We already know that there are tampon applicator options other than plastic—whether that's using digital tampons (without an applicator) or the tampons with cardboard applicators. (There are even applicators made from recycled cardboard!) Digital tampons (such as o.b.'s signature product) produce "58% less waste."[10]

I personally don't understand why anyone would not change to cardboard applicators or even using tampons without applicators once being made aware of the environmental impact. The only difference is the initial feeling of insertion, and any benefit from using a plastic applicator isn't enough to ever outweigh the environmental cost of throwing away more plastic.

TOXINS

Although we do not know exactly what is in our period products (which is a whole other issue discussed in the period policy chapter), many of the ingredients in nonorganic disposable period products are definitely bad for the environment. These include pesticide residue (that eventually winds up in "groundwater supplies, causing contamination") and toxic dioxins (that "end up in our soil and water supplies, which ends up hurting the entire ecosystem").[11] These toxins are expelled into our world both in the production and in the eventual disposal and decomposition of them.

Toxins also affect the user. Since the beginning of period product history, women have been encouraged to use various methods to hide the smell or to mitigate the chafing that comes from having a lump in your underwear made of cotton and a plastic-like film. Baby powder, for instance, has been used for these purposes for decades. In August of 2017, $417 million was awarded to a woman who'd used Johnson & Johnson's talcum powder during her period ever since she was eleven, not realizing until too late that it was linked to ovarian cancer. Talc is "a naturally occurring clay mineral . . . mined in proximity to asbestos, a known carcinogen." Though it's been shown to be linked directly to cancer *since 1971*, it continues to be sold as a component of menstrual products. The woman, who has terminal ovarian cancer, is just one of thousands who have sued Johnson & Johnson in recent years for the same reason.[12]

Similar to the scandal with TSS and Tampax, disposable period product manufacturers were able to continue selling product that caused major health damage, even though the companies understood the significant consequences. But we are beginning to hold companies accountable, and the victory against Johnson & Johnson was a warning to the whole industry—and a further call to arms to menstruators to fight for their rights and their health.

As an individual, I have chosen to work with some of these companies in the past, both as a spokesperson and as a collaborator on media campaigns. Every time I debut news of my collaboration with these companies, I am met with very understandable pushback: How can I be so progressive and want to work with these corporations, when I know the horror stories about what some of them have been responsible for over the last century? How can I speak about the need for change in the way these products are marketed, while also working on their team?

I choose to work with these companies because it is undeniable that when it comes to the period product industry, they hold the power and influence. Because of the unwavering demand for these products, these companies have been integral in the introduction and then development of these period products to the public over the last century. YES, I also support the call for transparency about product ingredients, and YES, I think that there is *so much more* that they could do to bolster the Menstrual Movement's efforts to get people thinking and talking about periods in a more inclusive and empowering way. I believe that the most efficient and effective way that I can contribute to that vision is by working with them and spurring change from the inside.

DON'T FLUSH YOUR TAMPON OR APPLICATOR

Flushing your tampon is extremely bad for the environment—but most menstruators don't know this. An estimated 1.4 billion tampons in the UK alone are "being flushed through our sewage systems every year." This 1.4 billion number comes from our knowing that "9.4 million women use tampons every month, which, according to the research, totals twenty tampons per period, per person—60% of which are being flushed."[13] More than twenty thousand "tampon applicators out of 4 million total pieces of reclaimed plastic waste" were collected by the Ocean Conservancy's International Coastal Cleanup project in 2009. These plastic applicators end up on beaches after being flushed through sewage systems and ending up in oceans. If they do not wash up on shores to be collected or aren't consumed by an animal, it can "take applicators 25 years to break down in the ocean."[14]

Unlike toilet paper, tampons are specially made to be durable and not break down in moisture. (It would be a big health risk if they did, since they'd be breaking down inside menstruators.) The cotton usually found in tampons "can expand up to 15x in water," so they frequently cause severe plumbing issues.[15,16] In order for a product to claim to be flushable, it has to pass something called the Brunelle Flushability Test, which is conducted in a lab to see if the product passes through the U-bend in the toilet waste pipe. However, even if it does pass this test, tampons most likely will not be able to pass through the rest of the pipes.[17]

Most sewage systems and general "water

treatment plants aren't made to filter out used tampons. So they end up in our rivers, drifting out into our oceans." Rather than disintegrating like toilet paper, "tampons degrade slowly, over many years, to form tiny micro-plastics that float, almost undetected." The micro-plastics that are expelled from the degrading tampons are consumed by "crustaceans and other filter feeders," and a 2015 study found that "the breeding capacity of oysters was almost halved following exposure to micro-plastics. Every other level of the food chain was quickly affected as a result."[18]

Besides being bad for the environment, flushing tampons also creates problems for local governments that have to keep fixing the disastrous effects. It's estimated that Canadians are "shelling out $250 million a year to clean" their water and "remove everyday items that people are flushing," including products such as tampons, applicators, condoms, and wet wipes. Even if there is equipment installed that is supposed to filter these items out, the equipment is overburdened because so many of these products are being flushed.[19]

Are you feeling appalled by the effects of disposable period products? Are you feeling conflicted because you've realized how much trash you might have put into the world? Whether you want to take the simple action of committing to using tampons with cardboard applicators, or switch to exclusively using reusable products, do all you can to cut down the waste and environmental impact, even if it's just a little change at a time. And for goodness' sake . . . please don't flush your tampons!

PERIOD now has an educational program called Cup & Cloth, which began in 2017 after we absorbed another nonprofit called UnTabooed, founded by Diandra Kalish. Like UnTabooed, Cup & Cloth's mission is to provide sustainable period products (menstrual cups and cloth pads) to people in need who can use them safely, and to offer menstrual health education to everyone about the different products available.

• MENSTRUATING AROUND THE WORLD •

In some parts of the world, menarche is a day that young menstruators may learn to dread. A first period can hold the weight of signifying the transition from girlhood to womanhood, and it is often the single event that leads to a girl's dropping out of school, getting married early, undergoing female genital mutilation, or in some places even being forced into social isolation.

In many countries the stigma around menstruation is deeply embedded into culture and practice, even more than it is in the United States. What is exciting about seeing the Menstrual Movement grow, though, is that more than ever before, people are paying attention to when the stigma hurts and even kills—and it seems that we are pushing toward a pivotal moment when people will yell, "Enough is enough!" That being said, it is challenging to work internationally on fighting the stigma, because we must be careful to not call another culture's practice wrong. It's just different, and from there, with mutual respect, we can keep talking about the Menstrual Movement internationally.

In 2017 headlines were made when a twelve-year-old girl in India committed suicide after she was scolded and punished for her menstrual blood soaking through her clothes. Reports say that after the teacher saw the stain, the girl was "forced by the teacher to leave her classroom." In a suicide note, she wrote that she felt confusion over why the teacher was "harassing and torturing me like this."

Young menstruators feel deep humiliation because of incidents like this. Menstruators similarly feel anxiety about staining clothes with menstrual blood, not having access to adequate wash facilities, or being able to cope with period pain, and these are all significant reasons why menstruators stay home from school. According to a United Nations

Educational, Scientific and Cultural Organization (UNESCO) report from 2016, "20 percent of girls in India drop out of school after starting their periods."[20] While it is uncommon for mainstream international news organizations to highlight incidents such as this young girl's suicide, these types of tragedies are not new. Hopefully this sort of coverage can act as a wake-up call for government officials, teachers, communities, and even families, showing that period shaming has real consequences.

The wild thing is that we don't actually have any product that can address periods in the most impoverished parts of the world where there is a lack of access to water and a lack of any sort of waste management system. Right now it's not a great idea to ship disposable products to places where they wouldn't normally have access to them, because soon enough the supply will run out, and without a waste management system, the products will likely be burned. Because of the harmful chemicals and toxins in many disposable products, this isn't good for anyone. A lack of access to water eliminates the viability of products such as menstrual cups, and in a lot of countries the intense stigma around wearing anything intra-vaginally also eliminates cups as a viable option.

There are many initiatives happening around the world to manufacture period products (specifically pads) at very low costs. Most notable is the enterprise begun by Arunachalam Muruganantham, a college dropout turned social entrepreneur and one of *TIME*'s 2014 100 Most Influential People. He is also known as the *Menstrual Man* (the title of the 2013 documentary film about him and his work) or, more recently, as *Pad Man* (the title of the Bollywood movie about him). After discovering that his wife was having to choose between purchasing food for his family or buying pads, he went to purchase some himself and was appalled by how expensive they were. He started on a mission to produce low-cost yet effective and comfortable pads—even testing them out himself with animal blood. He created an affordable machine that manufactures pads and started distributing these machines to rural women as a source of economic empowerment and menstrual hygiene. He has since started what he calls a "local sanitary pad movement" aimed at making India a "100-percent-sanitary-napkin-using-country" in his lifetime. (Right now only 2 percent of rural women in India use pads. Others have to turn to unclean methods of using anything from rags to sawdust).[21]

There are other places (such as South Korea, Japan, Indonesia, Taiwan, certain provinces in China, and some other Asian countries) that offer "menstrual leave"—paid leave for menstruators with painful symptoms. GREAT. Yes, it is great that companies and government officials are acknowledging that period pain is very real and can be debilitating for many. Women make up "nearly 40% of the global workforce, and up to 20% of women experience extreme [period] cramps." (Remember those conditions we learned about early on, such as endometriosis?) However, these practices have sometimes been met with criticism from activists who argue that the policies reinforce the concept that menstruation makes women less capable and unable to participate at the same level as their non-menstruating peers.

Not many women take full advantage of menstrual leave policies, though, out of fear of "sexual harassment or perceptions of weakness."[22] Menstrual leave has existed in Japan since 1947, and a study conducted in 1986 found that the percentage of women taking time off under the policy had declined, "largely because of societal pressures that frown upon its use." The number of workers using menstrual leave went down from 20 to 13 percent between 1960 and 1981. When menstrual leave was implemented in South Korea in 2001, it was met with criticism from men, who viewed it as reverse discrimination.[23]

In March 2017 the "Italian parliament considered introducing national period leave," but the concern was raised that this policy might discourage employers from hiring women. While enforcing company- or country-wide policies with the word "menstrual" in their titles does help to break stigma, these actions also associate menstruation with illness. Periods are a NATURAL part of life. We need to have these conversations about how to enforce gender equality in communities and workplaces, while also respecting and being understanding of very real experiences of pain. At the same time, the movement has to invest in finding ways to alleviate such intense period pain for so many menstruators.[24]

And compared to some European countries, the United States is very far behind in the fight against period poverty. In March 2018 the Welsh government pledged $1.4 million USD to go directly to combating period poverty, especially for girls in school.[25] The following month, leading politicians of Scotland declared their agenda to abolish period poverty after a report was released showing that "nearly one in five women in Scotland have been unable to afford" period products. Monica Lennon, a lawmaker in Scotland, announced that a six-month pilot program would begin in the summer of 2017 to test the positive effects of a bill to provide free period products "at food banks, schools, colleges and universities."[26]

CHAPTER NINE

•

TAKE ACTION

For those of you who saw a book with the word "period" on the front and thought, *Oh, cool,* and also for those of you who saw it, hesitated, and started reading anyway, I hope that you have learned a lot thus far and that you agree that the Menstrual Movement is not just necessary but is a huge priority in the fight to achieve gender equality. I hope you agree that it is a complex movement, one that needs to include everyone who has a unique perspective on the cause, and one that needs to include all issues that are affected by menstruation. SO LET'S DO SOMETHING!

The easiest and perhaps most effective first step that you can take as a supporter of the Menstrual Movement is to just GET PEOPLE TALKING about menstruation and the need for menstrual equity. Begin dialogues where people can become comfortable saying words like "period" and "tampon" and "menstrual blood" in the sphere of productive conversations. Jennifer Weiss-Wolf has said that "anyone can pull a roundtable together—do it in your house, your living room, in a church or community center. There's nothing more empowering than having women talk about this."[1] I would add that it is extremely empowering and eye-opening to include in these discussions a range of people of various ages, genders, and socioeconomic circumstances. Periods truly are a great equalizer because we all either menstruate or know someone who does—and it's (literally) a regular part of our lives that we need to bring out into the open.

Want to take it to the next level? DO IT. Contact your local legislator or representative and start asking questions or expressing your opinion about the need for period equity. Set up meetings and mobilize—it makes a difference. And because changing policy is a slower, long-term process, in the meantime you can collect period products to donate to menstruators. That is always an effective way to give back and also to start conversations about the need for more access to products for all people.

GET ANGRY. TAKE ACTION. For me, as a passionate young activist, one of the most disheartening things I hear—much too often—is my friends saying that they choose not to participate in politics or advocacy because they don't think that any of their actions will actually have a substantial impact. Or they say that they've lost hope in our government's ability to serve the people. NOOOO! Don't think that! It's very easy to become frustrated during tough political times and to become complacent about the responsibilities of active citizenship, but it is *so* important to keep hoping and keep fighting.

• ANSWER AND ENGAGE IN QUESTIONS •

A common question that I am asked when I'm making a public appearance as a #PERIODGirl is, "Why should we be thinking about periods when we have more important things to talk about, like hunger, economic development, or even gender equality in the first place?" One of the most powerful tactics in my arsenal as a menstrual activist is the ability to explain how these issues are directly related to the mission of the Menstrual Movement. And by reading this book, I hope you've seen firsthand how all of these important world issues are interrelated.

Politics is personal—rightfully so. People really care about what role government plays in their lives, how it influences their communities and the status of the surrounding cities, states, and countries. And people care about what taxes they're paying and where that money is going. Most individuals feel inspired to get involved in politics because of something that happened to them on a personal level. Maybe they witnessed or experienced something that made them feel angry and energized, or public service and political leadership are their way of realizing their own personal mission. Periods are also personal—to such an extent that they're treated as private and then as inherently *taboo*. Because of the lack of conversation about periods, most people are not aware of their privilege in either not having to worry about access to period products or not having to experience menstruation themselves.

It can be hard to start an uncomfortable conversation, and it can be even harder to calmly respond to statements that question the Menstrual Movement's importance. Below are some common arguments I've heard against the need for period policy, and quick tips on how to address them and begin a conversation.

TAX DOLLARS?!

When it's proposed that tax dollars should be used to fight period poverty, people often reply by saying one or more of the following:

Why should tax dollars cover period products if most people don't need them?

Why do men have to contribute to paying for someone else's tampons and pads?

The government should be prioritizing other things, like educational opportunities, rather than buying period products. Isn't toilet paper enough? Why take my hard-earned tax dollars?

Response

Our government prioritizes the health and well-being of its citizens—supporting the constitutional right to life, liberty, and the pursuit of happiness. In addition, our country prides itself on being a place that strives toward social equality (at least, it should). So, to start with, tax dollars support citizens in living out this mission of our country. Feeling confident, clean, capable, and dignified is a human right, but at the moment that right is unjustly treated as a privilege for people who naturally have periods. Also, the argument comparing period products to toilet paper works well here: going to the bathroom, and menstruating, are NATURAL!

LUXURY!

Many people think that it's not a necessity to be able to feel and be clean throughout menstruation; they see menstrual hygiene as a sort of luxury that should be earned. Most of the time I've heard this from cis men who have never experienced menstruation. They just sort of stare at me with this dazed and frustrated look in their eyes, communicating something like, *What's the big deal? Just shrug it off! You don't need tampons and pads. Just ignore your period. We have better things to talk about.* NYC Council Member Ferreras-Copeland reported having received some hate emails saying things like, "Well, why don't you just buy them cars? Why don't you just buy them jewelry?"

Response

Ferreras-Copeland said in response to those emails, and as we all should say, we are fighting against the idea that menstrual hygiene is a privilege because "This is not a luxury. . . . I want my young women and my women in general to be able to sit in any room next to a man and be able to focus on and think about the same things. That's it."[2] Frame your response to this argument within the context of how period equity is integral to achieving gender equality—even if haters are stuck on how expensive these products are, or can't seem to grasp why it's important for a person to feel clean on their period.

Gender equality is about providing equal opportunities to everyone, so that each person can discover and reach their full potential, regardless of their gender identity. This is not about helping menstruators feel clean on their period for the sake of feeling more "put together" or more comfortable. This is about ensuring that all people, regardless of whether or not they menstruate, are able to focus and go about their lives without having to worry about their periods. Nancy Kramer, the founder of the Free the Tampons campaign, has said that periods are an equality issue because "men walk into their restroom and they have everything in it that they need to take care of their normal bodily functions—women don't. I honestly believe that if men got periods we wouldn't be having this discussion."[3]

WE NEED TO FOCUS ON MORE IMPORTANT THINGS!

Some people argue that because only about half the population will experience menstruation, even if menstruators do need period products, we should focus on something that 100 percent of the population will need. Like food! Or education! In response to Jessica Valenti's 2014 article making the case that tampons should be free for all people who need them, a counter-argument op-ed was published in the *Washington Examiner* saying, "Food is something that 100 percent of the population needs, multiple times a day, every day of their lives. Shouldn't that be treated as health care?"[4] The author, Ashe Schow, writes articles with titles such as "Why the Popular Vote Is a Meaningless Statistic" and "A Fitting End to Hillary Clinton's Public Service Career."[5] In her op-ed "Should Tampons Be Free?" Schow calls Valenti's argument a plea to the government to "give me free stuff because, woman." Schow says that the belief that tampons should be "free just because women need them," as well as any argument that women should receive free birth control, "stops looking like equality and more like a new class of privilege."[6]

Response

The final line of Schow's response op-ed to Valenti is, "Full disclosure: I'm a woman," as if that validates her argument that period products should not be free and accessible. Clearly Schow is someone who has never had to struggle with not having access to period products.[7] It really becomes apparent that anyone who opposes granting people access to period products is probably someone who either does *not* get a period or has never been in a situation where they can't go to work or school because they can't afford menstrual products. In response to those who think that menstrual equity is not important—start by relating it to other issues that they might find important. Gender equality? Equality in education and employment opportunities? Access to health? Global development?

Breaking the cycle of poverty? Sustainability? Well, we need to address periods in order to better move toward progress on *all* of these things.

WHAT'S NEXT?!

Those against access to free period products might ask, *If women had access to free tampons, what would come next—cars and food? Don't you want the government out of your uterus?*[8]

Response

This pushback, which I hear too often, always makes me giggle. Somehow people think that providing free tampons and pads is going to be a sort of gateway to a flood of government spending on whatever women might want. The prevalence of comments like this highlights the lack of understanding about how necessary it is for menstruators to have access to period products to maintain adequate menstrual hygiene. People who don't menstruate are probably afraid that those of us who do menstruate are going to seize power and favor ourselves, the way those in control have always done.

WASTE OF MONEY

Some of the concern about making period products free to all menstruators is that people will take advantage of the supply. If dispensers are always stocked with an unlimited amount of tampons and pads, will people take more than they need?

Response

According to NYC Council Member Ferreras-Copeland, the best way to respond to questions like this is to compare the provision of free tampons and pads to that of toilet paper and condoms. "You'll never walk into a bathroom in a public office without toilet paper. You'd be like, 'What the hell?' . . . I have yet to hear someone say, 'Well, what's the budget on all these [free] condoms?'" Think about it. What other resources are there that are free to people and subsidized by the government where this concern isn't vocalized? Use that as a starting point for your response.[9]

FREE PRODUCTS? THAT'S UNFAIR!

Some opponents say that those of us fighting for free period products are whiny and weak women who are just complaining to get free products that we probably don't need. One comment that I saw in response to a student-written article in the *Daily Bruin* (a UCLA publication) really struck a nerve. The comment read, "Really? Give me more free stuff is your stance? By that rationale, why should men have to pay for razors or deodorant either. . . . Grow up. I put myself through college without whining about no one giving me free stuff, and I'm doing just fine now."[10]

Response

Policy change around period products accessibility is not about making these products free for EVERYONE. That isn't the goal at all. This is about menstrual equity and making period products available to people who would otherwise not have the resources to participate at an equal level with non-menstruating peers—whether for financial reasons or because they find themselves in a setting where there are no menstrual products.

The need for *period talk* and menstrual equity is a necessary one. Whether people like it or not, life is made possible because menstruation exists—it is literally the reason why pregnancy is possible and why we are all here. Of course, I am making some very broad and bold statements—and there are people who disagree. After press interviews, I have received phone calls during which complete strangers (usually women, actually) tell me that I am doing the "devil's work" by exposing the privacy of women across America—and that "periods exist to hold women in their place."

I frequently sit on panels to talk about my work

as a menstrual activist and to bring light to what my vision for the Menstrual Movement is. I am often asked by moderators what my goal is in my work with periods. When will I be satisfied? The honest answer, and I know it might sound sad, is that I don't know if I ever will be—but I sure hope so. I believe that my work in the Menstrual Movement can stop when something so natural as periods does not hinder any menstruator's experience of feeling confident, capable, and ready to discover and reach their own potential. When there is no opportunity for me to speak out against a menstrual taboo, because it no longer exists—that is when I will be done.

• HOW WE CAN USE SOCIAL MEDIA AND PRESS RELATIONS TO ADVANCE THE MENSTRUAL MOVEMENT? •

I am a *huge* fan of social media because I truly believe that it's the most potent tool we have for mobilizing and participating in (and even starting our own) movements.

People who are older and didn't grow up with social media as part of daily life will sometimes *hire* young people who know how to use it effectively, in order to help make their work known—but for us young fire starters, social media is already second nature, so it's only natural that we're able to use these tools to spread our message. Once you know what you're passionate about—whether it be a cause that you want to fight for or a business that you want to start—all you need to start taking action is (1) Google and (2) social media.

Google is to get the basic information you might need to know how to navigate the industry you're hoping to move into. When I was getting ready to start the organization that would become PERIOD, I literally googled questions like, "What is a nonprofit?" and "What is the IRS?" Of course, taking action and starting something requires more than just finding answers in quick Google searches, but this is an important first step to knowing what resources you have right in front of you. Once you figure out a business plan (you can Google what this is, if you're not sure), the next step is to build your team, gather resources, and start spreading the word about what you're trying to do—and all these steps can be done on social media if you know how to use it effectively.

Hashtags are powerful because they unify many voices across various groups around shared emotions, topics, or stories. #ThrowbackThursday or #FlashbackFriday? These are hashtags that I'm sure we young people are familiar with—the ones that we see often on social media, or maybe that even become part of our colloquial language. As twenty-first-century young people who most likely spend large amounts of time on social media, we know that these hashtags are associated with sharing old pictures of ourselves and others to honor and celebrate memories.

So how does this relate to the #MenstrualMovement? Because menstruation is currently such a taboo topic, the first step forward is to get people talking, and this can take place on social media platforms in addition to conversations in real life, especially by mentioning words in public that pertain to the Menstrual Movement. Here are some hashtags that I love:

#MenstrualMovement
#TamponTax
#FreetheTampons
#PeriodPoverty
#PeriodProud
#PeriodPower

And you can always start your own!

• CAMPUS POLICY •

Systemic change around period equity can also start on school campuses. It's more common to find free condoms on college campuses than it is to find free period products. In 2016 a junior at Barnard College wrote in the student newspaper, "Sure, I can easily find a free condom on Barnard and Columbia's campuses, but why can't I find a free tampon in the bathrooms? Why does the administration care about my sexual protective rights, but not how I handle my monthly menstrual cycle?"[11] Students across the United States have made similar arguments and have started petitions to get free period products in all restrooms on campus. In 2016 there was a *lot* of mobilization to get period products in schools, including on university campuses. And over the last couple of years many schools have launched pilot programs through student government initiatives to provide free and accessible period products to students.[12]

So why, at some of the most well-endowed universities in the world, is it important to have period products be free and available? Again, it's a matter of equality within a diverse set of students.

In the fall of 2016 Brown University started making tampons and pads free and accessible in campus bathrooms. This made Brown "one of the first higher-education institutions to implement such a widespread program." The initiative was entirely student-led, with student body president Viet Nguyen at the helm. Nguyen's motivation for having free period products on campus sprang from his mission to level the playing field for low-income students, who he said already "struggle with having the necessary funding for food, let alone tampons."[13]

For the 2016–2017 school year, between thirty and forty bathrooms were stocked with free menstrual products thanks to funding from the student-run undergraduate finance board. Another amazing thing about that? Not all of those bathrooms were women's bathrooms. Brown's new policy ensured that free tampons and pads would be made available on a weekly basis for student government representatives to refill the baskets. Nguyen "hopes that one day, the program will become 'an institutional part of Brown.'"[14] Nguyen's campaign on campus made national headlines as a trans-inclusive student initiative, placing products in "women's, men's and gender-inclusive bathrooms," and highlighting the "often ignored fact: Not all people who menstruate are women."[15]

Brown's work to make period products free, led by Viet Nguyen, was one of the first highly publicized instances of a university doing so. Nguyen said that within a couple of days his team was receiving "enthusiastic calls and emails from other universities, coast to coast, seeking guidance on how to kick-start their own programs." Of course, especially due to the trans inclusivity component of the initiative, they also received hate mail and press coverage from outlets such as Breitbart and Mediaite, who were angry about what they inaccurately reported was Brown's way of declaring that "both sexes menstruate." In my opinion, the fact that such opposition exists is the reason why we need to keep pushing trans-inclusive language and legislation across the country.[16]

In 2015 Rebekah Rennick, then a student at Grinnell College, had the experience of starting her period unexpectedly in public and not being able to find any period products in nearby restrooms. To protest the lack of products available, she took "two bobby pins to break into 'all the tampon and pad dispensers [she] could find' on campus," and she stacked the products "on top of the machines for others to use." In the open letter she wrote to her college, she said, "I freed your tampons kept behind lock, key and quarter. . . . When we menstruate, however unexpectedly, we should not feel fear in the pits of our stomachs because of your lack of foresight. We are a part of this college. Provide free menstrual products to students who need them so I can stop picking the locks on your bogus machines."[17]

YES, girl, YES! I am not condoning her method of breaking into the machines, but it was an effective tactic that got the attention of Raynard Kington, the president of Grinnell, who could only agree with her argument. Initially she faced the prospect of punishment, but the administration "instead decided to implement the changes she was asking for," most likely because of the national visibility that her open letter to the school had garnered.[18] And Kington, the "former deputy director of the National Institutes of Health," was open to talking about periods too. Following Rennick's open letter, Grinnell worked with the student government to ensure free access to period products in "at least one gender-neutral restroom in each campus building." Kington supported the idea of free period products on campus, saying, "we have free toilet paper, so wanting the same for menstrual products is not extreme. This is a normal human function."[19]

The hurdle that Grinnell faced in trying to get period products into restrooms was the same one that our PERIOD chapters and ambassadors run into all the time: money. Policy takes a long time even on campus, especially when it involves changes in funding. Most student governments, like Grinnell's, work from budgets that are "allocated a year in advance, so in order to enact swift change, SGA [the Student Government Association] needed to locate free, unrestricted money." Grinnell did this by securing money from a "combination of unallocated SGA and presidential funding. SGA and President Kington each paid for half of the cost of the new machines, while

FM [Facilities Management] agreed to pay for future upkeep costs." In total, making the products available in thirty-five restrooms cost almost fifteen thousand dollars. While Grinnell has not had any formal policy written to ensure that free period products will be available into the future, the policy was ratified in a series of verbal commitments. So, it is doable, but the logistics of providing free period products can be pretty discouraging. Nevertheless, the outcome in Grinnell's case was *free period products* in accessible restrooms, just as Rennick had called for.[20]

Very recently some campuses have started to talk about providing more sustainable period products as well. Usually this involves collaborations among student government, manufacturers of reusable products (menstrual cups and cloth pads), and the school's office of sustainability.

• MY JOURNEY TO TAKING ACTION •

When I first learned about the need to address period poverty, I was as angry as you are right now. I knew I had to do something. My mom had worked in nonprofit management, and she warned me about the heavy responsibilities that come with running an organization. She would remind me that heading a nonprofit is more than a project.

When you become an official organization and you make promises, you have to keep them. To run a nonprofit, new players have to be brought on to hold a leader accountable: the board, the IRS, volunteers, and more. Sort of to spite my mom—without having a business plan or any plan for action—I decided with 100 percent of my will to start a nonprofit. My one goal? To start, slowly but surely (twenty periods per week), addressing periods for the homeless women I had met in downtown Portland that year.

In the summer of 2014 I had the opportunity to participate in a program that was then called ANNpower. It has since been rebranded HERlead. The program was run by a partnership between Vital Voices and ANN INC. (of the Ann Taylor and LOFT stores). Every year they choose fifty young women from around the world with ideas to change the world or serve their communities, and the program hosts these young women for a four-day leadership conference. Those four days were life-changing for me. I had never felt so much passion and eagerness to act and serve. I had applied and been accepted with that simple idea—to bring period products to the homeless women in my local area, many of whom I had talked with and built relationships with.

The conference provided me with a lot of essential lessons to help me embrace my leadership potential— some of which I want to share with you. They are key lessons that I think every young woman (or any change maker, for that matter) should learn.

YOU'RE WORTH IT

I know that it's a simple thing to say, but this is so much harder to learn than it seems. Throughout my adolescent years I really struggled with feelings of self-worth (and experiencing domestic abuse and sexual assault does not help). At an early age, especially in middle school, even when I felt feelings of worth, the source was from my body. This conference was the first time that a larger entity (both in the form of a big network of strong women, and in the form of a corporation and a foundation) was making an investment in me because they felt like I had great potential. I mean, they flew us out to a fancy hotel in Dupont Circle in DC. How could you not look around and say, "Damn, I'm really grateful for this," and realize that someone must really believe in you?

YOU ARE NOT ALONE

YES, it is SCARY to put yourself out there and take big risks to follow your dreams. I AM SCARED OUT OF MY MIND ALL THE TIME, TBH. What will people think of me? What if what I'm trying to do doesn't work? Gathering together in circles of passionate people and young activists is so important because it reminds you that you're not alone. If you are passionate about something, talk about it! Because someone you know might be able to help you build a community, and as you embark on a pretty terrifying journey, you can do so together.

With PERIOD, I knew that in starting an organization, there was a lot that I was not going to be good at, and some aspects of it really gave me the heebie-jeebies—like the finances and paying attention to the small details and fine print. So, I chose a cofounder who not only liked looking into the finances and small details but was also really good at it. He was a classmate, and we had barely talked, but something about him (in how different he was from me but also in how outspoken he was) told me that we could be great complements for each other. I put my trust in him, my mom and his dad (who were our founding board members), my sisters (who kept me grounded), all the young women who pushed me, and the mentors who inspired me—and all together we held hands and LEAPT. We leapt toward a clear vision of *talking about periods* and *providing period products*, and I continue to hold tightly to the hands of people I care about and trust, and I take leap after leap—excited about what I might find.

There was another way in which I felt alone when I first started as an activist. "Try-hard" and "over-achiever" were labels that I was constantly teased with throughout my early education—and even now, in college. It was something I would respond to with, "Thank you?" I was confused about why striving to do my very best or go above and beyond with my work (as my parents had really instilled in me) was a bad thing, but somehow my enthusiasm became something that I was self-conscious about, especially with the ridicule from classmates.

By the end of middle school I wasn't vocal about my excitement to learn more or go above and beyond on homework assignments. I was afraid that I would receive that disapproving look from class-mates as they rolled their eyes and sighed a sort of, "GAWHHD, you try-hard!" The ANNpower confer-ence and the other young-leaders conferences that I've been to were the first time that I could be my unapologetically ambitious self. Unfortunately, we still live in this society that labels young women as "bossy" or "intimidating" when we dream big. For the first time, someone besides my mom was look-ing at me and sort of screaming "DREAM BIGGER." And the girls who sat beside me for those four days all echoed in a harmonious chorus an empowering, "I CAN DO IT! I WILL DO IT! I AM FEARLESS!"

• YOUR "WHY?" ONLY MAKES YOU *STRONGER* •

Jumping into activism and entrepreneurship was the gateway to my embracing my own "WHY?" Why do I care about service and giving back? Why am I so passionate about periods? Why does it matter to me to speak up? Why is it important to me that menstruators feel empowered at all times? Why am I hungry to make a difference? The Vital Voices curriculum calls this your "driving force," and many others will name this the "hook" to any strong, quick elevator pitch.

During a storytelling workshop at this leadership conference was the first time I said OUT LOUD that my family had just faced this confusing experience of housing and financial instability. I had volunteered to get up and simply answer the question, "Why do you care about the fight against homelessness?" I said my simple answer—the one I really thought they wanted to hear, like when every pageant contestant says they want "world peace." I said that everyone should care about homelessness, because security in where we live and our support networks is not something that should be taken for granted. The facilitator of the workshop sighed after I responded, and boldly asked, "But why YOU?" He asked me a few times, until I finally opened up about what my family had faced just that year—and within seconds I was crying and semi-hyperventilating in front of the whole room filled with forty-nine other young women leaders, amazing mentors, and executives.

As I was finishing, I stood at the podium, mascara streaming down my cheeks, trying to explain why I believed so strongly in the right to menstrual hygiene. The room burst out in applause, and as I looked up, I saw that the entire audience was in tears. That was the moment when I first felt that . . . maybe the things that I thought made me weak and less worthy were in fact the experiences that made me stronger—and perhaps there was something about my story and showing my own vulnerability that had resonated with so many.

That conference was also the first time that I witnessed girls my age stand up and, through tears, tell their stories of experiencing domestic violence or sexual assault. I sat there listening in awe, tears streaming down my own face, thinking about my own similar experiences—but without the courage yet to speak out myself on this topic. It wouldn't be until later, after four similar conferences, a few speaking gigs, and a year of therapy and self-reflection, that I would tell my own (more full) story in front of people. Our experiences fuel our passions, and our passions fuel our drive to dream, believe, and act.

MENTORSHIP IS POWERFUL (AND SO IS WOMEN SUPPORTING WOMEN)

Especially as I grew up and became a teenager, my mom was one of my biggest mentors. However, when it came to the professional world, I don't think I'd ever had a real mentor. Nor had I recognized the power and importance of having one— before this conference. Each fellow was assigned to a small group that had a mentor (a past recipient of the Vital Voices Global Leadership Awards). My two mentors were Kah Walla (the badass who ran for president in her home country of Cameroon) and Laura Alonso (an Argentine congresswoman fighting for transparency).[21,22] I furiously took notes when my group had a chance to meet them, because they both spoke so eloquently. It felt like every single one of their quotes should be pasted up on my wall to remind me why my voice matters as a young woman. Here I had the chance to see women in real life who were taking risks, fighting past criticism and hatred, and following their dreams to pursue justice and equality.

Hearing about their work and listening to their advice about needing to stay focused and committed to my larger mission (for my community as well as for my personal life) fueled me deeply as I started my own journey as a young activist. From that week on, I have continued to seek out mentorship wherever possible—especially with women of color. I think that's one of the reasons why I've been able to lead a fast-growing venture like PERIOD and participate in the Menstrual Movement at a higher level than I had ever anticipated. I push myself to always feel inspired by amazing humans that I know or have heard of—and to do this, I stay humble in who I am and what I have done, while believing strongly in both my own and others' potential.

I seek out conversations with role models in different industries, I ask questions about anything from career paths to self-care and relationships, and I look for any advice about how to stay resilient and true to my own values and goals. When I am feeling down or discouraged, I recall the stories of these mentors and the fiery look that they get in their eyes when they talk about their passion and work, and I remind myself of the courage and commitment that it took for them to raise their own voices and maximize their impact, and I keep going.

ASK QUESTIONS, ASK FOR HELP, AND ASK BIG

At the very beginning of leadership conferences or summits that I've been to, there is usually some sort of welcome session where the rules and expectations for the summit are defined. I have found that there are two that are pretty standard but immensely important: (1) respect others—in how you act and what you say—and (2) ask questions and participate. Though the latter is difficult for some, I have always been good at it. And although it did not make me many friends in school classes, it made me a lot of friends in these settings—I found my people. Suddenly I was with ambitious, like-minded young women in meetings and workshops that were facilitated by adults who were hungry to take our questions (and even encouraged questions that were out of the box and bold).

Humility is extremely important in life (especially as an entrepreneur, IMO) because you need to be humble to recognize that there is *so* much that you do *not* know. But you can learn if you own up to where you lack knowledge and skills, and commit yourself to asking questions and admiring others. I truly think that my ability to ask questions and to push everyone I collaborate with (or who works for PERIOD) to ask questions of me and others is what makes PERIOD a game-changer in the Menstrual Movement. I think that my personal experiences with financial instability, and with a mom who always prioritized my sisters' and my having access to quality education no matter what our living situation was, heavily influenced the high level of appreciation that I have for educational opportunities. Any chance I have to learn from others in interesting and entertaining ways, I am all there, ready to raise my hand and ask boldly.

PAY IT FORWARD

Truly effective leadership is when the leader's goal is to empower others to be leaders themselves—and together they all work toward a larger vision. This kind of leadership is effective because it catalyzes movement in so many different ways. On the one hand, from the leader's perspective, if I empower others by giving them opportunities to be leaders themselves and to think independently and act upon their own initiative, then our job is more fun. Suddenly, working together is more about collaboration toward a common goal than about one person simply giving directions—and at the same time, what we produce is often better because there were more perspectives considered (with equal weight). The team will also be more productive. When people feel ownership of certain tasks or projects, I truly believe that their commitment (even if at a subconscious level) is heightened because now there is obvious personal investment in having the end product be successful and effective. This type of leadership is also strong in movements because it's a chain reaction—the empowered leaders will seek out others to empower, and those will find others to empower, and suddenly you have a fast-growing network of passionate leaders.

I will admit, this chain is sometimes challenging because you could be at risk of having "too many cooks in the kitchen," and for me as a natural control freak, I had to learn to ask questions of others rather than simply giving out orders and criticisms. This way of leadership has allowed PERIOD to flourish because people are constantly innovating, respecting others, and creating spaces to thrive in our service work. This is why at PERIOD our one hard request (without exception) in the application process is that people explain to us why they care about the mission of the Menstrual Movement, and what they would do differently if they stepped into a leadership role.

As PERIOD grows, I am often asked, "How did you lead PERIOD to grow so fast?" My *honest* answer is, "It was not just me." PERIOD has become what it is as an organization because many different people, each one involved for their own (often very personal) reasons on why they care about periods, stand together and do work that amplifies our respective skill sets—and together, while having so much fun, we have simply pursued a mission that we truly care about. Not for the money or for the recognition but to fight for EVERY PERSON'S RIGHT TO FEEL CONFIDENT, CAPABLE, AND DIGNIFIED WHILE MENSTRUATING. And I'm proud to say that since its founding in December 2014, PERIOD has distributed more than 270,000 periods addressed and registered more than 200 chapters as of June 2018.

If you are reading this and feeling that passion for period brewing inside you and READY TO BURST, and you're ready to mobilize and get involved in the fight to end period poverty, here are some easy things you can do to start making a difference in your own community:

• RAISE AWARENESS! •

One of the main reasons why period poverty and the stigma around menstruation are perpetuated is that people avoid even thinking about it—so MAKE THEM. Use social media, social spaces, or even individual conversations with people you know to talk about period poverty and why we need to end it. You have plenty of statistics and facts about policy to arm you with knowledge to share. You may have already shared with friends some of the frustrating things you've learned!

• START A PERIOD CHAPTER! •

Our organization is committed to our model of three *Is*—invest, individualize, and incentivize. We have built tool kits and secured resources and staff to invest in all of our chapters, and we individualize our collaboration with and support for each one. We also have worked to find new ways to continue incentivizing the young leaders in our network to push the movement forward. Start a chapter so that we can bring PERIOD's mission to life on your campus or in your community group!

• HOST A DRIVE! •

Collect period products to donate. SHELTERS NEED PERIOD PRODUCTS. Yes, menstrual products are expensive (that's why period poverty is such a problem), so you may need to recruit some friends and spread the word, but try hosting a drive to collect period products from people around the community. This is also a great way to actively break the silence around menstruation, because you have to talk to people you know, strangers, and anyone else in your target audience about what you're doing and why. All you need to do is set up a donation location where you will collect period products. This can even be at a fun gathering of friends, or in a school hallway, in a staff lounge, at an office space, or at the front of a local business. Once you have a space, you can get started publicizing by word of mouth and digitally (USE SOCIAL MEDIA) to encourage people to donate unopened period products.

• MAKE PERIOD PACKS! •

At PERIOD we put together care packages of disposable period products. We then distribute the packages to a network of nonprofit organizations that give them to menstruators who need them. Our national office, along with as many chapters as possible, hosts monthly events to bring people together to assemble the packages. These events are great ways to mobilize volunteers, encourage healthy discussion about periods, and teach about the prevalence of period poverty—and spending time to make a beautiful package of period products creates a more positive experience for whoever ends up receiving it.

• EXPLORE POLICY! •

When studying period poverty through different lenses—whether in relation to homelessness, women in prison, or low-income menstruators—it becomes clear that policy is the most effective way to catalyze long-lasting change to ensure access to period products for all.

• FIND A LEADERSHIP CONFERENCE OF YOUR OWN! •

On a personal level as a leader and activist in the Menstrual Movement, and on a professional level as a cofounder of PERIOD, I see that the movement is working toward a world in which every human is empowered to discover and reach their full potential, without being held back by the fact that they menstruate. To be honest, I am not even sure if this is something that will be achieved in my lifetime, because it is such a global and universal issue, and the stigma that holds back progress is so deeply entrenched in custom and tradition. I often feel in over my head about the world and the industry I'm navigating, but I'm just trying to do whatever I can about this issue, and right now that means using social media platforms to start conversations, traveling and talking to people about the need for equitable access to period products, running this organization and mobilizing other young voices around the world, and starting to explore more potential legislation to end period poverty.

While PERIOD distributes the largest number of period products to people in need, we are just one of many organizations that do this. Interviewers often ask me how I feel about competitors in the same nonprofit arena. I'm asked how I deal with the competition or with criticism that PERIOD receives. Well, first of all, I don't think that there should be any sort of competition between different mobilized groups working toward the same goal. I mean, aren't we all on the same team? We all want to break down the stigma around menstruation and redefine the way our society views periods in the first place, and we're organizing to make sure that all people have equitable access to period products. We have our work cut out for us, and we need all hands on deck. I mean, it is *senseless* to me that even in the twenty-first century, 86 percent of "US women aged 18 to 54 say they have experienced the unexpected onset of their period in public without the supplies they needed,"[23] and 17 percent of women around the world say that they have "missed school, work or an event because they were afraid someone might find out they had their period."[24] That is UNACCEPTABLE. This is a large and universal movement, and we all need to speak out if we want things to change.

Some other organizations besides PERIOD that you can donate to, support, or get involved with include:

DISTRIBUTING DIGNITY

Founded in 2009 in New Jersey, this organization distributes new bras, pads, and tampons, enhancing the dignity of women in need.[25] They currently serve menstruators in need through seventy partners in fifty-two cities across the United States.[26]

I SUPPORT THE GIRLS

Founded by Dana Marlowe, who has been called the "Bra Fairy" for her work, I Support the Girls collects donations of new and gently used bras, and new sealed packages of tampons and maxi pads. The organization distributes these items nationally and internationally to women and girls, "whether they be homeless, refugees, in transitional housing, or fleeing domestic violence."[27]

#HAPPYPERIOD

This organization, founded in early 2015 by Chelsea VonChaz and her mother, is based in Los Angeles and describes itself as a "social movement of girlfriends providing menstrual hygiene kits" to support "anyone that is homeless, low-income, and/or living in poverty."[28]

I want to end this book by saying that if any of this has inspired or empowered you to act, DO IT. Whether it be simply starting a conversation or hosting something larger to collect period products to be donated to people who need them, just GO FOR IT. Every voice and every effort makes a difference, and within this larger social movement, every action counts. I think we'll get there, eventually. I'm optimistic about it . . . but we need all hands on deck.

I'm ready. Are you?

NOTES

Introduction
1. Femme International, "The Issue."
2. Valenti, "Case for Free Tampons."
3. Yan, "Donald Trump's 'Blood.'"
4. Yan, "Donald Trump's 'Blood.'"
5. Trump, "Re Megyn Kelly."
6. Trump, "So Many 'Politically Correct.'"

Chapter One
1. WebMD, "Why Is My Period."
2. NHS Choices, "Periods."
3. Krause, "Menstruation."
4. Krause, "Menstruation."
5. Mayo Clinic, "Menorrhagia."
6. Thinx, "How Heavy Is Too Heavy?"
7. Krause, "Menstruation."
8. McWeeney, "Period Blood Color."
9. McWeeney, "Period Blood Color."
10. Brief, "Period De-Coding."
11. Florio, "What You Need to Know."
12. Coughlin, "Here's Why Your Period."
13. Coughlin, "So That's Why."
14. KidsHealth, "All about Menstruation."
15. Crosta, "What's to Know."
16. WebMD, "Vaginal Discharge: What's Abnormal."
17. Olson, "Age of Woman's First Period."
18. Rose, "NYC School Offers Free Tampons."
19. Planned Parenthood, "Menstruation."
20. Stöppler, "Menopause."
21. Mayo Clinic, "Uterine Fibroids."
22. Nordqvist, "What Are Menstruation."

23. Mayo Clinic, "Amenorrhea."

24. Mayo Clinic, "Premenstrual Syndrome."

25. Mayo Clinic, "Premenstrual Syndrome."

26. Mayo Clinic, "Premenstrual Syndrome."

27. PubMed Health, "Premenstrual Dysphoric Disorder (PMDD)."

28. Yuko, interview.

29. WebMD, "Menstrual Pain."

30. Women's Health Concern, "Period Pain."

31. WebMD, "Menstrual Pain."

32. TrueMedCost.com, "Endometriosis."

33. Crosta, "What's to Know."

34. Crosta, "What's to Know."

35. United States Food and Drug Administration, "The Benefits and Risks."

36. Crosta, "What's to Know."

37. Mavrelos, "Treatment Options."

38. Crosta, "What's to Know."

39. Kennedy, et al., "ESHRE Guideline."

40. Kennedy, et al., "ESHRE Guideline."

41. Mayo Clinic, "Endometriosis."

42. Office on Women's Health, "Endometriosis."

43. Mayo Clinic, "Endometriosis."

44. Brotherton, interview.

45. Kennedy, et al., "ESHRE Guideline."

46. Kennedy, et al., "ESHRE Guideline."

47. Office on Women's Health, "Endometriosis."

48. Office on Women's Health, "Endometriosis."

49. Brotherton, interview.

50. Telfer and Bell, "How Common Is Endometriosis?"

51. Meuleman et al., "High Prevalence of Endometriosis."

52. Eunice Kennedy Shriver, "How Many People Are Affected."

53. Louis et al., "Incidence of Endometriosis."

54. Culley et al., "Social and Psychological Impact."

55. Rizk et al., "Reoccurance of Endometriosis."

56. Center for Young Women's Health, "Endometriosis."

57. Meuleman et al., "High Prevalence of Endometriosis."

58. Office on Women's Health, "Endometriosis."

59. Suresh, P. K. et al, "Complementary and Alternative Medicine."

60. Medline Plus, "Uterine Artery Embolization."

61. Mayo Clinic, "Adenomyosis."

62. Nordqvist, "Fibroids."

63. National Women's Health Network, "Fibroids Medications."

64. Mayo Clinic, "Uterine Fibroids."

65. Mayo Clinic, "Uterine Fibroids."

66. National Women's Health Network, "Hysterectomy."

67. Grunebaum, "Getting Pregnant after a Hysterectomy."

68. National Women's Health Network, "Fibroids Medications."

69. University of California, "Myomectomy."

70. Medline Plus, "Uterine Artery Embolization."

71. National Women's Health Network, "Fibroids Medications."

72. Stewart et al., "Burden of Uterine Fibroids."

73. Stewart et al., "Burden of Uterine Fibroids."

74. National Women's Health Network, "Fibroids Medications."

75. Seely, interview.

76. Nordqvist, "What Is Pelvic Inflammatory Disease?"

77. Centers for Disease Control and Prevention, "Pelvic Inflammatory Disease."

78. Centers for Disease Control and Prevention, "Pelvic Inflammatory Disease.

79. Center for Young Women's Health, "Pelvic Inflammatory Disease."

80. Zepeda, interview.

Chapter Two

1. Gottlieb, panel.

2. Henig, "Dispelling Menstrual Myths."

3. Thorpe, "7 Crazy Period Myths."

4. Grahn, *Blood, Bread, and Roses*, 3–23.

5. Kim, interview.

6. Henig, "Dispelling Menstrual Myths."

7. Henig, "Dispelling Menstrual Myths."

8. Druet, "How Did Menstruation Become Taboo?"

9. Druet, "How Did Menstruation Become Taboo?"

10. L. Smith, "Kahun Gynaecological Papyrus."

11. Druet, "How Did Menstruation Become Taboo?"

12. Druet, "How Did Menstruation Become Taboo?"

13. Quranic Path, "Glorious Qur'an on Menstruation."

14. Druet, "How Did Menstruation Become Taboo?"

15. Shamoun, "Muhammad and Menstruation."

16. Open Bible, "Menstruation."

17. Gottlieb, interview.

18. Linton, interview.

Chapter Three

1. Rubli, "History of the Sanitary Pad."

2. Staley, "Tampon."

3. Center for Young Women's Health, "Using Your First Tampon."

4. Center for Young Women's Health, "Using Your First Tampon."

5. Shure, "Why Has It Taken."

6. Shure, "Why Has It Taken."

7. Shure, "Why Has It Taken."

8. Lunette, "How to Clean."

9. Tsjeng, "The Forgotten Black Woman Inventor."

10. Finley, "'Classic' Sanitary Napkin Belt."

11. Kvatum, "Period Comes to an End."

12. Finley, "'Classic' Sanitary Napkin Belt."

13. Eschner, "Surprising Origins of Kotex Pads."

14. C. Adams, "Who Invented Tampons?"

15. Staley, "Tampon."

16. Fetters, "Tampon: A History."

17. C. Adams, "Who Invented Tampons?"

18. Jones, "Fight to End."

19. Fetters, "Tampon: A History."

20. Staley, "Tampon."

21. Fetters, "Tampon: A History."

22. Fetters, "Tampon: A History."

23. Finley, "Part of the Tampax."

24. C. Adams, "Who Invented Tampons?"

25. Fetters, "Tampon: A History."

26. Fetters, "Tampon: A History."

27. Finley, "Kotams First Kotex Stick."

28. Fetters, "Tampon: A History."

29. Finley, "Kotams First Kotex Stick."

30. Fetters, "Tampon: A History."

31. Fetters, "Tampon: A History."

32. Coughlin, "We Now Know."

33. Hematy, "Invention of the Menstrual Cup."

34. Shure, "Why Has It Taken."

35. Shure, "Why Has It Taken."

36. Shure, "Why Has It Taken."

37. Hematy, "Invention of the Menstrual Cup."

38. Finley, "Menstrual Cup."

39. Hematy, "Invention of the Menstrual Cup."

40. Hematy, "Invention of the Menstrual Cup."

41. Finley, "History of the Menstrual Cup."

42. Hematy, "Invention of the Menstrual Cup."

43. Finley, "History of the Menstrual Cup."

44. Hematy, "Invention of the Menstrual Cup."

45. Chambers, interview.

46. Chambers, interview.

47. Lunette, "Short History of Menstrual Cups."

48. Adamé, email.

49. Hoeger, email.

50. Puhl, interview.

51. Schulte, interview.

52. Thinx, "Period-Proof Underwear."

53. P. Kennedy, "Tampon of the Future."

54. P. Kennedy, "Tampon of the Future."

55. DAME, "D. The First Reusable."

56. Luu, "Creator of Period Panties."

57. Menstrual Cup Reviews, "Sea Sponge Tampons."

Chapter Four

1. Health and Hygiene Pamphlet Collection.

2. HISTORY, "Great Depression."

3. Freidenfelds, *Modern Period*, 1.

4. Freidenfelds, *Modern Period*, 43.

5. HISTORY, "Great Depression."

6. HISTORY, "American Women in World War II."

7. CNN, "American Generation Fast Facts."

8. Khan Academy, "Women in the 1950s."

9. Khan Academy, "Women in the 1950s."

10. Khan Academy, "Women in the 1950s."

11. Daily History, "Second Wave Feminist Movement."

12. Khan Academy, "Women in the 1950s."

13. Napikoski, "*Griswold v. Connecticut.*"

14. Lewis, "*Roe v. Wade.*"

15. Walsh, "1960s: A Decade of Change."

16. Daily History, "Second Wave Feminist Movement."

17. Daily History, "Second Wave Feminist Movement."

18. Digital History, "Overview of the 1960s."

19. Freidenfelds, *Modern Period*, 56.

20. Freidenfelds, *Modern Period*, 53–56.

21. Edelstein, "Menstruating in the Age of Mad Men."

22. Freidenfelds, *Modern Period*, 53–56.

23. Edelstein, "Menstruating in the Age of Mad Men."

24. Freidenfelds, *Modern Period*, 57.

25. Freidenfelds, *Modern Period*, 57.

26. Ellingham, "'You're a Young Lady Now.'"

27. Health and Hygiene Pamphlet Collection.

28. Freidenfelds, *Modern Period*, 87.

29. Freidenfelds, *Modern Period*, 88–89.

30. Health and Hygiene Pamphlet Collection.

31. Health and Hygiene Pamphlet Collection.

32. Health and Hygiene Pamphlet Collection.

33. Stamets, "1940's Pamphlet on Periods."

34. Edelstein, "Menstruating in the Age of Mad Men."

35. Stamets, "1940's Pamphlet on Periods."

36. Health and Hygiene Pamphlet Collection.

37. Marland, *Health and Girlhood in Britain*, 59.

38. Freidenfelds, *Modern Period*, 93.

39. Freidenfelds, *Modern Period*, 93.

40. Edelstein, "Menstruating in the Age of Mad Men."

41. Edelstein, "Menstruating in the Age of Mad Men."

42. Freidenfelds, *Modern Period*, 57.

43. Bobel, interview.

44. Jones, "Fight to End Period Shaming."

Chapter Five

1. Weiss-Wolf, "New York."

2. Mukuria, interview.

3. Kane, "Here's How Much."

4. Collective Evolution, "What All Women Need to Know."

5. Allen, "The Fight."

6. Upadhye, "This Is How Homeless Women."

7. Bustle, "How Do Homeless Women," Facebook.

8. Bustle, "How Do Homeless Women," YouTube.

9. Bustle, "How Do Homeless Women," YouTube.

10. Bustle, "How Do Homeless Women," YouTube.

11. L. Moore, "What It's Like."

12. Upadhye, "This Is How."

13. Jones, "Free Tampons and Pads."

14. Cawthorne, "Straight Facts."

15. Kosin, "Getting Your Period."

16. Tucker and Lowell, "National Snapshot."

17. Tucker and Lowell, "National Snapshot."

18. Cawthorne, "Straight Facts."

19. Murdoch, "Turns Out."

20. Plank, "Secret Tax."

21. Plank, "Secret Tax."

22. Murdoch, "Turns Out."

23. Murdoch, "Turns Out."

24. Goldman, "Why Women Pay More."

25. Cawthorne, "Straight Facts."

26. Cawthorne, "Straight Facts."

27. Weiss-Wolf, "Helping Women and Girls."

28. Cawthorne, "Straight Facts."

29. Tucker and Lowell, "National Snapshot."

30. Miller, "Simple Truth."

31. Miller, "Simple Truth."

32. Cawthorne, "Straight Facts."

33. BBC, "Girls 'Too Poor.'"

34. Tsjeng, "Activists Making Sure."

35. Scaccia, "Price Young Girls Pay."

36. Mays, "She Put Newspaper."

37. Greenberg, "In Jail."

38. Kosin, "Getting Your Period."

39. Schenwar, "In Prison."

40. Schenwar, "In Prison."

41. Greenberg, "In Jail."

42. Greenberg, "In Jail."

43. Greenberg, "In Jail."

44. Greenberg, "In Jail."

45. Greenberg, "In Jail."

46. Scaccia, "Women in Jail."

47. Goodman, Dawson, and Burlingame, "Reproductive Health Behind Bars."

48. Goodman, Dawson, and Burlingame, "Reproductive Health Behind Bars."

49. Goodman, Dawson, and Burlingame, "Reproductive Health Behind Bars."

50. Goodman, Dawson, and Burlingame, "Reproductive Health Behind Bars."

51. Kraft-Stolar, *Reproductive Injustice.*

52. Kraft-Stolar, *Reproductive Injustice.*

53. Kraft-Stolar, *Reproductive Injustice.*

54. Kraft-Stolar, *Reproductive Injustice.*

55. Rabuy and Kopf, "Prisons of Poverty."

56. *Guardian*, "Woman Enters Court."

57. Sidahmed, "Woman Enters Court."

58. Bever, "'She Has No Pants.'"

59. Bozelko, "Prisons That Withhold."

60. Ronan, "Menstruation Can Become Humiliation."

61. Bozelko, "Prisons That Withhold."

62. Bozelko, "Prisons That Withhold."

63. Kloosterman, "Michigan ACLU."

64. ACLU Michigan, "ACLU of Michigan."

65. Scaccia, "Women in Jail."

Chapter Six

1. Kosin, "Getting Your Period."

2. Valenti, "Case for Free Tampons."

3. Valenti, "Case for Free Tampons."

4. Weiss-Wolf, "Helping Women and Girls."

5. Jones, "Free Tampons and Pads."

6. Scaccia, "Price Young Girls Pay."

7. Jones, "Free Tampons and Pads."

8. Roy, "Hero Councilwoman."

9. Rinkunas, "One NYC High School."

10. Campanile and Gartland, "Councilwoman."

11. Scaccia, "Women in Jail."

12. Rinkunas, "One NYC High School."

13. BBC, "'Menstrual Equity.'"

14. Ferreras-Copeland, "Over 20 Women."

15. Rinkunas, "One NYC High School."

16. Maunz, "Meet the Women."

17. Rinkunas, "One NYC High School."

18. Jones, "Free Tampons and Pads."

19. New York City Council, "Provision of Feminine Hygiene Products."

20. BBC, "'Menstrual Equity.'"

21. Rinkunas, "One NYC High School."

22. Scaccia, "Women in Jail."

23. Kraft-Stolar, *Reproductive Injustice*.

24. New York City Council, "Provision of Feminine Hygiene Products."

25. BBC, "'Menstrual Equity.'"

26. Dane County Government, "2015 RES-317."

27. Conner, *"Atkins v. County of Orange."*

28. Conner, *"Atkins v. County of Orange."*

29. Garcia, "Assembly Bill No. 10."

30. Cruz, "Having a Period."

31. Koseff and Cadelago, "Poor Students."

32. Garcia, "Assembly Bill No. 10."

33. Mays, "She Put Newspaper."

34. Garcia, "Assembly Bill No. 10."

35. Mays, "She Put Newspaper."

36. Koseff and Cadelago, "Poor Students."

37. Valenti, "Case for Free Tampons."

38. Gupta, "Why the Hell."

39. Hillin, "These Are the U.S. States."

40. Poppick, "More States Tax Tampons."

41. Sagner, "More States Move."

42. Mettler, "Free Tampons for All."

43. Cart, "Barbie's in Bonn."

44. Dillon, "A Proposal."

45. Dillon, "A Proposal."

46. Calfas, "Most States Charge."

47. Calfas, "Most States Charge."

48. Dillon, "A Proposal."

49. Mettler, "Free Tampons for All."

50. Feuerherd and Campanile, "Lawmaker Wants to Wipe."

51. Campanile, "Assemblyman Says Tampon."

52. Feuerherd and Campanile, "Lawmaker Wants to Wipe."

53. Campanile, "Assemblyman Says Tampon."

54. Jones, "Free Tampons and Pads."

55. Jones, "New York Terminates."

56. North, "Welcome End."

57. New York State Governor, "Governor Cuomo Signs Legislation."

58. Jones, "New York Terminates."

59. Associated Press, "New York Legislature."

60. Blain, "New York State."

61. New York State Governor, "Governor Cuomo Signs Legislation."

62. Jones, "New York Terminates."

63. New York State Governor, "Governor Cuomo Signs Legislation."

64. Kabas, "New York Abolished."

65. Jones, "New York Terminates."

66. Illinois Department, "Drugs, Medicines."

67. Maloney, "Which States."

68. Jones, "Fight to End Period Shaming."

69. United States Congresswoman, "Meng: FEMA to Permit."

70. Jones, "Fight to End Period Shaming."

71. Jones, "New York Terminates."

72. M. Smith, "'Periods for Pence.'"

73. Jones, "New York Terminates."
74. Twitter, "#PeriodsforPence."
75. Domonoske, "Periods as Protest."
76. M. Smith, "'Periods for Pence.'"
77. Gupta, "Why the Hell."
78. Supreme Court of Illinois, "*Geary v. Dominick's*."
79. Gupta, "Why the Hell."
80. Illinois Department of Revenue Regulations. "Drugs, Medicines."
81. Gupta, "Why the Hell."
82. Illinois Department of Revenue Regulations, "Drugs, Medicines."
83. Wisconsin State Legislature, "Assembly Bill 555."
84. Gupta, "Why the Hell."
85. Maunz, "Meet the Women."
86. Obama, "Let Girls Learn."
87. Jones, "Free Tampons and Pads."
88. Collective Evolution, "What All Women Need to Know."
89. Jones, "Free Tampons and Pads."
90. Collective Evolution, "What All Women Need to Know."
91. Wasser, "Model Lauren Wasser."
92. Wasser, "Model Lauren Wasser."
93. Lippo, "Model Who Lost Leg."
94. Lippo, "Model Who Lost Leg."
95. Green Feminine Hygiene Queen, "Amy Elifritz."
96. Wasser, "Model Lauren Wasser."
97. Brown, "Model Loses Remaining Leg."
98. Wasser, "Model Lauren Wasser."
99. Jones, "Fight to End Period Shaming."
100. Rix, "Toxic Shock Syndrome."
101. Jones, "Fight to End Period Shaming."
102. Jones, "Free Tampons and Pads."
103. Jones, "Free Tampons and Pads."
104. Center for American Women and Politics, "Women in Elective Office."

105. Oh and Kliff, "The US Is Ranked."

106. Lawless and Fox, "Men Rule."

107. Lawless and Fox, "Men Rule."

108. Lawless and Fox, "Men Rule."

Chapter Seven

1. Yuko, "Why It Matters."

2. Squier, "In 10 Years."

3. Pearson, "What Hollywood Gets Wrong."

4. Yuko, interview.

5. Moeschen, "Shameless: Broad City."

6. Yuko, "2017 Was a Big Year."

7. Velocci, "Why Are We Suddenly."

8. Yuko, "2017 Was a Big Year."

9. Chaney, "On TV."

10. Chaney, "On TV."

11. Chaney, "On TV."

12. Farley, "Vulvas Are Funny, Too."

13. Chaney, "Talking Puberty."

14. Chaney, "On TV."

15. Farley, "Vulvas Are Funny, Too."

16. Chaney, "On TV."

17. Yuko, interview.

18. Zabczynski, "Period Humor on 'Broad City.'"

19. Zulch, "Most Body Positive Moment."

20. Zulch, "Most Body Positive Moment."

21. Gallagher, "Abbi & Ilana's Tampon Search."

22. Gallagher, "Abbi & Ilana's Tampon Search."

23. Moeschen, "Shameless: Broad City."

24. Farley, "Vulvas Are Funny, Too."

25. Yuko, "2017 Was a Big Year."

26. Blay, "'OITNB' Exposed."

27. Hawkins, "'Orange Is The New Black' Tampon."

28. Truong, "What It's Like."

29. Bozelko, "Prisons That Withhold."
30. *New Yorker*, "Video: Vintage Tina Fey."
31. *Saturday Night Live*, "Kotex Classic—SNL."
32. Linton, "Tina Fey's Menstrual Musings."
33. S. Moore, "Let's See Menopausal."
34. Quality Logo Products, "History of TV Ads."
35. Ziv, "Periods Are Normal."
36. Period, "Tampon History."
37. Tampax, "Courteney Cox 1985 Tampax Commercial."
38. R. Adams, "Tampon-Makers."
39. DiBranco, "Terms 'Vagina' and 'Down There.'"
40. Chyr, "Always Maze."
41. Chyr, "Always Maze."
42. Ziv, "Periods Are Normal."
43. Jardine, "This Powerful Bodyform."
44. Rodulfo, "Finally, a Period Commercial."
45. Moss, "Bodyform's 'Red.Fit' Campaign."
46. Kutner, "Will the New York City Subway."
47. Rinkunas, "Women's Underwear Company."
48. Rinkunas, "Women's Underwear Company."
49. Kutner, "Will the New York City Subway."
50. Kutner, "Will the New York City Subway."
51. Malone, "Panty Raid."
52. Lonergan, interview.
53. del Rosario, interview.
54. Merlan, "Celebration of the Beautiful."
55. Leibow, interview.
56. Hello Flo, "About Us."
57. Hello Flo, "FAQs."
58. Hello Flo, "Camp Gyno."
59. Hello Flo, "First Moon Party."
60. Reflect, "Ingrid Nilsen Interviews Obama."
61. Reflect, "Ingrid Nilsen Interviews Obama."
62. AJ+, "We Are Being Taxed."

63. L. Moore, "Instagram Apologizes."

64. Gray, "Removal of Rupi Kaur's Instagram Photos."

65. L. Moore, "Instagram Apologizes."

66. L. Moore, "Instagram Apologizes."

67. Kaur, "Thank You Instagram."

68. Moore, "Instagram Apologizes."

69. Gray, "Removal of Rupi Kaur's Instagram Photos."

70. *Cosmopolitan*, "Why Do Men Accuse."

71. As/Is, "Guys Experience Periods."

72. As/Is, "Guys Test Maxi Pads."

73. *Glamour*, "This Is Your Period."

74. Sanghani, "This Woman."

75. Feng, "Uninhibited Chinese Swimmer."

76. Gandhi, "Going with the Flow."

77. London, "Runner Who Completed."

78. Feng, "Uninhibited Chinese Swimmer."

79. Feng, "Uninhibited Chinese Swimmer."

80. Feng, "Uninhibited Chinese Swimmer."

Chapter Eight

1. Muller, "Emma Watson."

2. Toni the Tampon, "Y'all Know I'm Trans."

3. Smothers, "How This Trans."

4. Kosin, "Getting Your Period."

5. Rastogi, "Greening the Crimson Tide."

6. Spinks, "Disposable Tampons Aren't Sustainable."

7. Bolen, "Are Disposable Pads."

8. Garewal, "Perils of Plastic Applicator Tampons."

9. Earth Eclipse, "Effects of Plastic Pollution."

10. Garewal, "Perils of Plastic Applicator Tampons."

11. Bolen, "Are Disposable Pads."

12. Rabin, "$417 Million Awarded."

13. Eden, "Here's Why."

14. Garewal, "Perils of Plastic Applicator Tampons."

15. Garewal, "Perils of Plastic Applicator Tampons."
16. Eden, "Here's Why."
17. Sheffield, "Can You Flush."
18. Bishop, "We Need to Talk."
19. Rohmann, "PSA: Don't Flush."
20. Kale, "12-Year-Old Reportedly."
21. Muruganantham, "How I Started."
22. Lampen, "Can 'Period Leave' Ever Work?"
23. Pattani, "In Some Countries."
24. Lampen, "Can 'Period Leave' Ever Work?"
25. Llywodraeth Cymru/Welsh Government, "£1 Million."
26. Onyanga-Omara, "Women Get Their Periods."

Chapter Nine

1. Maunz, "Meet the Women."
2. Rinkunas, "One NYC High School."
3. Rinkunas, "One NYC High School."
4. Schow, "Should Tampons Be Free?"
5. Schow, "Should Tampons Be Free?"
6. Schow, "Should Tampons Be Free?"
7. Schow, "Should Tampons Be Free?"
8. Jones, "Fight to End Period Shaming."
9. Jones, "Fight to End Period Shaming."
10. Freedman, "Zoey Freedman: Free Tampons."
11. Frej, "Colleges Are the Next."
12. Scaccia, "Free Bleeding."
13. Jones, "Fight to End Period Shaming."
14. Mettler, "Free Tampons for All."
15. Jones, "Fight to End Period Shaming."
16. Mettler, "Free Tampons for All."
17. New, "If Condoms Are Free."
18. Friedlander, "College Bathrooms."
19. New, "If Condoms Are Free."
20. Friedlander, "College Bathrooms."

21. Vital Voices, "Kah Walla."
22. Vital Voices, "Politics Innovator."
23. Goldber, "U.S. Women Push Back."
24. Goldber, "U.S. Women Push Back."
25. Distributing Dignity, "Home."
26. Distributing Dignity, "Our Partners."
27. I Support the Girls, "About Us."
28. Hashtag Happy Period, "Our Story."

BIBLIOGRAPHY

ACLU Michigan. "ACLU of Michigan Sues Muskegon County over Unconstitutional Policies, Hazardous Conditions at Jail." December 4, 2014. http://aclumich.org/article/aclu-michigan-sues-muskegon-county-over-unconstitutional-policies-hazardous-conditions-jail.

ACLU Michigan. "Mistreatment of Women at the Muskegon County Jail." October 7, 2015. https://www.aclumichigan.org/article/abhorrent-conditions-confinement-muskegon-county-jail.

Adamé, Jane. Email with author. February 26, 2018.

Adams, Cecile. "Who Invented Tampons?" Straight Dope, June 6, 2006. http://www.straightdope.com/columns/read/2252/who-invented-tampons/.

Adams, Richard. "Tampon-Makers Can't Mention the V-word. Period." *Guardian*, March 17, 2010. https://www.theguardian.com/world/richard-adams-blog/2010/mar/16/tampon-vagina-kotex-advertising.

AJ+. "We Are Being Taxed for Being Women." Facebook, January 16, 2016. https://www.facebook.com/ajplusenglish/videos/672845842856926/.

Allen, Samantha. "The Fight to Give Homeless Women a Dignified Period." *The Daily Beast*, July 25, 2016. https://thedailybeast.com/the-fight-to-give-homeless-women-a-dignified-period.

As/Is. "Guys Experience Periods for the First Time." YouTube, April 5, 2016. https://www.youtube.com/watch?v=tciKSzVZro4&t=16s.

As/Is. "Guys Test Maxi Pads." YouTube, May 13, 2017. https://www.youtube.com/watch?v=wn3LP90-fPo.

Associated Press. "New York Legislature Cuts Taxes on Tampons and Other Feminine Hygiene Products." *New York Times*, May 25, 2016. https://www.nytimes.com/2016/05/26/nyregionew-york-legislature-cuts-taxes-on-feminine-hygiene-products.html?rref=collection%2Fsectioncollection%2Fhealth.

BBC. "Girls 'Too Poor' to Buy Sanitary Protection Missing School."
March 14, 2017. http://www.bbc.com/news/uk-39266056.

BBC. "'Menstrual Equity': Free Tampons for New York City
Schools and Jails." June 22, 2016. http://www.bbc.com/news
/world-us-canada-36597949.

Bever, Lindsey. "'She Has No Pants and She Is in Court': Judge
Outraged over Inmate's Appearance." *Washington Post*, August
1, 2016. https://www.washingtonpost.com/news/morning-mix
/wp/2016/08/01/am-i-in-the-twilight-zone-a-judges-reaction-to
-a-bare-legged-defendant-in-court/?utm_term=.ab001d62594d.

Bishop, Caitlin. "We Need to Talk about What We Are Doing with
Tampons." MamaM!a, September 27, 2016. https://www.
mamamia.com.au/flushing-tampons/.

Blain, Glenn. "New York State Set to Repeal Tax on Tampons and
Other Feminine Hygiene Products." *Daily News*, May 25, 2016.
http://www.nydailynews.com/news/politics/gov-cumo-pushes
-tax-free-feminine-hygiene-products-bill-article-1.2650036.

Blay, Zeba. "'OITNB' Exposed the Frustrating Realties of Getting
Your Period in Prison." Huffington Post, June 22, 2016.
https://www.huffingtonpost.co.uk/entry/oitnb-exposed
-the-frustrating-realties-of-getting-your-period-in-prison
_us_576a951de4b 09926ce5d1ffaf.

Bobel, Chris. Interview with author. December 11, 2017.

Bodyform Channel. "Blood." YouTube, May 27, 2016. https://www
.youtube.com/watch?time_continue=2&v=8Q1GVOYIcKc.

Bolen, Jackie. "Are Disposable Pads and Tampons Harmful to the
Environment?" Earth Eclipse, accessed December 20, 2017.
https://www.eartheclipse.com/environment/disposable
-pads-and-tampons-harmful-environment.html.

Bozelko, Chandra. "Prisons That Withhold Menstrual Pads
Humiliate Women and Violate Basic Rights." *Guardian*, June
12, 2015. https://www.theguardian.com/commentisfree/2015
/jun/12/prisons-menstrual-pads-humiliate-women-violate-rights.

Brief. "Period De-Coding: All About Period Blood Consistency."

Accessed December 1, 2017. http://monthlygift.com/blog
/period/period-decoding-period-blood-consistency/.

Brown, Vanessa. "Model Loses Remaining Leg after Tampon
Mishap." *New York Post*, January 15, 2018. https://nypost.com
/2018/01/15/model-loses-remaining-leg-after-tampon-mishap/.

Bustle. "How Do Homeless Women Cope with Their Periods?"
Facebook, October 18, 2016. http://www.facebook.com
/bustledotcom/videos/1456778941002334.

Bustle. "How Do Homeless Women Cope with Their Periods? |
NSFWomen." YouTube, October 18, 2016. https://www
.youtube.com/watch?v=ABch4VYOJZ0&feature=youtu.be.

Calfas, Jennifer. "Most States Charge a Tax on Tampons. This
Lawmaker Has a Brilliant Solution." *Money*, March 15, 2017.
http://time.com/money/4701623/california-tampon-tax/.

Campanile, Carl. "Assemblyman Says Tampon and Toilet Paper
Taxes Should Be Flushed Away." *New York Post,* May 18,
2015. https://nypost.com/2015/05/18/assemblyman-says
-tampon-and-toilet-paper-taxes-should-be-flushed-away/.

Campanile, Carl, and Michael Gartland. "Councilwoman
Wants to Make Tampons Free for Teens." *New York
Post*, June 9, 2015. https://nypost.com/2015/06/09/
councilwoman-wants-to-make-tampons-free-for-teens/.

Cart, Julie. "Barbie's in Bonn with Assemblywoman Garcia."
CALmatters, November 13, 2017. https://calmatters.org
/articles/blog/barbies-bonn-assemblywoman-garcia/.

Cawthorne, Alexandra. "The Straight Facts on Women in Poverty."
Center for American Progress, October 8, 2008. https://www
.americanprogress.org/issues/women/reports/2008/10/08/5103
/the-straight-facts-on-women-in-poverty/.

Center for American Women and Politics. "Women in Elective
Office Fact Sheet." Rutgers Eagleton Institute of Politics.
Accessed January 25, 2018. http://www.cawp.rutgers.edu
/current-numbers.

Center for Young Women's Health. "Endometriosis: Hormonal

Treatment Overview." Updated August 29, 2016. https://
youngwomenshealth.org/2014/08/01/endometriosis-hormonal
-treatment-overview/.

Center for Young Women's Health. "Pelvic Inflammatory Disease
(PID)." Accessed July 13, 2017. https://youngwomenshealth
.org/2013/02/21/pelvic-inflammatory-disease/.

Center for Young Women's Health. "Using Your First Tampon."
Accessed July 25, 2016. https://youngwomenshealth.org/2012
/09/27/tampons/.

Centers for Disease Control and Prevention. "Pelvic Inflammatory
Disease (PID)—CDC Fact Sheet." Accessed January 25, 2018.
https://www.cdc.gov/std/pid/stdfact-pid-detailed.htm.

Chambers, Carinne. Interview with the author. December 22, 2017.

Chaney, Jen. "On TV, a Girl's First Period as a Mark of Female
Power." Vulture, November 13, 2017. http://www.vulture.com
/2017/11/blackish-alias-grace-big-mouth-period-episodes.html.

Chaney, Jen. "Talking Puberty with *Big Mouth*'s Jessi Klein and
Andrew Goldberg." Vulture, November 7, 2017. http://www
.vulture.com/2017/11/big-mouth-jessi-klein-andrew-goldberg
-interview.html.

Chyr, William. "Always Maze, or: How to Break Taboos in Feminine
Hygiene Advertising." November 3, 2011. http://willychyr.com
/2011/11/always-maze-or-how-to-break-taboos-in-feminine
-hygiene-advertising/.

CNN. "American Generation Fast Facts." Accessed August 27,
2017. https://www.cnn.com/2013/11/06/us/baby-boomer
-generation-fast-facts/index.html.

Collective Evolution. "What All Women Need to Know about Pads &
Tampons." Accessed March 15, 2016. http://www.collective
-evolution.com/2016/03/15/what-all-women-need-to-know-about
-pads-tampons/.

Conner, William C. "*Atkins v. County of Orange*." June 3, 2015. https://
scholar.google.com/scholar_case?case=2513628061483569234&hl
=en&as_sdt=6&as_vis=1&oi=scholarr.

Cosmopolitan. "Why Do Men Accuse Women of Being on Their
    Periods?" YouTube, August 14, 2015. https://www.youtube
    .com/watch?v=WPuy94tqqfg.

Coughlin, Sara. "Here's Why Your Period Blood Smells."
    Refinery29, July 15, 2016. https://www.refinery29.com/2016
    /07/116837/period-blood-smell?bucketed=true.

Coughlin, Sara. "So That's Why You Have to Poop So Much
    During Your Period." Refinery29, March 6, 2017. https://
    www.refinery29.com/2016/02/103078/strange-period
    -questions.

Coughlin, Sara. "We Now Know What the Very First Menstrual
    Cup Looked Like." Refinery29, June 12, 2015. https://www
    .refinery29.com/2015/06/89096/first-menstrual-cup-history.

Crosta, Peter. "What's to Know about Menstrual Cramps?"
    Medical News Today, November 24, 2017. https://www
    .medicalnewstoday.com/articles/157333.php.

Cruz, Araceli. "Having a Period Will No Longer Affect California's
    Female Students Ability to Get an Education." Fierce, October
    16, 2017. https://fierce.wearemitu.com/fierce/california
    -public-schools-will-now-offer-free-tampons/.

Culley, Lorraine, Caroline Law, Nicky Hudson, Elaine Denny,
    Helene Mitchell, Miriam Baumgarten, and Nick Raine-
    Fenning. "The Social and Psychological Impact of
    Endometriosis on Women's Lives: A Critical Narrative
    Review." Human Reproduction Update, Volume 19, Issue 6 (1
    November 2013): 625–639, https://doi.org/10.1093/humupd
    /dmt027.

Daily History. "What Was the Second Wave Feminist Movement?"
    Last modified May 17, 2018. https://dailyhistory.org/What
    _was_the_Second_Wave_Feminist_Movement%3F.

DAME. "D. The First Reusable Tampon Applicator." Indiegogo,
    March 29, 2018. https://www.indiegogo.com/projects
    /d-the-first-reusable-tampon-applicator#/.

Dane County Government Legislative Information Center. "2015

RES-317." November 3, 2015. https://dane.legistar.com
/LegislationDetail.aspx?ID=2511915&GUID=9671AEA0
-521C-4D5B-BC0E-8472A3F5B263&Options=&Search=.

del Rosario, Veronica. Interview with author. March 5, 2018.

DiBranco, Alex. "Terms 'Vagina' and 'Down There' Banned from
T.V. Ads." Fractals, March 17, 2010. https://adibranco
.wordpress.com/2010/03/17/terms-vagina-and-down-there
-banned-from-t-v-ads/.

Digital History. "Overview of the 1960s." Accessed December 1,
2017. http://www.digitalhistory.uh.edu/era.cfm?eraID
=17&smtid=1.

Dillon, Liam. "A Proposal to Eliminate Sales Taxes on Tampons
and Diapers in California Fails." *Los Angeles Times*, May 8,
2017. http://www.latimes.com/politics/la-pol-sac-tampon-tax
-dies-20170508-story.html.

Distributing Dignity. "Give Dignity." Accessed January 15, 2018.
http://www.distributingdignity.org/give-dignity.

Distributing Dignity. "Home." Accessed January 15, 2018. http://
www.distributingdignity.org/.

Distributing Dignity. "Our Partners." Accessed January 15, 2018.
http://www.distributingdignity.org/our-partners/.

Do Something. "Power to the Period." Accessed December 3, 2017.
https://www.dosomething.org/us/campaigns/power-period.

Domonoske, Camila. "Periods as Protest: Indiana Women Call
Governor to Talk about Menstrual Cycles." NPR, April 8,
2016. https://www.npr.org/sections/thetwo-way/2016/04/08
/473518239/periods-as-protest-indiana-women-call-governor
-to-talk-about-menstrual-cycles.

Druet, Anna. "How Did Menstruation Become Taboo?" Clued In,
September 8, 2017. https://medium.com/clued-in/how-did
-menstruation-become-taboo-3c626585c87.

Earth Eclipse. "Effects of Plastic Pollution." Accessed December 20,
2017. https://www.eartheclipse.com/pollution/fatal-effects
-of-plastic-pollution.html.

Edelstein, Sally. "Menstruating in the Age of Mad Men."
    Envisioning the American Dream, April 25, 2016. https://
    envisioningtheamericandream.com/2016/04/25/menstruating
    -in-the-age-of-mad-men/.

Eden, Nellie. "Here's Why You Should Never Flush Your Tampon
    Down the Toilet." Refinery29, July 12, 2016. https://
    www.refinery29.uk/2016/07/116505/flushing-tampons
    -toilet-bad-environment-tampon-tax-toxic.

Egozi, Arielle. "Life after Thinx: Chelsea Leibow on Her New
    Business, Sex Positivity and Healing Trauma." Mic, August 24,
    2017. https://mic.com/articles/183807/life-after-thinx-chelsea
    -leibow-on-her-new-business-sex-positivity-and-healing
    -trauma#.HBaqBiRF8.

Ellingham, Erin. "'You're a Young Lady Now': Menstrual
    Education through Advertising." Radcliffe Institute for
    Advanced Study, July 17, 2014. https://www.radcliffe.harvard
    .edu/schlesinger-library/blog/youre-young-lady-now.

Eschner, Kat. "The Surprising Origins of Kotex Pads." *Smithsonian*
    magazine, August 11, 2017. https://www.smithsonianmag
    .com/innovation/surprising-origins-kotex-pads-180964466/.

Eunice Kennedy Shriver National Institute of Child Health and
    Human Development. "How Many People Are Affected by
    or at Risk for Endometriosis?" Accessed January 31, 2017.
    https://www.nichd.nih.gov/health/topics/endometri
    /conditioninfo/at-risk.

Farley, Rebecca. "Vulvas Are Funny, Too—How This Show Does
    Puberty Humor Right." Refinery29, October 4, 2017. https://
    www.refinery29.com/2017/10/175012/netflix-big-mouth
    -review-jessi-klein-period-episode-2.

Femme International. "The Issue." Accessed January 15, 2018.
    https://www.femmeinternational.org/our-work/the-issue/.

Feng, Emily. "Uninhibited Chinese Swimmer, Discussing Her Period,
    Shatters Another Barrier." *New York Times*, August 16, 2016.
    https://www.nytimes.com/2016/08/17/world/asia/china-fu

-yuanhui-period-olympics.html?mtrref=undefined&gwh
=21DAB887762ED1FDF330FAD56E57EFA8&gwt=pay.

Ferreras-Copeland, Julissa. "Over 20 Women Joined My
Roundtable." Facebook, June 10, 2015. https://www.facebook
.com/Julissa.Ferreras/posts/916555208387957.

Fetters, Ashley. "The Tampon: A History." *Atlantic*, June 1, 2015.
https://www.theatlantic.com/health/archive/2015/06/history
-of-the-tampon/394334/.

Feuerherd, Ben, and Carl Campanile. "Lawmaker Wants to Wipe
Toilet Paper Tax off the Books." *New York Post*, May 16,
2015. https://nypost.com/2015/05/16/lawmaker-wants-to
-wipe-toilet-paper-tax-off-the-books/.

Finley, Harry. "A History of the Menstrual Cup (continued)."
Museum of Menstruation, accessed December 3, 2017. http://
www.mum.org/CupTaset.htm.

Finley, Harry. "'Classic' Sanitary Napkin Belt, U.S.A., about 1945."
Museum of Menstruation, accessed December 10, 2017.
http://www.mum.org/beltclass.htm.

Finley, Harry. "Kotams First Kotex Stick Menstrual Tampons."
Museum of Menstruation, accessed December 3, 2017. http://
www.mum.org/kotams.htm.

Finley, Harry. "Part of the Tampax Menstrual Tampon Patent."
Museum of Menstruation, accessed December 8, 2017. http://
www.mum.org/Tampaxpatent.htm.

Finley, Harry. "The Menstrual Cup in the Intimate Side of a Woman's
Life, by Leona W. Chalmers." Museum of Menstruation, accessed
December 4, 2017. http://www.mum.org/chalmbok.htm.

Florio, Gina. "What You Need to Know about the Way Your
Period Smells." Hello Giggles, July 26, 2016. https://
hellogiggles.com/lifestyle/need-know-way-period-smells/.

Freedman, Zoey. "Zoey Freedman: Free Tampons Would Slow
Flow of Gender Inequality." *Daily Bruin*, July 20, 2015. http://
dailybruin.com/2015/07/20/free-tampons-would-slow-flow-of
-gender-inequality/.

Freidenfelds, Lara. *The Modern Period: Menstruation in Twentieth-Century America.* Baltimore: JHU Press, 2009.

Frej, Willie. "Colleges are the Next Battleground in the Fight for Free Tampons." Huffington Post, March 11, 2016. Updated January 4, 2017. https://www.huffingtonpost.com/entry /colleges-free-tampons-equality_us_56e2dd98e4b065e2e3d5a09a.

Friedlander, Emma. "College Bathrooms Provide Free Pads and Tampons: Student Activist Rebekah Rennick Inspired Action." *Scarlet and Black*, September 9, 2016. http://www.thesandb .com/article/college-bathrooms-provide-free-pads-and -tampons-student-activist-rebekah-rennick-inspired-action.html.

Gallagher, Caitlin. "Abbi & Ilana's Tampon Search on 'Broad City' Shows Just How Much Women Have to Deal With." Bustle, April 21, 2016. https://www.bustle.com/articles/155752 -abbi-ilanas-tampon-search-on-broad-city-shows-just-how -much-women-have-to-deal.

Gandhi, Kiran. "Going with the Flow." Endless, July 20, 2015. https://medium.com/endless/going-with-the-flow-blood -sisterhood-at-the-london-marathon-f719b98713e7.

Garcia, Cristina. "Assembly Bill No. 10." California Legislative Information, October 13, 2017. http://leginfo.legislature .ca.gov/faces/billTextClient.xhtml?bill_id=201720180AB10.

Garewal, Komal. "The Perils of Plastic Applicator Tampons." Maxim Hygiene, October 28, 2016. http://www.maximhy.com /blog/2016/10/28/the-perils-of-plastic-applicator-tampons-the -need-to-go-green/.

Glamour. "This Is Your Period in 2 Minutes." YouTube, December 6, 2016. https://www.youtube.com/watch?v=WOi2Bwvp6hw.

Goldber, Barbara. "U.S. Women Push Back against Stigma, Cost of Menstruation." Reuters, March 8, 2016. https://www.reuters .com/article/us-usa-menstruation/u-s-women-push-back -against-stigma-cost-of-menstruation-idUSKCN0WA1RG.

Goldman, Lea. "Why Women Pay More." *Marie Claire*, March 15, 2012. https://www.marieclaire.com/career-advice/news/a6999

/why-do-women-pay-more/.

Goodman, Melissa, Ruth Dawson, and Phyllida Burlingame. "Reproductive Health Behind Bars in California." California: ACLU of California, January 2016. https://www.aclunc.org /ReproductiveHealthBehindBars_Report.

Gottlieb, Alma. PERIOD CON Menstrual Education Panel #3. August 2017.

Grahn, Judy. *Blood, Bread, and Roses: How Menstruation Created the World.* Boston: Beacon Press, 1994. http://bailiwick.lib .uiowa.edu/wstudies/grahn/chapt01.htm.

Gray, Emma. "The Removal of Rupi Kaur's Instagram Photos Shows How Terrified We Are of Periods." Huffington Post, March 27, 2015. https://www.huffingtonpost.co.uk/entry /rupi-kaur-period-instagram_n_6954898.

Green Feminine Hygiene Queen. "Amy Elifritz: Toxic Shock Syndrome Awareness." Maxim Hygiene, May 4, 2011. https:// www.maximhy.com/blog/2011/05/04/amy-elifritz-toxic-shock -syndrome-awareness/.

Greenberg, Zoe. "In Jail, Pads and Tampons as Bargaining Chips." *New York Times*, April 20, 2017. https://www.nytimes.com /2017/04/20/nyregion/pads-tampons-new-york-womens -prisons.html.

Grunebaum, Amos. "Getting Pregnant after a Hysterectomy." BabyMed, October 8, 2008. https://www.babymed.com /getting-pregnant-after-hysterectomy.

Guardian. "Woman Enters Court Without Pants After Jail 'Fails to Provide Hygiene Products.'" August 1, 2016. https://www .theguardian.com/us-news/2016/aug/01/Louisville-jail-woman -no-pants-court.

Gupta, Prachi. "Why the Hell Are Tampons Still Taxed?" *Cosmopolitan*, October 15, 2015. https://www.cosmopolitan .com/politics/news/a47780/abolish-tampon-tax-america/.

Hashtag Happy Period. "Our Story." Accessed January 15, 2018. http://hashtaghappyperiod.org/index.php/our-story/.

Hawkins, Kayla. "The 'Orange Is the New Black' Tampon Storyline Gives Periods Much Needed Attention." Bustle, July 3, 2016. https://www.bustle.com/articles/168222-the-orange-is -the-new-black-tampon-storyline-gives-periods-much-needed -attention.

Health and Hygiene Pamphlet Collection. Schlesinger Library, Radcliffe Institute, Harvard University. Accessed December 22, 2017.

Hello Flo. "About Us." Accessed December 15, 2017. http://helloflo .com/about-us/.

Hello Flo. "The Camp Gyno." YouTube, July 28, 2013. https:// www.youtube.com/watch?v=0XnzfRqkRxU.

Hello Flo. "FAQs." Accessed December 15, 2017. http://helloflo .com/faq/.

Hello Flo. "First Moon Party." YouTube, June 17, 2014. https:// www.youtube.com/watch?v=NEcZmT0fiNM.

Hematy, Mandana. "Invention of the Menstrual Cup." Menstrual Cup.co, accessed September 30, 2017. https://menstrualcup .co/invention-of-the-menstrual-cup/.

Henig, Robin Marantz. "Dispelling Menstrual Myths." *New York Times Magazine,* March 7, 1982. https://www.nytimes .com/1982/03/07/magazine/dispelling-menstrual-myths .html?pagewanted=all.

Hillin, Taryn. "These Are the U.S. States That Tax Women for Having Periods." *Splinter*, June 3, 2015. https://splinternews .com/these-are-the-u-s-states-that-tax-women-for-having -per-1793848102.

HISTORY. "American Women in World War II." Accessed December 9, 2017. https://www.history.com/topics/world -war-ii/american-women-in-world-war-ii.

HISTORY. "The Great Depression." Accessed December 9, 2017. https://www.history.com/topics/great-depression.

Hoeger, Cherie. Email to author. February 12, 2018.

Illinois Department of Revenue Regulations. "Drugs, Medicines,

Medical Appliances and Grooming and Hygiene Products."
August 1, 2017. http://tax.illinois.gov/LegalInformation/regs
/part130/130-311.pdf.

IMDb. "*The Cosby Show*: The Infantry Has Landed (and They've
Fallen off the Roof)." Accessed January 5, 2018. https://www
.imdb.com/title/tt0547083/.

I Support the Girls. "About Us." Accessed January 15, 2018. http://
isupportthegirls.org/.

Jardine, Alexandra. "This Powerful Bodyform Commercial Is All
About Blood." *Ad Age*, May 27, 2016. http://creativity-online
.com/work/bodyform-blood/47429.

Jones, Abigail. "The Fight to End Period Shaming Is Going
Mainstream." *Newsweek*, April 20, 2016. http://www.newsweek
.com/2016/04/29/womens-periods-menstruation-tampons
-pads-449833.html.

Jones, Abigail. "Free Tampons and Pads Are Making Their Way to
U.S. Colleges, High Schools and Middle Schools." *Newsweek*,
September 6, 2016. http://www.newsweek.com/free-tampons
-pads-us-schools-496083.

Jones, Abigail. "New York Terminates the Tampon Tax."
Newsweek, July 21, 2016. http://www.newsweek.com/new
-york-tampon-tax-cuomo-periods-tampons-menstruation
-donald-trump-482918.

Kabas, Marisa. "New York Abolished Its Tampon Tax—So Why
Are Some Stores Still Bloating the Price?" *Splinter*, September
2, 2016. https://splinternews.com/new-york-abolished-its
-tampon-tax-so-why-are-some-store-1793861649.

Kale, Sirin. "A 12-Year-Old Reportedly Killed Herself after Being
Shamed for Getting Her Period." Broadly, September 1, 2017.
https://broadly.vice.com/en_us/article/paa4yv/a-12-year-old
-reportedly-killed-herself-after-being-shamed-for-getting-her
-period.

Kane, Jessica. "Here's How Much a Woman's Period Will Cost Her
over a Lifetime." Huffington Post, December 6, 2017. https://

www.huffingtonpost.com/2015/05/18/period-cost-lifetime_n _7258780.html.

Kaur, Rupi. "Thank You Instagram." Facebook, March 25, 2015. https://www.facebook.com/rupikaurpoetry /photos/a.523823527711928.1073741828 .513614775399470/821302664630678/?type=1&theater.

Kennedy, Pagan. "The Tampon of the Future." *New York Times*, April 1, 2016. https://www.nytimes.com/2016/04/03/opinion /sunday/the-tampon-of-the-future.html.

Kennedy, Stephen, Agneta Bergqvist, Charles Chapron, Thomas D'Hooghe, Gerard Dunselman, Robert Greb, Lone Hummelshoj, Andrew Prentice, and Ertan Saridogan. "ESHRE Guideline for the Diagnosis and Treatment of Endometriosis." *Human Reproduction*, Volume 20, Issue 10 (1 October 2005): 2,698–2,704. https://doi.org/10.1093/humrep/dei135.

Khan Academy. "Women in the 1950s." Accessed December 20, 2017. https://www.khanacademy.org/humanities/ap-us-history /period-8/apush-1950s-america/a/women-in-the-1950s.

KidsHealth. "All about Menstruation." Accessed December 5, 2017. https://kidshealth.org/en/kids/menstruation.html.

Kim, Annabel. Interview with author. April 4, 2018.

Kloosterman, Stephen. "Michigan ACLU Files Lawsuit against Muskegon County on Behalf of Female Jail Inmates." MLive, December 4, 2014. http://www.mlive.com/news/muskegon /index.ssf/2014/12/michigan_aclu_files_lawsuit_ag.html.

Koreff, Alexei, and Christopher Cadelago. "Poor Students Will Get Free Tampons and Pads at California Schools." *The Sacramento Bee*, October 12, 2017. https://www.sacbee.com/news/politics -government/capitol-alert/article178479851.html.

Kosin, Julie. "Getting Your Period Is Still Oppressive in the United States." *Harper's Bazaar*, October 9, 2017. https://www .harpersbazaar.com/culture/features/a10235656/menstrual -period-united-states/.

Kraft-Stolar, Tamar. *Reproductive Injustice: The State of*

Reproductive Health Care for Women in New York State Prisons. New York: Women in Prison Project of the Correctional Association of New York, 2015. http://www .correctionalassociation.org/wp-content/uploads/2015/03 /Reproductive-Injustice-FULL-REPORT-FINAL-2-11-15.pdf.

Krause, Stephanie. "Menstruation: How Much Do We Bleed?" Eco Femme, accessed January 30, 2018. https://ecofemme.org /menstruation-much-bleed/.

Kutner, Jenny. "Will the New York City Subway Ban These Ads for Using the Word 'Period'?" Mic, October 20, 2015. https://mic .com/articles/127022/will-the-new-york-city-subway-ban -these-thinx-ads-for-using-the-word-period#.VWsEYVwJR.

Kvatum, Lia. "A Period Comes to an End: 100 Years of Menstruation Products." *Washington Post,* April 25, 2016. https://www.washingtonpost.com/national/health-science /a-period-comes-to-an-end-100-years-of-menstruation -products/2016/04/25/1afe3898-057e-11e6-bdcb -0133da18418d_story.html?utm_term=.a13aff34e670.

Lampen, Claire. "Can 'Period Leave' Ever Work?" BBC, September 8, 2017. http://www.bbc.com/capital/story/20170908-can -period-leave-ever-work.

Lawless, Jennifer L., and Richard L. Fox. "Men Rule: The Continued Under-Representation of Women in U.S. Politics." Washington, DC: Women & Politics Institute, January 2012. https://www.american.edu/spa/wpi/upload/2012-Men-Rule -Report-web.pdf.

Leibow, Chelsea. Interview with author. February 28, 2018.

Lewis, Jone Johnson. "*Roe v. Wade* Supreme Court Decision: An Overview." ThoughtCo., updated August 31, 2017. https:// www.thoughtco.com/roe-v-wade-overview-3528244.

Linton, David. "Tina Fey's Menstrual Musings." Society for Menstrual Cycle Research, January 31, 2012. http://www .menstruationresearch.org/2012/01/31/tina-feys-menstrual -musings/.

Lippo, Carlynn. "Model Who Lost Leg to Toxic Shock Syndrome in 2012 Says She Will Lose Her Other One Soon Too." Little Things, accessed December 10, 2017. https://www.littlethings.com/toxic-shock-syndrome-losing-2nd-leg-lauren-wasser/.

Llywodraeth Cymru/Welsh Government. "£1 Million to Tackle Period Poverty and Dignity." March 23, 2018. https://gov.wales/newsroom/people-and-communities/2018/180323-tackle-period-poverty-dignity/?lang=en.

London, Bianca. "Runner Who Completed the London Marathon During Her Period without a Tampon Says She Did It to 'Break the Stigma' after Receiving Support—and Criticism—for Her Actions." *Daily Mail,* August 10, 2015. http://www.dailymail.co.uk/femail/article-3192039/Woman-26-ran-marathon-WITHOUT-tampon-break-stigma-surrounding-women-s-periods.html.

Lonergan, Siobhan. Interview with author, December 20, 2017.

Louis, Germaine M. Buck, Mary L. Hediger, C. Matthew Peterson, Mary Croughan, Rajeshwari Sundaram, Joseph Stanford, Zhen Chen, Victor Y. Fujimoto, Michael W. Varner, Ann Trumble, Linda C. Giudice, and ENDO Study Working Group. "Incidence of Endometriosis by Study Population and Diagnostic Method: The ENDO Study." *Fertility and Sterility*, Volume 96, No. 2 (August 2011): 360–5. https://doi.org/10.1016/j.fertnstert.2011.05.087.

Lovestory, Kim, and Amanda Lovestory. "Does It Work? A Look at the FLEX Menstrual Disc." Put a Cup in It, accessed December 3, 2017. https://putacupinit.com/about-the-movement/.

Lunette. "How to Clean Your Lunette Cup." Accessed February 10, 2018. https://www.lunette.com/blogs/news/how-to-clean-your-lunette-cup.

Lunette. "Short History of Menstrual Cups." Accessed December 2, 2017. https://www.lunette.com/blogs/news/short-history-of-menstrual-cups.

Luu, Christopher. "The Creator of Period Panties Just Revolutionized Your Period Again." Refinery29, January 13, 2017. https://www.refinery29.com/2017/01/136199/thinx-reusable-tampon-applicator.

Malone, Noreen. "Panty Raid." The Cut, accessed January 15, 2018. https://www.thecut.com/2016/01/thinx-miki-agrawal-c-v-r.html.

Maloney, Alli. "Which State Will Slash the Tampon Tax Next?" *Splinter*, July 28, 2016. https://www.splinternews.com/which-states-will-slash-the-tampon-tax-next-1793860652.

Mangaldas, Leeza. "Why Bollywood's 'PadMan' Is Getting India Talking about Periods." *Forbes*, February 9, 2018. https://www.forbes.com/sites/leezamangaldas/2018/02/09/why-bollywoods-pad-man-is-getting-india-talking-about-periods/#5737f75f4879.

Marland, Hilary. *Health and Girlhood in Britain, 1874–1920*. New York: Springer, 2013.

Maunz, Shay. "Meet the Women Who Helped Repeal New York's Tampon Tax." *Glamour*, September 1, 2016. https://www.glamour.com/story/meet-the-women-who-helped-repeal-new-yorks-tampon-tax.

Mavrelos, Dimitrios, and Ertan Saridogan. "Treatment Options for Primary and Secondary Dysmenorrhea." *Prescriber*, November 2017. https://onlinelibrary.wiley.com/doi/pdf/10.1002/psb.1624.

Mayo Clinic. "Adenomyosis." Accessed April 2, 2018. https://www.mayoclinic.org/diseases-conditions/adenomyosis/symptoms-causes/syc-20369138.

Mayo Clinic. "Amenorrhea." Accessed August 26, 2018. https://www.mayoclinic.org/diseases-conditions/amenorrhea/symptoms-causes/syc-20369299.

Mayo Clinic. "Endometriosis." Accessed April 2, 2018. https://www.mayoclinic.org/diseases-conditions/endometriosis/symptoms-causes/syc-20354656.

Mayo Clinic. "Menopause." Accessed August 7, 2017. https://www.mayoclinic.org/diseases-conditions/menopause/symptoms-causes/syc-20353397.

Mayo Clinic. "Menorrhagia (Heavy Menstrual Bleeding)." Accessed July 15, 2017. https://www.mayoclinic.org/diseases-conditions/menorrhagia/symptoms-causes/syc-20352829.

Mayo Clinic. "Premenstrual Syndrome (PMS)." Accessed April 5, 2018. https://www.mayoclinic.org/diseases-conditions/premenstrual-syndrome/symptoms-causes/syc-20376780.

Mayo Clinic. "Uterine Fibroids." Accessed March 6, 2018. https://www.mayoclinic.org/diseases-conditions/uterine-fibroids/symptoms-causes/syc-20354288.

Mays, Mackenzie. "She Put Newspaper in Her Underwear Because Her School Charged for Pads. A New Law Ends That." *Fresno Bee*, October 22, 2017. http://www.fresnobee.com/news/local/education/article180114836.html.

McWeeney, Claire. "Period Blood Color: Brown, Black, or Dark—Does It Matter?" Hello Clue, accessed October 18, 2017. https://helloclue.com/articles/cycle-a-z/period-blood-color-brown-black-dark-does-it-matter.

Medline Plus. "Uterine Artery Embolization." Accessed April 30, 2018. https://medlineplus.gov/ency/article/007384.htm.

Menstrual Cup Reviews. "Sea Sponge Tampons: Product Reviews." Accessed August 1, 2016. https://menstrualcupreviews.net/sea-sponge-menstrual-soft-tampons-product-reviews/.

Merlan, Anna. "A Celebration of the Beautiful, Lightly Deranged PR Emails We Get from Period Undie-Makers." Jezebel, August 9, 2016. https://jezebel.com/a-celebration-of-the-beautiful-lightly-deranged-pr-ema-1784978795.

Mettler, Katie. "Free Tampons for All at Brown University This School Year—Even in the Men's Room." *Washington Post*, September 9, 2016. https://www.washingtonpost.com/.

Meuleman, Christel, Birgit Vandenabeele, Steffen Fieuws, Carl

Spiessens, Dirk Timmerman, and Thomas D'Hooghe. "High Prevalence of Endometriosis in Infertile Women with Normal Ovulation and Normospermic Partners." *Fertility and Sterility*, Volume 92, No. 1 (July 2009): 68–74. https://www.fertstert.org/article/S0015-0282(08)00975-8/pdf.

Miller, Kevin. "The Simple Truth about the Gender Pay Gap." American Association of University Women, accessed December 9, 2017. https://www.aauw.org/research/the-simple-truth-about-the-gender-pay-gap/.

Moeschen, Sheila. "Shameless: *Broad City* Takes on Period Shaming." Huffington Post, May 18, 2016. https://www.huffingtonpost.com/sheila-moeschen/shameless-broad-city-take_b_10008046.html.

Moore, Lane. "Instagram Apologizes for Removing Poignant Photos of a Woman on Her Period." *Cosmopolitan*, March 27, 2015. https://www.cosmopolitan.com/sex-love/news/a38309/instagram-apologizes-for-removing-poignant-photos-of-a-woman-on-her-period/.

Moore, Lane. "What It's Like to Get Your Period When You're Homeless." *Cosmopolitan*, October 13, 2015. https://www.cosmopolitan.com/sex-love/news/a47596/what-its-like-to-get-your-period-when-youre-homeless/.

Moore, Suzanne. "Let's See Menopausal Women on Screen—in All Their Glory." *Guardian*, March 15, 2018. https://www.theguardian.com/commentisfree/2018/mar/15/menopausal-women-screen-glory-representation-menopause-popular-culture.

Moss, Rachel. "Bodyform's 'Red.Fit' Campaign Stops Periods Being 'The Last Taboo' in Women's Sport." Huffington Post, March 6, 2016. https://www.huffingtonpost.co.uk/entry/bodyform-redfit-campaign-periods-in-sport_uk_575175abe4b0b23a261a286b.

Muller, Marissa. "Emma Watson Addresses Her White Privilege and 'White Feminism' in Letter to Her Book Club." W magazine, January 9, 2018. https://www.wmagazine.com/story

/emma-watson-white-privilege-feminism.

Murdoch, Cassie. "Turns Out Being Born a Woman Is a Major Financial Mistake." Jezebel, March 20, 2012. https://jezebel .com/5894744/turns-out-being-born-a-woman-is-a-very-costly -mistake.

Muruganantham, Arunachalam. "How I Started a Sanitary Napkin Revolution." Ted Talk, May 2012. https://www.ted.com/talks /arunachalam_muruganantham_how_i_started_a_sanitary _napkin_revolution#t=541838.

Napikoski, Linda. "*Griswold v. Connecticut.*" ThoughtCo., March 18, 2017. https://www.thoughtco.com/griswold-v-connecticut -3529463.

National Women's Health Network. "Fibroids Medications." Accessed December 5, 2017. https://www.nwhn.org /uterine-fibroids-medications/.

National Women's Health Network. "Hysterectomy." Accessed December 5, 2017. https://www.nwhn.org/hysterectomy/.

New, Jake. "If Condoms Are Free, Why Aren't Tampons?" Inside Higher Ed, March 11, 2016. https://www.insidehighered.com /news/2016/03/11/students-demand-free-tampons-campus.

New York City Council. "Provision of Feminine Hygiene Products in Schools." Accessed January 5, 2018. http://legistar.council.nyc.gov /LegislationDetail.aspx?ID=2637114&GUID=834E4DFC -7F14-4E1E-812F-2CD862A4FC1D&Options=ID%7CText %7C&Search=menstrual.

New York City Council. "Requiring That the DOC Issue Feminine Hygiene Products to Inmates." Accessed January 5, 2018. http://legistar.council.nyc.gov/LegislationDetail.aspx?ID =2637117&GUID=4D97B9EE-4986-4B87 -B846-2E52A329695A&Options=ID%7CText %7C&Search=menstrual.

New Yorker. "Video: Vintage Tina Fey." March 4, 2011. https:// www.newyorker.com/news/news-desk/video-vintage-tina-fey.

New York State Governor Andrew M. Cuomo Press Office.

"Governor Cuomo Signs Legislation to Exempt Sales and Use Taxes on Feminine Hygiene Products." News release, July 21, 2016. https://www.governor.ny.gov/news/governor-cuomo -signs-legislation-exempt-sales-and-use-taxes-feminine -hygiene-products.

NHS Choices. "Periods." Accessed October 21, 2017. https://www .nhs.uk/conditions/periods/.

Nordqvist, Christian. "Fibroids: Everything You Need to Know." Medical News Today, November 30, 2017. https://www .medicalnewstoday.com/articles/151405.php.

Nordqvist, Christian. "What Are Menstruation, Periods, and PMS?" Medical News Today, February 20, 2018. https://www .medicalnewstoday.com/articles/154699.php.

Nordqvist, Christian. "What Is Pelvic Inflammatory Disease?" Medical News Today, October 23, 2017. https://www .medicalnewstoday.com/articles/177923.php.

North, Anna. "A Welcome End to New York's 'Tampon Tax.'" Taking Note, New York Times, May 26, 2016. https://takingnote .blogs.nytimes.com/2016/05/26/a-welcome-end-to-new -yorks-tampon-tax/.

Obama, Michelle. "Let Girls Learn." Atlantic, November 2, 2015. https://www.theatlantic.com/international/archive/2015/11 /girls-education-michelle-obama/413554/.

O'Brien, Sara Ashley. "Period Underwear Brand Thinx Names New CEO after HR Issues." CNN Tech, July 27, 2017. http:// money.cnn.com/2017/07/27/technology/startups/thinx-names -new-ceo/index.html.

Office on Women's Health. "Endometriosis." Updated March 16, 2018. https://www.womenshealth.gov/a-z-topics /endometriosis#references.

Oh, Soo, and Sarah Kliff. "The US Is Ranked 104th in Women's Representation in Government." Vox, March 8, 2017. https:// www.vox.com/identities/2017/3/8/14854116/women -representation.

Olson, Samantha. "Age of Woman's First Period Linked to Heart
      Disease Risk: Menstruation's Impact on Heart Health."
      Medical Daily, December 15, 2014. https://www.medicaldaily
      .com/age-womans-first-period-linked-heart-disease-risk
      -menstruations-impact-heart-health-314460.

Onyanga-Omara, Jane. "Women Get Their Periods Every Month—
      and It's Incredibly Expensive." USA Today, April 18, 2018.
      https://eu.usatoday.com/story/news/world/2018/04/18
      /scotland-end-period-poverty-tampon-tax/502020002/.

Open Bible. "Menstruation." Accessed December 8, 2017. https://
      www.openbible.info/topics/menstruation.

Planned Parenthood. "Menstruation." Accessed December 5, 2017.
      https://www.plannedparenthood.org/learn/health-and
      -wellness/menstruation.

Pattani, Aneri. "In Some Countries, Women Get Days Off for
      Period Pain." New York Times, July 24, 2017. https://www
      .nytimes.com/2017/07/24/health/period-pain-paid-time-off
      -policy.html?mtrref=www.google.co.jp.

Pear, Robert. "Gender Gap Persists in Cost of Health Insurance." New
      York Times, March 19, 2012. https://www.nytimes.com/2012/03
      /19/health/policy/women-still-pay-more-for-health-insurance
      -data-shows.html?_r=1&partner=rss&emc=rss&mtrref=undefined
      &gwh=EFE31792AC9E03A4A97B3504F2568ABB&gwt=pay.

Pearson, Catherine. "What Hollywood Gets Wrong about Your Period."
      Huffington Post, July 17, 2012. https://www.huffingtonpost
      .com/2012/07/17/menstruation-movies_n_1676551.html.

Period. "Tampon History." January 29, 2016. http://www.period
      .media/factsfigures/tampon-history/.

Picard, Caroline. "Women Everywhere Are Still Debating about
      Whether You Should Flush Tampons or Not." Good
      Housekeeping, February 12, 2018. https://www.goodhousekeeping
      .com/health/news/a43348/tampon-disposal/.

Plank, Elizabeth. "The Secret Tax Screwing Women Out of
      Thousands of Dollars Over a Lifetime." Mic, April 22, 2015.

https://mic.com/articles/115922/the-secret-tax-screwing-women
-out-of-thousands-of-dollars-over-a-lifetime#.wDFdNnVKo.

Playtex. "How to Use a Tampon." Accessed January 15, 2018.
http://www.playtexplayon.com/tampon-faq/how-to-use.

Poppick, Susie. "More States Tax Tampons Than Candy in
America." *Money*, June 3, 2015. http://time.com/money
/3907775/states-tax-tampons-candy-america/.

PubMed Health. "Premenstrual Dysphoric Disorder (PMDD)."
U.S. National Library of Medicine, accessed December 1,
2017. https://www.ncbi.nlm.nih.gov/pubmedhealth
/PMHT0024721/.

Puhl, Tracy. Interview with author. December 29, 2017.

Quality Logo Products. "History of TV Ads." Accessed January 15,
2018. https://www.qualitylogoproducts.com/promo-university
/history-of-tv-ads.htm.

Quranic Path. "Glorious Qur'an on Menstruation." Accessed
January 15, 2018. http://www.quranicpath.com
/misconceptions/menstruation_islam.html.

Rabin, Roni Caryn. "$417 Million Awarded in Suit Tying
Johnson's Baby Powder to Cancer." *New York Times*, August
22, 2017. https://www.nytimes.com/2017/02/22/health/417
-million-awarded-in-suit-tying-johnsons-baby-powder-to
-cancer.html?mcubz=3.

Rabuy, Bernadette, and Daniel Kopf. "Prisons of Poverty:
Uncovering the Pre-incarceration Incomes of the Imprisoned."
Prison Policy Initiative, July 9, 2015. https://www.prisonpolicy
.org/reports/income.html.

Rastogi, Nina. "Greening the Crimson Tide." Slate, March 16,
2010. http://www.slate.com/articles/health_and_science/the
_green_lantern/2010/03/greening_the_crimson_tide.html.

Reflect. "Ingrid Nilsen Interviews Obama." YouTube, January 16,
2016. https://www.youtube.com/watch?v=K2OaaWjB6S8&t
=18s.

Rinkunas, Susan. "One NYC High School Now Offers Free

Tampons." The Cut, September 22, 2015. https://www.thecut
.com/2015/09/free-tampons-new-york-city-high-school.html.

Rinkunas, Susan. "Women's Underwear Company Getting Hassled
over Subway Ads." The Cut, October 21, 2015. https://www
.thecut.com/2015/10/womens-underwear-company-hassled
-by-mta.html.

Rix, Catie. "Toxic Shock Syndrome: Amy's Story." Her Campus,
February 27, 2018. https://www.hercampus.com/school/iu
/toxic-shock-syndrome-amys-story.

Rizk, B., A. S. Fischer, H. A. Lotfy, R. Turki, H. A. Zahed, R. Malik,
C. P. Holliday, A. Glass, H. Fishel, M. Y. Soliman, and D.
Herrera. "Recurrence of endometriosis after hysterectomy."
Facts, Views & Vis Obgyn 6, No. 4 (2014): 219–227. https://
www.ncbi.nlm.nih.gov/pmc/articles/PMC4286861/pdf
/FVVinObGyn-6-219-227.pdf.

Rodulfo, Kristina. "Finally, a Period Commercial That's Not Afraid
to Show Blood." Elle, June 7, 2016. https://www.elle.com
/culture/news/a36911/bodyform-feminine-hygiene-ad/.

Rohmann, Emma. "PSA: Don't Flush Your Tampons down the
Toilet." Green Moms Collective, June 29, 2017. https://www
.greenmomscollective.ca/can-you-flush-tampons/.

Ronan, Alex. "Menstruation Can Become Humiliation in Prisons."
The Cut, June 16, 2015. https://www.thecut.com/2015/06
/menstruation-can-become-humiliation-in-prisons.html.

Rose, Jenn. "NYC School Offers Free Tampons for Students, & It's
Just the First Step in a Broader Initiative to Expand Access for
All Women." Bustle, September 23, 2015. https://www.bustle
.com/articles/112546-nyc-school-offers-free-tampons-for
-students-its-just-the-first-step-in-a-broader.

Roy, Jessica. "Hero Councilwoman Wants to Make Tampons Free
for NYC Teens." New York magazine, June 10, 2015. http://
nymag.com/daily/intelligencer/2015/06/councilwoman-wants
-to-make-tampons-free.html.

Rubli, Sabrina. "The History of the Sanitary Pad." Femme

International, June 24, 2013. https://www.femmeinternational
.org/the-history-of-the-sanitary-pad/.

Sanghani, Radhika. "This Woman Ran the London Marathon on
Her Period without a Tampon." *Telegraph*, August 10, 2015.
https://www.telegraph.co.uk/women/womens-life/11793848
/Free-bleeding-This-woman-ran-the-London-Marathon-on
-her-period-without-a-tampon.html.

Sagner, Ema. "More States Move To End 'Tampon Tax' That's Seen
As Discriminating Against Women." NPR, March 25, 2018.
https://www.npr.org/2018/03/25/564580736/more-states
-move-to-end-tampon-tax-that-s-seen-as-discriminating
-against-women.

Saturday Night Live. "Kotex Classic—SNL." YouTube, September
23, 2013. https://www.youtube.com/watch?v=aBlR7qVQ0X8.

Scaccia, Annamarya. "Free Bleeding: NYC Public Schools to Give
Out Pads and Tampons to Students." Broadly, March 17,
2016. https://broadly.vice.com/en_us/article/nz8xqx/free
-bleeding-nyc-public-schools-to-give-out-pads-and-tampons
-to-students.

Scaccia, Annamarya. "The Price Young Girls Pay When Tampons
Aren't Free." Free the Tampons, February 29, 2016. https://
www.freethetampons.org/the-price-young-girls-pay-when
-tampons-arent-free.html.

Scaccia, Annamarya. "Women in Jail Are Being Denied Tampons,
Pads, and Basic Human Dignity." Broadly, March 28, 2016.
https://broadly.vice.com/en_us/article/qkgyyb/women-in-jail
-are-being-denied-tampons-pads-and-basic-human-dignity.

Schenwar, Maya. "In Prison, Toilet Paper Is the New Tampon." *Ms.*
magazine, April 12, 2010. http://msmagazine.com/blog/2010
/04/12/in-prison-toilet-paper-is-the-new-tampon/.

Schow, Ashe. "Should Tampons Be Free?" *Washington Examiner*,
August 11, 2014. https://www.washingtonexaminer.com
/should-tampons-be-free/article/2551894.

Schulte, Lauren. Interview with author. January 12, 2018.

Seely, Linda. Interview with author. April 10, 2018.

Shamoun, Sam. "Muhammad and Menstruation." Answering Islam, accessed December 10, 2017. http://www.answering -islam.org/Muhammad/Inconsistent/menstruation.htm.

Sheffield, Toria. "Can You Flush Tampons down the Toilet? We Investigated So You Don't Have To." Hello Giggles, September 22, 2017. https://hellogiggles.com/lifestyle/can-you-flush-tampons -down-the-toilet/.

Shure, Natalie. "Why Has It Taken the Menstrual Cup So Long to Go Mainstream?" *Pacific Standard*, July 6, 2016. https:// psmag.com/news/why-has-it-taken-the-menstrual-cup-so-long -to-go-mainstream.

Sidahmed, Mazin. "Woman Enters Court without Pants after Jail 'Fails to Provide Hygiene Products.'" *Guardian*, August 1, 2016. https://www.theguardian.com/us-news/2016/aug/01 /louisville-jail-woman-no-pants-court.

Smith, Lesley. "The Kahun Gynaecological Papyrus: Ancient Egyptian Medicine." *BMJ Sexual & Reproductive Health*, Volume 37, No. 1 (2011): 54–55. http://dx.doi.org/10.1136 /jfprhc.2010.0019.

Smith, Mitch. "'Periods for Pence' Campaign Targets Indiana Governor over Abortion Law." *New York Times*, April 7, 2016. https://www.nytimes.com/2016/04/08/us/periods-for -pence-campaign-targets-indiana-governor-over-abortion-law .html.

Smothers, Hannah. "How This Trans Activist's Free-Bleeding Photo Fights Period Stigma." *Cosmopolitan*, July 31, 2017. https://www.cosmopolitan.com/sex-love/a10372747 /cass-clemmer-trans-inclusive-period/.

Spinks, Rosie. "Disposable Tampons Aren't Sustainable, but Do Women Want to Talk about It?" *Guardian*, April 27, 2015. https://www.theguardian.com/sustainable-business/2015/apr/27 /disposable-tampons-arent-sustainable-but-do-women-want-to -talk-about-it.

Squier, Chemmie. "In 10 Years, 'Friends' Only Mentioned Periods Once." *Grazia*, January 22, 2016. https://graziadaily.co.uk/life/tv-and-film/10-years-friends-mentioned-periods/.

Staley, Willy. "Tampon." *New York Times Magazine*, June 7, 2013. http://archive.nytimes.com/www.nytimes.com/packages/html/magazine/2013/innovations-issue/#/?part=tampon.

Stamets, Maggie. "1940's Pamphlet on Periods Shares the Secret to an Easy Flow: Keep Smiling." *Bust*, accessed December 4, 2017. http://bust.com/entertainment/15492-1940-s-pamphlet-on-periods-shares-the-secret-to-an-easy-flow-keep-smiling.html.

Stewart, Elizabeth A., Wanda K. Nicholson, Linda Bradley, and Bijan J. Borah. "The Burden of Uterine Fibroids for African-American Women: Results of a National Survey." *Journal of Women's Health*, Volume 22, No. 10 (October 2013): 807–816. https://doi.org/10.1089/jwh.2013.4334.

Stöppler, Melissa. "Menopause." MedicineNet, last modified January 29, 2018. https://www.medicinenet.com/menopause/article.htm#antidepressants_and_other_medications_for_menopause.

Supreme Court of Illinois. "*Geary v. Dominick's Finer Foods, Inc.*" Justia, June 19, 1989. https://law.justia.com/cases/illinois/supreme-court/1989/67049-7.html.

Suresh, P. K., Panda Roshni, A. Suneetha, and Susan Cleave. "Complementary and Alternative Medicine (CAM) Therapies for Management of Pain Related to Endometriosis." *International Research Journal of Pharmacy*, Volume 3, No. 3 (March 2012): 30–34. http://www.irjponline.com/admin/php/uploads/897_pdf.pdf.

Tampax. "Courteney Cox 1985 Tampax Commercial." YouTube. https://www.youtube.com/watch?v=kOHCtQfFn7E.

Telfer, Nicole, and Jen Bell. "How Common Is Endometriosis?" Hello Clue, March 26, 2018. https://helloclue.com/articles/cycle-a-z/how-common-is-endometriosis.

Thinx. "How Heavy Is Too Heavy? Breaking down Period Flows." Accessed March 15, 2017. https://www.shethinx.com/blogs /womens-health/how-heavy-is-too-heavy-breaking-down -period-flows.

Thinx. "Period-Proof Underwear That Works." Accessed December 5, 2017. https://www.shethinx.com/.

Thorpe, J. R. "7 Crazy Period Myths from History, Because People Once Thought Menstrual Blood Could Kill Crops." Bustle, May 1, 2015. https://www.bustle.com/articles/80289-7-crazy -period-myths-from-history-because-people-once-thought -menstrual-blood-could-kill-crops.

Thorpe, J. R. "What the Age You Got Your First Period Says about You, According to Science." Bustle, August 27, 2015. https:// www.bustle.com/articles/106308-what-the-age-you-got-your -first-period-says-about-you-according-to-science.

Toni the Tampon. "Y'all Know I'm Trans and Queer." Instagram, July 12, 2017. https://www.instagram.com/p/BWdC4UEgAzj.

Tsjeng, Zing. "The Activists Making Sure Kids Don't Miss School Because of Their Periods." Broadly, June 13, 2017. https:// broadly.vice.com/en_us/article/qv4z7m/the-activists-making -sure-kids-dont-miss-school-because-of-their-periods.

Tsjeng, Zing. "The Forgotten Black Woman Inventor Who Revolutionized Menstrual Pads." Broadly, March 8, 2018. https://broadly.vice.com/en_us/article/mb5yap/mary-beatrice -davidson-kenner-sanitary-belt.

TrueMedCost.com "Endometriosis Could Lead to Medical Complications If Left Untreated." July 2, 2014. https://www .truemedcost.com/endometriosis-lead-medical-complications -left-untreated/.

Trump, Donald (@realDonaldTrump). "Re Megyn Kelly." Twitter, August 8, 2015. https://twitter.com/realdonaldtrump /status/629997060830425088.

Trump, Donald (@realDonaldTrump). "So Many 'Politically Correct'." Twitter, August 8, 2015. https://twitter.com

/realdonaldtrump/status/629992743788523520.

Truong, Kimberly. "What It's Like to Get Your Period in Prison."
Refinery29, June 23, 2016. https://www.refinery29.uk
/2016/06/114921/orange-is-the-new-black-period-prison.

Tucker, Jasmine, and Caitlin Lowell. "National Snapshot: Poverty
among Women & Families, 2015." National Women's Law
Center, September 14, 2016. https://nwlc.org/resources
/national-snapshot-poverty-among-women-families-2015/.

Twitter. "#PeriodsforPence." Accessed April 4, 2018. https://twitter
.com/hashtag/periodsforpence?src=hash.

United States Congresswoman Grace Meng Media Center. "Meng:
FEMA to Permit Homeless Assistance Providers to Purchase
Feminine Hygiene Products—Such as Tampons and Pads—
with Federal Grant Funds." Press release, March 1, 2016.
https://meng.house.gov/media-center/press-releases/meng
-fema-to-permit-homeless-assistance-providers-to-purchase
-feminine.

United States Food and Drug Administration. "The Benefits and
Risks of Pain Relievers: Q & A on NSAIDs with Sharon
Hertz, M.D." Updated September 24, 2015. https://www.fda
.gov/ForConsumers/ConsumerUpdates/ucm107856.htm.

University of California San Francisco Health. "Myomectomy."
Accessed December 3, 2017. https://www.ucsfhealth.org
/treatments/myomectomy/.

Upadhye, Janet. "This Is How Homeless Women Cope with Their
Periods." Bustle, October 18, 2016. https://www.bustle.com
/articles/190092-this-is-how-homeless-women-cope-with-their
-periods.

Valenti, Jessica. "The Case for Free Tampons." Guardian, August
11, 2014. https://www.theguardian.com/commentisfree/2014
/aug/11/free-tampons-cost-feminine-hygiene-products.

Velocci, Carli. "Why Are We Suddenly Seeing Period Blood on
TV?" The Wrap, July 13, 2017. https://www.thewrap.com
/periods-on-tv/.

Virmani, Amit. "*Menstrual Man* Trailer." Accessed February 15, 2018. http://www.menstrualman.com/.

Vital Voices. "Kah Walla." Accessed January 15, 2018. https://www.vitalvoices.org/people/kah-walla-2/.

Vital Voices. "Politics Innovator: Laura Alonso, Argentina." Accessed January 15, 2018. https://www.vitalvoices.org/2012/08/politics-innovator-laura-alonso-argentina/.

Walsh, Kenneth. "The 1960s: A Decade of Change for Women." *U.S. News & World Report*, March 12, 2010. https://www.usnews.com/news/articles/2010/03/12/the-1960s-a-decade-of-change-for-women.

Wasser, Lauren. "Model Lauren Wasser Lost Her Leg to TSS— Here's What She Wants You to Know about the Tampon Disease." *InStyle*, November 29, 2017. http://www.instyle.com/celebrity/amputee-model-lauren-wasser-tss.

WebMD. "Menstrual Pain." Accessed December 1, 2017. https://www.webmd.com/women/guide/menstrual-pain#1-2.

WebMD. "Vaginal Discharge: What's Abnormal." Accessed December 1, 2017. https://www.webmd.com/women/guide/vaginal-discharge-whats-abnormal#1.

WebMD. "Why Is My Period So Heavy?" Accessed December 1, 2017. https://www.webmd.com/women/heavy-period-causes-treatments#2.

Weiss-Wolf, Jennifer. "Helping Women and Girls. Period." *New York Times*, January 28, 2015. https://kristof.blogs.nytimes.com/2015/01/28/helping-women-and-girls-period/.

Weiss-Wolf, Jennifer. "New York, Time to Shelve the Tax on Tampons." *Daily News*, June 1, 2015. http://www.nydailynews.com/opinion/jennifer-weiss-wolf-shelve-tampon-tax-article-1.2242455.

Wisconsin State Legislature. "Assembly Bill 555." April 13, 2016. https://docs.legis.wisconsin.gov/2015/proposals/ab555.

Women's Health Concern. "Period Pain." Accessed June 28, 2018. https://www.womens-health-concern.org/help-and-advice

/factsheets/periodpain/.

Yan, Holly. "Donald Trump's 'Blood' Comment About Megyn Kelly Draws Outrage." CNN. Updated August 8, 2015. https://www.cnn.com/2015/08/08/politics/donald-trump-cnn -megyn-kelly-comment/index.html.

Yuko, Elizabeth. Interview with author. December 5, 2017.

Yuko, Elizabeth. "2017 Was a Big Year for Periods on TV." SheKnows, December 29, 2017. http://www.sheknows.com /health-and-wellness/articles/1137604/periods-on-tv-2017.

Yuko, Elizabeth. "Why It Matters That 'Anne with an E' Has a Period Episode." *Pacific Standard*, May 22, 2017. https:// psmag.com/social-justice/half-the-population-suffers -through-it.

Zabczynski, Veronica. "The Period Humor on 'Broad City' Is Both Revolutionary and Important." Hello Giggles, April 29, 2016. https://hellogiggles.com/news/broad-city-period-humor/.

Zepeda, Mara. Interview with author. January 12, 2018.

Ziv, Stav. "Periods Are Normal, Says First U.K. Commercial to Use Red Liquid on a Pad." *Newsweek*, October 19, 2017. http:// www.newsweek.com/periods-are-normal-says-first-uk -commercial-use-red-liquid-pad-688699.

Zulch, Meg. "The Most Body Positive Moment on 'Broad City' Season 3 Tackled Natural Bodily Functions." Bustle, May 15, 2016. https://www.bustle.com/articles/159673-the-most-body -positive-moment-on-broad-city-season-3-tackled-natural -bodily-functions.

INDEX

gender equality, 48, 56, 230–232
    intersectional feminism and, 228
    progress of, 106
    taking action, 253–289
    Weiss-Wolf on, 176
menstrual transaction, 57
Modess brand, 113
Moore, Suzanne, 202–203
mucus, vaginal, 24
Mukuria, Megan White, 118
Muruganantham, Arunachalam, 250
myolysis, 40
myomectomy, 40
Myovant Sciences, 41

national government, period policy and, 170–173, 251–252
New York Times, 141–142, 153
Nguyen, Viet, 267–269
Nilsen, Ingrid, 184, 215–216, 218
NSAIDs, 31, 34
NSFWomen (documentary series), 122–123

Obama, Barack, 177, 184, 215–216
Obama, Michelle, 176–177
Ocean Conservancy, 245
Oldfield-Parker, Tara, 141
On the Ground blog, 153
Optimized Woman, The (Gray), 43–44
Oreck, Robert, 89
Outfront Media (company), 209
ovarian cysts, 35
ovaries (diagram), 20–21
ovulation, 21, 37

impact on education, 137–139

    medical risk, 139–140

    scale of problem, 131–137

    women in prisons and, 140–150, 158, 200

period products

    about, 59–60

    access to, 6–11

    costs of using, 76, 119

    distribution of, 9–10, 53–54, 96

    history of, 79–81, 100–101

    innovation in, 94–97

    as luxury items, 9, 152–153, 165–168, 184–185, 196, 257–258

    makeshift alternatives to, 7, 120, 123–126, 128–130, 250

    menstrual cups, 22, 73–78, 85–93

    sanitary napkins. *See* sanitary napkins

    sustainability in, 240–247

    tampons. *See* tampons

    taxation of, 9, 133, 153, 163–170, 173–174, 216–217, 256–257

periods, difference between menstrual cycle and, 20–21

#PeriodsforPence campaign, 172–173

Periods Gone Public (Weiss-Wolf), 152

Periods in Pop Culture (Rosenwarn), 190

Period Warriors, 12, 55–57

PID (pelvic inflammatory disease), 42–44

"pink tax." *See* taxation of period products

planning around periods, 43–44

Playtex brand, 85, 178

PMDD (premenstrual dysphoric disorder), 31

PMS (premenstrual syndrome), 30–31

policy, period. *See* period policy

polyps, 23

polyvinyl alcohol (PVA), 40

poverty, period. *See* period poverty

Tenderich, Gertrude, 83–84

Thinx underwear brand, 93–94, 123, 208–212

toxic shock syndrome (TSS), 70–71, 128, 139, 178–184, 243

trichomoniasis, 25

Trump, Donald, 13–14, 172

TSS (toxic shock syndrome), 70–71, 128, 139, 178–184, 243

TV, menstruation discussions on, 191, 193–203

#TweetTheReceipt campaign, 170

UAE (uterine artery embolization), 40

underwear, period, 93–94

UNESCO report, 248–249

United Nations, 153, 230

University of Central Florida study, 133–134

UnTabooed (NGO), 247

urethra, 70

urinary tract infections (UTIs), 62

uterine artery embolization (UAE), 40

uterine fibroids, 23, 38–41

uterus (diagram), 20–21

UTIs (urinary tract infections), 62

vagina (diagram), 20

vaginal discharge, 24, 26

Valenti, Jessica, 152–153, 164, 259–260

videos, period-related, 206–207, 212–214, 219–222

VonChaz, Chelsea, 288

Voting Rights Act (1965), 104

Walker, Emma, 113

Walla, Kah, 278

washing out blood stains, 64

Washington Examiner (newspaper), 259–260

Wasser, Lauren, 179–182